Japan: the childless society?

CW00418614

Disillusioned by long hours at home and by demands from the older generation, Japanese women are marrying later, resulting in a sharp decline in the Japanese birthrate.

Muriel Jolivet considers the reasons why Japanese women are finding it increasingly difficult to accept the terms and conditions of motherhood, exploring the major factors of malaise in Japan today. These include:

- the 'ten commandments of the good mother'
- the changing role of the father
- education and careers
- pressure from older generations

Drawing on extensive interviews with Japanese women and translated into English for the first time, this innovative study examines the implications for the declining birthrate and looks towards the future of a country that is in danger of becoming a 'childless' society.

Muriel Jolivet is Professor of French Studies and Sociology, Sophia University, Tokyo.

By the same author

L'université au service de l'economie japonaise, Economica, 1985

Japon le consensus: mythe et réalités (collaborative work), Economica, 1984

Childcare Values of Five Countries: Cross-cultural Content Analysis of Childcare Manuals (in collaboration with Sarane Boocock and Tsuneyoshi Ryôko)

Japan: the childless society?

The crisis of motherhood

Muriel Jolivet

Translated by Anne-Marie Glasheen

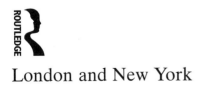

London and New York

First published in English in 1997
by Routledge
11 New Fetter Lane, London EC4P 4EE

Simultaneously published in the USA and Canada
by Routledge
29 West 35th Street, New York, NY 10001

Originally published in French as
Un pays en mal d'enfants by Éditions La Découverte

© 1993, Éditions La Découverte

This edition © 1997 Routledge

Translated by Anne-Marie Glasheen

Publié avec le concours du Ministère Français de la Culture

Typeset in Times by Keystroke, Jacaranda Lodge, Wolverhampton
Printed and bound in Great Britain by Redwood Books,
Trowbridge, Wiltshire

All rights reserved. No part of this book may be reprinted
or reproduced or utilized in any form or by any electronic,
mechanical, or other means, now known or hereafter
invented, including photocopying and recording, or in any
information storage or retrieval system, without permission
in writing from the publishers

British Library Cataloguing in Publication Data
A catalogue record for this book is available from the British Library

Library of Congress Cataloging in Publication Data
Jolivet, Muriel.
  [Pays en mal d'enfants. English]
  Japan: the childless society / Muriel Jolivet.
    p. cm.
  Includes bibliographical references.
  1. Motherhood–Japan. I. Title.
HQ759.J6813 1997
306.874'3'0952–dc20   96–26036
                                           CIP

ISBN 0–415–14646–1
     0–415–14647–X (pbk)

To Erika and Julia
without whom this book would not have been possible

Contents

Figures

Introduction

Women who have nothing better to do have a child.
(Words of the poetess Tomioka Taeko, from *Fuji no koromo ni asa no fusuma*, quoted by Tanaka Kimiko, in *Hataraku josei no kosodateron* ('The educational theories of working women'), 1988, p. 84)

Japan's political leaders are constantly deploring the fact that the fall in the birthrate will mean that by the twenty-first century Japan will have the oldest population in the world. In 1989 they referred to the '1.57 crisis' in the same grave tones as when they spoke of the oil crisis in the 1970s. Little did they know that the record was lying in wait for them, for in 1993 the average was 1.46 children per woman. Forecasts for 1996 are between 1.4 and 1.45.

Some reacted quickly and accused young women of being selfish epicureans bent on prolonging the break between university and employment, which gave them (too many) opportunities to enjoy the good things of life. Even the Prime Minister Hashimoto Ryûtarô, could not refrain from criticizing in public the harmful effects of higher education which distracted women from their primary duty in life.

Do all these complaints with which the press was inundated, point to a more deep-seated reason as to why these 'bellies are on strike'? The drop in the birthrate shows that Japanese women are finding it increasingly difficult to accept the terms and conditions of motherhood. How reluctant they are appears in the press and on television, where a growing number of women admit that they find motherhood tedious, exhausting and exasperating. Solitude and isolation would seem to be the common denominator behind what the 'nuclear' family has sadly become.

In order to gain a better understanding of this malaise, Chapter 1 gives a voice to those anguished young mothers. As a demonstration of the extent of the damage, just after the appearance in Japan of a baby help line, another help line for parents of potential battered children was set up. 'Is my child in danger of becoming a battered child?' is the main preoccupation of callers, who frequently say: 'I am an unworthy mother . . .', or 'I should never have been a mother . . .'

While parents unsympathetically remind their daughters that 'every normal woman must eventually cope with motherhood', it became necessary to carry out a survey to ascertain the cause of young women's low morale.

Chapter 2 describes several factors which have had an impact. First, couples are marrying later. Second, it is difficult to get parents to look after the children or to find places for children in a crèche. A third factor is the high cost of financing their studies. Moreover, young women are finding the freedom which studies and a job brings them increasingly attractive.

Chapter 3 deals with the sensitive issue of Japanese fathers. Trapped in a career structure where competition is fierce they have had to relinquish their traditional role and thus the family unit has become unstable. Completely destabilized themselves, they are unable to offer their wives any kind of support.

Another factor is the influence of paediatricians (through their books on childcare) who have given prominence to the 'ten commandments of the good mother' (Chapter 4). Paediatricians have put so much pressure on women that the latter have ended up losing their profession; their child is often the first baby they have ever touched in their lives. The paediatricians then perpetuate this harm by idealizing their own mothers and by holding up mothers during the Meiji period as a model. Chapter 5 discusses these 'pelican' mothers, who were also capable of killing, abandoning or selling their children, since small girls ended up – on occasion – as prostitutes, *geisha* or children's nursemaids (*komori*). By agreeing to sacrifice themselves for a 'good' cause, these children carried out the most exquisite act of filial piety that exists. Though infanticide has not theoretically been practised since the First World War, half a million foetuses continue to be aborted each year in Japan and official sources suggest that this figure should be multiplied by three. Chapter 6 describes the sinister ritual inspired by the new religions for the appeasement of the souls of aborted foetuses and then establishes the inevitable connection between the rise in the number of abortions and the drop in the birthrate, to illustrate the lack of enthusiasm on the part of women, to procreate.

Chapters 7 and 8 could be seen as a prospective. Are young women from the big cities, considered to be astute and disinclined to have children, not in fact the first to fall back into stereotypes? Is it not after all the men who are in danger of being unable to find a wife? If Japanese farmers are notorious for no longer being able to find anyone to marry them, it is a less well-known fact that 12 per cent of the male population is in danger of remaining single for life. Dismayed by the demands which Japanese women make on them these days, and incapable of emulating the changes that women have undergone, some have gone in search of a wife beyond their national borders. An underground network has developed, 'importing' Asian women from Korea, Taiwan, the Philippines or (more recently) from mainland China. That some Japanese men still resort to this alternative (suggestive of a disturbing trade in Asians) highlights their resistance to change.

The concluding chapter presents (as at the beginning of the book) real-life accounts of couples. These families have gradually found a new equilibrium of good will and role-sharing which has allowed these few women to present their child(ren) with a father who is actually present.

But, if all change necessarily implies a transformation in the way men think, it also requires a maturation in the way women think, for they sometimes restrain more than they encourage the evolution which has begun. In order to anticipate criticism from those who might suggest that I am ignoring the women who claim to be fulfilled, while maintaining that those who find motherhood fulfilling are not exempt from having an identity crisis, we close with three 'snapshots', which could be regarded as a glimmer of hope but also a possible resistance to change.

This work is based exclusively on Japanese sources (books, reviews, interviews, newspaper articles) as well as discussions held with a study group made up of some thirty Japanese women, who gave me the opportunity of inviting various eminent Japanese paediatricians, as well as many others referred to in this book, for example the psychiatrist Saito Satoru, who specializes in women's problems, and the paediatrician Môri Taneki. I should like to thank them all for having so generously taken the time to discuss their work with me. Just as important was the role of my fellow researchers who, through their enthusiasm and regular comments, were an unparalleled source of inspiration and encouragement. I am also grateful to them for having allowed me to test out reactions to my reading and personal observations. I thank them all most sincerely.

My gratitude goes especially to Elisabeth Badinter, Hara Hiroko, Philippe Pons, Catharina Blomberg, Corinne Quentin, Maurice Bairy, Tani Shizuko and Hayashi Mizue, who took the trouble to read and comment on the manuscript while it was being prepared and when it was finished. The editor-in-chief of the review *Wife*, Tanaka Kimiko, was a constant source of inspiration as well as a good friend who never once curtailed a discussion however long it was. I should also like to thank the Japanese Foundation which honoured me by contributing to the publication of this book.

I shall never forget Yûki Misae, who after allowing me to become her friend passed away and whose moving book touched my heart, nor Tottori Kinuko, who has been patient enough to translate this book into Japanese. All my thanks to Anne-Marie Glasheen, who went to the trouble of translating this book into English. May it help to alleviate our common destiny.

AUTHOR'S NOTE

The author has respected the Japanese tradition of always placing the family name or surname before the given or first names.

Sums of money referred to are in yen with no indication as to what their equivalent would be in pounds sterling. On 21 June 1996 that rate of exchange was one pound sterling to 167 yen and one US dollar to 108 yen.

1 Young mothers in a dilemma

Here is a real-life account taken from *Asahi* (13 September 1989) which seems fairly typical of the malaise experienced by many women. It provoked over forty responses from readers expressing their sympathy with this woman, whose experience they shared or had shared.

THE 'ANGUISH' OF ORDINARY WOMEN

It is said of today's women that they are either too relaxed with their children or that they lavish too much care and attention on them. Personally I find it extremely difficult to find the right balance when it comes to my own 2 and 4 year olds. When I make a proper job of it we make dough together or I play the piano and sing or read them stories. However there are times when the emptiness of my life leaves me reeling. They get upset when I ask them to leave me alone so that I can have an hour to myself. When my husband has a day off I sometimes leave them with him so that I can go out on my own.

I love my children dearly but while I lie down with them to get them off to sleep, I can't help looking at my watch. I can't bear it either when they won't leave me alone to read the paper. I don't mind so much when I'm doing the housework! But when it's finished, I long to have some time to myself but the children won't let me.

No one ever disturbs men when they're working and people always presume that mothers 'are enjoying themselves' even though their work is never done and they often feel that they're going around in circles. Although caring for my children takes up all my time and wears me out physically, I also end up feeling emotionally drained. There are so many things I'd like to be doing!

Even though I tell myself repeatedly that it won't last for ever, I can't help thinking that I shall never be able to make up the time I've lost.

I know it's absurd even to entertain the idea that I could do something else while I still have the children to bring up, but when we apply ourselves solely to caring for our children, we do still sometimes regard them as a nuisance. Years ago people used to say that children brought themselves up, but it's no longer the case today. What can we do to ensure that childcare regains its human face?

This confession is fairly representative of the national average inasmuch as this woman finds her children 'lovable' and goes to a lot of trouble to look after them as best she can. However, the fact that it is full-time and relentless is what she finds so daunting. We sense that this mother is in a dilemma since she cannot rid herself of the notion that she is the only one capable of looking after her children. When we see how difficult it is for her to forgive herself for 'abandoning' them to their father on a Sunday, we realize how unthinkable it would be to leave them in a crèche or to call on the services of a baby-sitter.

Her 'anguish' also stems from the empty, alienating and thankless nature of housework whose value is never fully appreciated. Where she seems to founder, though, is when at the end she says it is a delusion to entertain the hope of doing anything else when you have children to bring up. And yet, however painful and stressful the alternative might be, the only way out is to try to do several things at the same time.

It is this overly *amai* aspect of childrearing – now no longer the prerogative of men – which works against women.[1] Relieved by their mothers from performing menial tasks so that they can fully devote themselves to their studies, they are so helpless when their time comes, that the idea of doing more than one thing at a time does not occur to them.

This woman's problem springs from the fact (although she tells herself it will not be for much longer) that she finds these negative feelings difficult to cope with, because at that precise moment it is time which seems interminable to her. However, even though she can tolerate the situation, she never questions the soundness of her decision. It is hard but it is irrevocable.

Another determining factor emerges from her deliberations: never before has childcare been as alienating as it is today. In fact, not so long ago people used to say that children raised themselves; many people in their forties remember having grown up in the pervading philosophy of *'laissez-faire'*, now referred to as 'moral abandon'. Previously, mothers did not have time to devote themselves unreservedly to their children, their main mission being 'productive' rather than educational. The custom of putting their children under the protection of the Shinto deities was also destined to absolve parents from the countless mishaps which lay in wait for them. Since a mother these days is responsible for everything, including the child's psychological well-being, it is not surprising if she ends up reeling.

The following selection of reactions which the preceding confession provoked, places the problem in its social context.

I was also left reeling when I was confronted by the vision of the monotonous insipidity of life stretching out before me.

You say you are incapable of restraining yourself but this is a problem we all have. However, compared to some mothers who are not prepared to make the smallest sacrifice for their children, I have great admiration for you. Begin by believing in yourself. Then relax a little.

We live in a society of information technology which bombards us with advice on the art and manner in which we should bring up our children and are constantly striving to be perfect parents. Yet, instead of wearing ourselves out trying to be perfect, wouldn't it be better to accept ourselves for what we are . . . and be happy. Raising your children should not be a struggle, if you want a quiet read, why not just simply say to them: 'Right, now it's time for *us* to read!' Or: 'Right, now mummy wants to read the paper, so you go and draw me a picture!' Make it seem as though you're having fun together, and for your part, if you're asking them to wait a while make sure you keep your word.

I think it's an excellent idea for your husband to help out so that you go out for a breath of fresh air. In fact I think that cinemas and museums should have childminding facilities so that young mothers can go out more often. It is always a good thing for parents to take it in turns to look after the children or occasionally for them to call upon outside help.

If you enjoy looking after them they will sense this and be all the happier for it.

You say that while a mother's work is never done and altogether unfulfilling she gives everyone the impression that she is enjoying herself. Personally, when I gave up work to devote myself to the children, the prospect of the monotonous insipidity of life stretching out before me also left me reeling. But when I was out collecting insects with the children or was drawing pictures with them, I realized how enriching their company was.

So stop ruining your life by forcing yourself to do this or that: not only will your life become easier but you will feel more relaxed especially if you can persuade yourself that you are not losing out.

Bringing up children is not what it's cracked up to be.

Don't worry, I was just like you! I now have a daughter of 7 and a son of 3, but I have to admit that two years ago I was feeling and behaving in exactly the same way as you! The nuclear family has created a situation where we learn by trial and error. But it is essential never to lose your temper.

All the time I had only one child, I was able to continue using my foreign languages by doing translations from home. But after the birth of the second, I had to give up. I was far too tired or exasperated but because I was absolutely determined to look after the children myself I did everything I could, alternating between the ideal mother I aspired to be and the unnatural mother which, unbeknownst to me, I sometimes became.

How to escape these anxieties is no secret however; you must be strong and not feel too guilty. The reality of bringing up children has nothing to do with what we read in childcare manuals. It is better to be yourself than live haunted by the fear of compromising their psychological well-being.

There is nothing wrong with wanting a social life in order to have a break from household chores and childcare. If you have an activity you are keen to pursue, your child will be only too happy to co-operate and the support of your partner will be indispensable.

Is there anything more wonderful than bringing up your children yourself?

Reading of your distress took me back to how I was ten years ago.

I am a housewife with two children of 14 and 18, and it is true that however much we devote ourselves to housework and children, the results are far from being immediately tangible. Moreover, even if we were paid to do the work we do, we would still not be congratulated. There is nothing more disheartening, sterile or exasperating.

To be quite honest, I seriously considered returning to work so that I could put the children in a crèche and rely on the expertise of others, but taking everything into account, I decided it would be better to bring them up myself.

I had to wait a few years – until they were toilet-trained – before being able to go out, but once they are out of nappies why not try to do something interesting together? I enrolled mine in a club where they could play with other children so that I could go to the library or a culture centre where I was initiated in the art of putting on a kimono.

When my child was 3, he was capable of sitting through a whole concert or piano recital without making a sound. I also took him to children's theatres. If the mother is contented this is bound to reflect on the children.

With a life expectancy of 80 these days, the few years we spend bringing up our children represent a tiny fraction of our lives. We live in a world where money can buy you everything. However, like home-made cakes, not everything can be bought, is there anything more wonderful than bringing up your children yourself?

These three responses come from the 'Keep going, Mother!' ideology (*okâsan gambareron*). What they have in common is that none suggests that having a job can be a way out.

The first reply, with its reference to busy women 'who are not prepared to make the smallest sacrifice for their children', mirrors current opinion for it claims that a working woman is selfish, and therefore automatically a bad mother.

The advantages of the mother being responsible for her child's education remains in effect the leitmotif behind each of the responses, which, while remaining sympathetic, endorse her decision and the price she is paying for coping with her negative feelings since it is for a limited period of time only.

This attitude reflects the theory that there is nothing more fulfilling for a woman than motherhood, linked to the – very Japanese – notion that in devoting ourselves wholeheartedly and applying ourselves as best we can to accomplishing our duty, we could not fail but find the kind of contentment which would give our lives (or sacrifices) a meaning.

In the words of the third response, what are two or three years in relation to present-day life expectancy? This moralizing stance, taken up by – among others – the Oketani School of Breastfeeding with a view to encouraging mothers to breastfeed their child every three hours for a year (see Chapter 4) is often used to convince women of their selfishness. The only innovative concepts to be found in these responses are the ideas that 'slow and steady wins the race' and that there is no point in striving to be perfect.

Without actually answering her question, she is advised to substitute her pursuit of perfection for a more sound *laissez-faire* approach by replacing intimidation and threat with a more gentle manipulation of the children. In other words she must cleverly dupe them in order to shield them from any source of frustration, an art in which Japanese mothers excel particularly well.

Moreover, it would appear that if the mother has a need to be patient, she also has a need to be well balanced since her child's stability depends on it. The success of so-called cultural centres – some of which include a crèche – is understandable, since they give mothers the chance to be adequately entertained: they do not need to invest too much of themselves or neglect their responsibilities. If the aim of these centres is to offer mothers a beneficial distraction from their solitude, the superficial and barely stimulating nature of the courses, specially conceived for amateurs, would not however be very satisfying to the more demanding.

Drawing upon the father's services certainly meets with their approval, though resorting to outside assistance should be the exception rather than the rule – affirming the repugnance that Japanese parents have of entrusting their children to a stranger. (My baby-sitter's own parents had told her that more than a hint of thoughtlessness was required to entrust a child to her.)

Much could be said on the subject of the father's contribution which, given the nature of everyday life, averages eight minutes a day. A government survey revealed that rather than spend time with the family and look after their children, Japanese fathers preferred to decamp on a Sunday (see Chapter 3). If their wives do manage to coerce them into participating more actively, few volunteer to baby-sit and those who do, do so due to force of circumstance rather than pleasure.

If the leitmotif echoed by the readers repeatedly brings us back to the famous *gambatte!* ('keep going!'), it is only because it reflects a social climate which demands that nothing should be achieved too easily, any reward residing in the amount of effort expended.

TOTAL ISOLATION AND THE MALAISE OF NEW RESIDENTIAL DEVELOPMENTS

Geographic isolation is particularly hard for people to bear. Dropped into one of these dormitory towns inoffensively named *beddo town*, women find themselves far from their close family, without any ties or contacts with the outside world. The newly acquired nuclear family comes with a high price tag. Here is a case which could be entitled 'the road to childrearing neurosis':

> As I am nearing the end of my pregnancy, we have just moved into a flat on the eighth floor of an eleven-storey block. We have a lot more space and room at last for the baby's cot. And yet, when I look out over the alien landscape outside my window, I cannot hold back my tears when I see the sky. I must confess that once my husband has left for work, no one ever comes to see me and I never go out. The day goes by without my having an opportunity to talk to anyone at all. As I am in the habit of doing all my shopping on a Sunday there is no reason for me to go out. All day I am subconsciously waiting for my husband to return. My only chance to open my mouth is when I telephone the baby help line. You are my one and only contact.[2]

Devastating through its banality, this testimony exposes the dangers of new residential developments, some of which, like those at Takashimadaira, were infamous for their suicide rate. (This is no longer the case since bars have been fitted to every storey.)

The solitude these women experience is sometimes so intense that it can develop into aphasia, like this 24 year old who, having married a man from her native province as soon as she finished her studies, contacted the baby help line when her child was 14 months old, telling them that she was becoming aphasic.

> My husband, a business man, always comes home late and I can go all day without speaking to anyone. Since I became pregnant I have been permanently shut up at home and feel completely cut off from the outside world. All my friends work and my husband comes home so tired that he falls asleep without saying a word to me; it is so bad that I can go the whole day without having occasion to open my mouth and utter a single word.
>
> My child is good and fairly undemanding, but as I cannot go on like this, once a week I take him with me to a class in the art of putting on a kimono.[3]

This young woman's isolation is aggravated by the fact that she has become marginalized as a result of her early marriage at the age of 22 (25 is the age said to be the most propitious to marry). She says as much herself, for at 24, her former friends are still single and have demanding professional lives which has resulted in their no longer having anything in common. This case underlines the danger which exists in Japan of becoming marginalized: marrying three years earlier than is the norm alienates you from your peer group.

Most young women – whose pregnancies are more or less fortuitous outcomes rather than planned ones – do not have the slightest idea what awaits them after the birth of their child, who arrives without an instruction manual. The forming of the nuclear family, together with fewer brothers and sisters, means that more often than not the first baby they hold is their own – as the following comments confirm:

> Having remained childless for the first four years of marriage, I suddenly discovered I was pregnant at the age of 30. When I was discharged from hospital I went straight to my parents. The malaise I endured at that time is still imprinted on my memory. I felt as though I had brought an extraterrestrial being home. It was fortunate that my mother was there, even though what she remembered – she was going back over thirty years! – was a little rusty. I have to admit to never having had the slightest contact with a child as I am the youngest in the family and there were never any around me, not even in the neighbourhood. Hence this was my first encounter with a child. If only an opportunity had presented itself earlier or if only there had been a beautiful little baby around, I might perhaps have felt more relaxed with mine.[4]

Few young girls now go to school with a younger brother or sister strapped to their backs (see pp. 125–6), and the rudimentary advice given to new mothers – by the duty nurse – on how to bath a newborn baby or how to sterilize bottles was quite inadequate once they are back home. The only option they have is to stay with their own mothers for as long as possible,[5] although this often entails putting off the evil day, as revealed in the second part of the above testimony:

> I felt quite out of my depth when Yûichi cried all the time for no apparent reason. Babies have a particularly frustrating way of crying which makes you want to run away.
>
> While I was with my parents it was just about bearable, as my mother would help out or give me advice, but it was all very well my staying there for as long as possible; at the end of a month I had to resign myself to going home. When my mother had left after bringing me back, I have to confess to having felt utterly isolated at finding myself alone with Yûichi in a house that was a total mess.
>
> My husband adores children and was happy to look after the

child, but as he doesn't work set hours, he was never home before midnight. Consequently the only time I could rely on him was when he had a day off.

Once I was home I found I couldn't get anything done. Whenever I tried to get on with the housework, Yûichi would start screaming and I was always having to stop what I was doing to take advantage of the rare moments when he was asleep. I just about had time to do the shopping. He got into the habit of crying at the end of the day or during the night. And if we ignored him once he had started, we could do nothing to calm him; he would become quite hysterical, it was as though a siren had got stuck.[6]

In Yûki Misae's case,[7] disillusionment came much sooner. Disappointed when she realized – with the onset of demands and difficulties – how different a real baby was from how she had imagined it would be; she conceded that the factor which triggered the baby blues for her (ridiculous though this might seem) was her son's inability to burp, together with his unfortunate habit of bringing up over half the feed which had been so time-consuming to administer.

'It begins well enough,' she stated and then went on to ask herself how he managed to be 'the only one' who could not do it properly.

Feeding time very soon turned into a nightmare, made worse by the fact that she had not mastered the technique of feeding him. The next moment she was blaming herself and became quite exasperated when the only suggestion those around her could come up with was the repeated refrain: *gambatte* ('keep going!'). The impact of these exhortations, however, was such that she ended up wondering whether she was a bad mother, devoid of maternal instinct. She admits that there were times when she harboured the darkest of thoughts towards her son.

In fact she would dispute the word instinct, for the truth is: either she is abnormal or it is a myth – skilfully perpetuated in order to manipulate women – in need of urgent eradication, given the harm it has already done them.

Although the trigger did not work automatically for her, she was appalled when she realized that those around her – especially her parents – saw her as being only a mother, a condition mercilessly confirmed by her mirror which reflected the image of a stocky figure (8 kilos overweight) with a bloated face. Why bother to wear makeup, do her hair or get dressed even? Indeed, for whom? She had lost the will and the energy. 'Am I in the process of losing "me"?' she wondered horrified, before going on to ask herself how 'all the others managed', especially 'those who seemed so confident'.

'Whenever my baby cries, I too feel like crying'

If tears are particularly troublesome to the delicate nerves of the young mother, the lack of understanding displayed by those around her are sometimes even more so. Here is an example:

> When your infant is babbling his first words or your child is taking his first steps, you cannot hope to get anything done because you have to keep a watchful eye on him. If there is no one to rely on, you have to give up any thoughts of putting your nose outside. Moreover, reading, an afternoon nap or anything requiring concentration is quite out of the question. But as it is also true that there are no pressures on you, for me it was the beginning of hell. I envied those mothers who enjoyed playing with their children but it was in vain that I waited for my maternal instinct to surface.
>
> One day my father turned up unexpectedly to find my child bawling his head off in his playpen. He rushed over and picked him up saying he couldn't understand how I could stay on the balcony, head propped in my hands while any mother 'worthy of that name' would console a crying child.[8]

This account is revealing in more ways than one. First, here is the lifting of a taboo inasmuch as women now have the courage to admit their innermost thoughts to a third party. They speak quite openly to the baby help line or the battered child help line of the boredom and exasperation, the tyranny of children, the monotony of the routine or the debilitation of being constantly alone with a child, they are no longer sublimated as their parents' generation was. The child is seen as a handicap and motherhood is in danger of degenerating into malediction.

Co-author of a book on childrearing neurosis, Jimba Yukiko, who spent twenty years answering calls made to the baby help line, confirmed: 'They have barely opened their mouths than they pour out their hearts, namely: 'Ah, if only he weren't there . . . ' '.[9] Another interesting element, which returns like a leitmotif, is the feeling of not being good enough or of actually being 'abnormal' for lacking that famous instinct which makes caring and sacrifice natural to everyone else. Instead of reassuring her, the afore-mentioned father plunges her further into a state of doubt by accusing her of being an unworthy mother.

'Tell me, are you affected by your child's tears?'

A survey carried out by the baby help line reveals that it is a child's tears which contribute the most to the levels of stress experienced by mothers. Among those who admitted that they sometimes hated their children (74 per cent), 54 per cent replied that it was when they cried, 10 per cent when they would not go to sleep, 5 per cent when they would not eat and 5 per cent in 'other situations'.

Bearable by day, at night a child's tears become a nightmare. Mothers reacted by: putting them to the breast (60 per cent), picking them up (51.6 per cent), putting them to bed (31.6 per cent), giving them a drink (18.3 per cent), opening the window (5 per cent), taking them out (3.3 per cent) or all of these (3.3 per cent). They complain of lack of sleep (73.3 per cent), of chronic exhaustion (35 per cent), of irritability (23.3 per cent), of fear of disturbing others (10 per cent), of constipation (6.6 per cent) or of other ailments (5 per cent).

Fear of disturbing the neighbours (63 per cent of women questioned), fear of disturbing the whole family (36.1 per cent) and especially that of jeopardizing her husband's professional performance (15 per cent) are the three principal concerns. This no doubt explains why over half of Japanese husbands do not react, 15.1 per cent pretend not to hear, 3.3 per cent even complain that their sleep has been disturbed.[10] There are many fathers who, when this happens, move into the next room, feeling diminished by the mother–child dyad. It must be said in their defence that through lack of any flexibility on the part of their employers, their working conditions do not give them much opportunity to co-operate. One woman's husband did not know of the birth of his daughter until twenty-four hours after the event. For a company to insist that an employee whose wife is about to go into labour should work at night, illustrates the priorities given to profitability. It is not surprising that 72 per cent of mothers whose child cries at night find the task of childcare exhausting, with 4.5 per cent even admitting that they consider their children to be burdens which erode all their self-esteem. Those who claim they are not disturbed by their crying (36 per cent) declare that they find them a great pleasure to look after.[11] Thus the growth or otherwise of neurosis is more or less predetermined by the mother's susceptibility or resistance to her child's tears.

'The most depressing thing about the mother's condition,' Yûki Misae adds,

is that beneath the veneer of having absolute freedom lurks an enslavement which is far worse than that of a busy schedule, for what with the sterilization of feeding bottles and the washing, the days go by, each one more insipid than the last without ever being aware of their passing.

Individual and group solitude

It takes only one step to move from this state to one of revolt, and it was one that Yûki Misae had no hesitation in taking. 'Whether they be fathers or not, how do their lives change when they have all the time in the world while they're at work to forget their other "subsidiary" role?' She states that from the very outset of pregnancy, inequality sets in, 'for it is always the same person who suffers from nausea, puts on weight and works hard'. And yet, what seemed to be the hardest for her to accept was the sudden change of attitude she observed in her husband, who seemed to say – just like all the rest – that it was not his fault if she was the mother.

Yûki Misae's experience of this painful solitude was even more distressing because she was not alone: in theory at least, she had her son to keep her company. Fortunately some of her friends had admitted to experiencing the same torment, one of them – a teacher by profession – had even confessed that she could never have taken her maternity leave had it not been for the fact that she knew she would be returning to work in a year's time.[12]

Of course women do have the chance of getting together to fill those lonely hours which was the option Yûki Misae chose (for want of any other alternative) when, to her horror, she found herself yearning for 'idle chat with the neighbours', she who had always found this kind of thing so abhorrent. 'Anything rather than stay at home alone with my son! I wanted to talk about my husband, my child, anything. A chance to pour out my soul, that was all I wanted.'

While acknowledging their undeniable therapeutic value, she admits that these superficial chats, constantly interrupted by crying babies, 'leaks' or feeds, had also had the opposite effect; for what could be more depressing than to be told by one's experienced elders, that getting up in the middle of the night to give your child the breast is nothing compared to what is in store for you. Of all the prognoses: 'Ah, just you wait until he starts moving around!' is the one which exasperated her the most.

To live with one's mother-in-law is no solution either

If the nuclear family has meant solitude then living with one's mother-in-law produces other tensions, notably a certain rivalry over the child, as in the following example:

We live with my in-laws. When my son was born my mother-in-law made it very clear that she had no intention of looking after her grandchildren. I found this quite shocking. Our relationship has never been the same since. And yet, the moment he starts crying, she runs to pick him up, a look of utter contempt in her eyes for me.

A child with a delicate constitution with several allergies, he has always cried a lot and needs so much attention that I have had to wrap him in cotton wool. I became so attached to him that he became a part of me.

It is for this reason that I find it difficult when he goes downstairs in search of his grandmother. This exasperates me and makes me wonder what useful purpose I am serving. If I scold him for refusing to eat what I have spent hours lovingly preparing, she gives him a banana. I resent her for encouraging him in this way not to eat his meals. I sometimes wonder whether he isn't doing it on purpose to provoke me and this irritates me beyond belief. I have to admit that I am no longer sure how to bring him up.[13]

This account reflects the universal conflicts which exist between mother-in-law and daughter-in-law, which Ariyoshi Sawako aptly describes in her novel based on the dramatic rivalry between the wife and the mother of the first Japanese surgeon, Hanaoka Seishû (1760–1835).[14]

These days, it is relatively rare for newly-weds to live with in-laws except in the country, where this tradition remains one of the main stumbling blocks in a farmer's search for a wife (see Chapter 7). Living with mother is more common when the grandfather dies since his wife is likely to survive him by around six years (Ministry of Health statistics, 1989). Conflict can arise between the two women when the grandmother looks after the grandchildren so that the daughter (it is unusual for it to be the daughter-in-law) can go out to work, sometimes giving the latter the impression that her children are no longer hers.

If this woman's obsession with her son appears 'disconcerting', it does not seem to worry her counsellor unduly who tells her to turn the situation to her advantage by skilfully transforming her rival into a 'baby-sitter'. This advice is interesting as it reveals that despite the many material advantages of two generations living together, it is an alternative seldom embraced.

FROM 'BABY-BLUES' TO NEUROSIS

Let us return to Yûichi's mother:

> Whenever I had nothing to do – how was that possible? – I lived on my nerves. Looking after my child, the cramped conditions in which we lived began to get me down. In my exasperation, I would tell him off for no apparent reason. I would rage when I realized how unjust I was being, accusing myself of being an unworthy mother. The idea that I would never get on with him grieved me so much that I ended up having uncontrollable bouts of crying.
>
> I would waylay my husband the moment he came through the door and pour out everything that was in my heart. Exhausted by his day at work we would end up arguing. Sometimes he even beat me. 'What do you expect me to do? You're his mother, aren't you?' he would invariably hurl in my face. I searched desperately for something to hang on to. Even in the toilet I could get no peace for the child would bang incessantly at the door, which made me feel really uptight. I would dream of half an hour on my own so that I could recharge my batteries.[15]

It would seem that here is the same cry of desperation: 'I am an unworthy mother!', but it is questionable who, under similar circumstances, would not end up neurotic.

The husband's attitude is quite appalling: instead of reaching out to save her from drowning, he pushes her back under the water. Never having needed to think of anyone but themselves, many husbands are apparently incapable of the least selflessness. They would rather throw themselves into their work in order to escape domestic problems they cannot deal with. That 'You're his mother, aren't you?' is an annihilating remark but it does embody their innermost thoughts, the biological argument serving to justify that a woman's place is in the home. After all, is it men's fault if women produce the milk? They just have to accept the consequences!

However, though men might blame nature for the fact that they desert their wives at this critical time, women are finding their enforced isolation and sacrifice increasingly 'unnatural'.

I should never have had a child

Here is another account, recorded by the baby help line.

Last night, however hard I tried, I couldn't get my child off to sleep. He even refused to take his bottle. Only when I held him did he calm down a little, but the moment I tried to put him down, he immediately began to bawl his head off. You would have thought his bed had caught fire. Propped up against the wall I was just beginning to doze off when I was jolted awake by the child falling to the ground. I am not coping at all well. When I wake up in the morning my head aches. No matter how often I gaze at the bucket of filthy nappies waiting to be washed, I can't find the energy to do the laundry.

Moreover my child has recently started drinking less milk during the day. If it continues like this I'm worried he'll end up undernourished.

I am an unworthy mother; I should never have had a child. I'll never be able to bring him up properly [*sobs and tears*]. Everyone else seems to manage except me. In fact my mother keeps telling me that there is no reason why I should be the only one who cannot cope since even animals manage to raise their offspring.

I see no sign of my maternal love appearing either. I no longer have the strength to go on living like this. My husband appears increasingly more remote. Speaking to him would achieve absolutely nothing for he is quite incapable of understanding me. In any case I could never tell him all that is in my heart.[16]

This young woman's sense of isolation is exacerbated by her impression that everyone else in the world copes except her: she is convinced that she will never conform to the norm, that she is in fact 'abnormal'. Instead of reassuring her, her mother reinforces this fear by emphasizing that even animals manage better. As for her husband, who is preoccupied with his own world, she knows that it would be useless to confide in him.

Such an atmosphere is ripe terrain for the cultivation of the darkest of thoughts concerning marriage, husbands, even relationships. Some young women actually contemplate killing themselves and their child.

I think I'm going mad from always being alone with my child!

It would appear that those who practise *tenuki*, that is those who manage to reduce the amount of housework they do to an absolute minimum, have a strong sense of self-preservation. However, the same cannot be said of those perfectionists who are hypersensitive to cleanliness and incapable of tolerating the disorder their children make, especially when it is left to them to clear up.

Mrs F, for example, is obsessed with cleanliness and cannot help becoming exasperated by the mess her child leaves in his wake. She follows Qchan everywhere and clears up behind him. An extremely meticulous woman, she admits to the baby help line that cleanliness has become an obsession. 'I'm frightened I might harm my child', she confides, adding that he is constantly washing his hands.

In the course of the telephone conversation she disclosed that she was totally isolated in her apartment and that her son had no friends of his own age. In the end she admitted: 'I think I'm going mad from always being alone with my child'. It was suggested that she should break out from her isolation by going to a 'playgroup' where she would meet other mothers.

The baby help line cites the case of a 31-year-old woman who called thirty-three times to reassure herself over the circumference of her child's head. This woman possessed – as do most women who call the help line – three books on childcare. These simply fed her neurosis for she believed that every other child was more 'standard' than her own. Her anxiety developed from her husband's professional moves. As a result of having no one to whom she could pour out her feelings, she formed the habit of phoning the baby help line to tell them that her child was vomiting or that he was restless or to report her anxiety that he was still unable to hold his head up by himself. Could he have hydrocephalus? Her doctor had assured her he had not, but she was still troubled.

She called many times to ask the same question, admitting she had been back to the doctor but that he had confirmed once more that the circumference of her child's head was absolutely normal.

When her child was 4 months old she called four times to say that he could now hold his head up by himself for thirty seconds but that the circumference of his head was one centimetre above the average quoted in her childcare manuals. Or she would call to say that, although everything was still fine (he was smiling and gurgling), she could not help but worry that there was still the possibility that he could have hydrocephalus, for although people kept telling her not to worry, there was nothing she could do about this obsession of hers. Were they keeping the truth from her?

When he was 5 months old, she called twice to express her concern over her child's faeces and because she was worried he was suffering from malnutrition. Although she was once again reassured by a visit to the doctor, she was no nearer to being freed from her obsession. She also wanted to know at what age babies started to roll over, for 'it's really maddening but all the children in the neighbourhood can roll over except mine.'

When he was 7 months old the circumference of his head was 45.2 cm. She had consulted the doctor again but had not dared insist in case he made fun of her. She went on to say that the child could remain seated but that he was still unable to sit up by himself.

She rang again to say that he was the only child who could not wave 'bye bye' while 'all the other children of his age can'; that he could do *banzai* (lift his arms in the air), but that he still could not wave 'bye bye'; or she would ask if he might not be a late talker.

However pathological this case might seem, here are a few more which will be commented on afterwards.

Mrs X, aged 29, has a child with a harelip. For the first three months of his life she did not dare go out, in case the people from her neighbourhood noticed his handicap. The only time she went out was to take the rubbish down; her husband did the shopping on a Sunday.

She described how she spent her days staring at her son's harelip and admitted that she was on the verge of a nervous breakdown. She was terrified that someone might open the front door.[17] Her husband advised her to force herself to go out, but she did not think she was brave enough. Her dream was to buy a house 'so that they could get out of their unlucky council flat as quickly as possible'. She told the help line that she had never sought medical advice for herself.

Mrs J, aged 28, was very shaken when the doctor announced that her daughter – then aged 2 months – might have a heart condition. All motivation to do anything disappeared and, frightened of harming the child, she found she could not look after her any longer and even lost interest in her.

Having worked for two years after obtaining her *tandai* diploma, she realized that since giving up work she had become prone to depression.[18] She phoned again the following day to say that she had become completely obsessed with what the doctor had told her. She changed the child's nappy mechanically, no longer able to feel anything for her.

Her husband advised her to have a good sleep and forget all about it but she felt guilty at the thought she might be wasting her time and could not bring herself to have an afternoon nap.

Even though she had been strongly recommended to consult a specialist, she called again a few days later to say that her husband had assured her that in time everything would sort itself out. However, she wondered whether he might not be averse to the idea of her seeking medical advice.

Five months later she called again to say that she had been so desperate that she had taken an overdose of sleeping pills. Her husband was taken completely by surprise.

They have now moved and 'things were better'. When her little girl cries she forces herself into action. However, she cannot find the energy to redecorate the flat and she is far from being as happy and lively as she would like to be.

No matter how often she repeats that she is cured, she still gives the impression that she is extremely depressed. 'No', she replies, she hasn't started therapy 'but things are better'. Her parents call her every day and she occasionally visits her in-laws.[19]

This depression is all the more alarming since it was triggered by a doctor telling this woman that her daughter had a 'bad' heart without elaborating on the subject. Though somewhat vague, this statement was enough to remove the mother's will to live, while jeopardizing her relationship with the daughter whose life she saw, in the long or short term, to be in danger, thus preventing her unconsciously from investing too much in it.

This case strongly reflects a doctor's blatant disregard for the patient's state of mind. In Japan a paediatrician is a paediatrician and that is all: the mother's mental state is of no concern. Moreover, since doctors are revered, they tend to patronize their patients (evidence of this can be seen in the way they dispense different remedies without explaining what they contain).

Besides, what chance do patients have to be candid when they are instructed to be brief, to trust their doctors and do as they say.[20] To ask questions would be to challenge the doctor's knowledge. Furthermore, the production line medical care practised in Japanese hospitals does not provide an environment where the patient can confide in the doctor, because the symbolic curtain, which so often separates the patient being attended from those who are waiting, makes the consultation quasi-public – gynaecological and psychiatric consultations are no exception. One general practitioner had a door between the waiting room and the consulting room but saw his patients four at a time.

To return to the above-mentioned cases, it is impossible not to feel a sense of outrage when paediatricians desert these distressed women, when a minimum of tact or understanding would no doubt have helped to reassure them, especially in the third case, where the diagnosis was hypothetical rather than definite.

Another recurring theme is the social stigma attached to neurosis, which in Japan is considered to be the most shameful illness: the fact that the 'mentally ill' are shunned is what prevents this woman from consulting a specialist.[21]

It might be common practice in the United States to consult a psychotherapist, but in Japan people are expected to call upon their inner resources to deal with their problems. That a husband should discourage his wife from seeing a specialist, assuring her that in time everything will sort itself out, is symptomatic of the universally held *laissez-faire* attitude.[22]

'The angrier I get the more he stutters'

When R-kun was 2, his 28-year-old mother called in to say he had developed a stammer. As the youngest in her family, this woman had always been very spoiled. Never having had to help out at home, she felt completely overwhelmed by her situation. She could not cope because she had had a child without ever having experienced independence or self-sufficiency. She was no more talented at cooking than she was at childcare and she is still haunted by the nightmare memory of the day her husband brought home some colleagues for dinner; one of them asked how he could put up with such food.[23] Since then she has lived in dread that he might repeat the experience for their home is untidy and disorganized.

When he was about 4 years old the problem of the child's stammer was exacerbated when he developed nervous twitches to the face. She feels that this is in some ways her fault and has resulted in her losing all her self-confidence, which is why she now dislikes both her children. The housework depresses her and she has reached the point where she no longer wants to live in the accommodation provided by her husband's company. But unless she were to go back to work they would need another source of income to have a house built. She cannot reconcile herself to doing this, however, as she does not like the idea of putting the children in a crèche. 'Everything would be fine if only I could enjoy being a housewife', she sighs. Unfortunately she is not made that way. She cannot bring herself to admit to her husband that she feels trapped. This feeling is reflected in her other phone calls regarding her son's stammer, which she finds increasingly more irritating. She calls again to say that he is constantly bickering with his younger brother, that he does not tell her when he needs to go to the toilet, that he cries for no apparent reason or that he is always being bullied by other children.

In the end, encouraged by the help line, she goes to a specialist who advises her 'not to let herself get angry'. And the day she stops badgering her son he stops stammering.

Nevertheless she calls a few days later to report that he has begun to stammer again, that he can never keep still, that he allows his little friends either to push him around or ignore him completely, that his perpetual whys and hows are driving her crazy, or to declare that she can take no more, that she thinks her head is going to explode and that she will never survive motherhood. She ends by wondering whether her son might be suffering from phimosis (constriction of the foreskin). Over a period of three years, until the child was 5 years old, she made twenty similar phone calls.[24]

Here is an example of a woman, obviously frustrated from having to stay at home and who, if she were able to be a part-time mother, would unquestionably make a much better job of it. Her dilemma is that she cannot bring herself to put her children in a crèche; her ambivalence reflects society's disapproval, not to mention that of her husband and in-laws (for further details see pp. 53–6).

'TO THINK I COULD HAVE KILLED HIM!'

One evening, when Yûki Misae was extremely tired, her child kept crying for no apparent reason since he had a full stomach and had just been changed. In her book she remembers:

> Murderous thoughts flashed through my mind. I told myself that if I were to smash him against the wall he would shatter! Good riddance! A job well done! There would still be time to have another but I didn't want to have anything more to do with this wretched child who was poisoning my life!
>
> Yes, I can honestly say that I did entertain such thoughts and I don't know by what miracle I was able to control myself. It was probably because I didn't fancy being locked up in prison not to mention seeing my photo in the paper with the headline: 'Degenerate mother assassinates child!'
>
> Neither did I have any desire to feel guilty for the rest of my life.
>
> With a kick I woke my husband who was sleeping soundly, as oblivious to Kôhei's screams as he was to my state of mind, and threw the child over to him. His eyes puffy with sleep, he looked at me, flabbergasted, unable to comprehend why on earth I was sobbing.
>
> I had hit rock bottom. How could I have sunk this low? But I

was also shedding tears of resentment because I was not up to the task which had been bestowed upon me and because I was feeling desperately engulfed by a life which had led to my having to sacrifice my identity.[25]

The sincerity of this account resulted in its author being inundated with letters from women thanking her for having been their spokesperson. It is also striking because it reveals that no one is above having such loathsome thoughts, which become repellent the moment they pass from the unconscious to the conscious mind. Another woman admitted that whenever she gave her baby a bath, 'crazy ideas' would filter into her mind, suggestions that she should stop supporting the baby's head so that he would 'slowly' drown, unknown, unseen.

Yûki Misae might well joke about her anxious husband constantly phoning her the next day to check 'whether everything is all right', recommending that she 'humour the child', but she breaks into a cold sweat whenever she remembers how close she was to taking her child's life. In fact she dares not even think about what she would have done had her husband not been there. Filled with remorse she is also filled with compassion for all those lonely women unable to prevent that desperate act because there was no one there. 'Those driven to kill their children', she explains, 'are no worse than me. They are ordinary women, exhausted from lack of sleep, who have reached the end of their tethers. Indeed', she adds, 'are we not each one of us potential criminals?'

This account is reminiscent of a passage from Adrienne Rich's book *Of Woman Born*, which recalls the rage and murderous fantasies experienced by her fellow poets who met in 1975 to sign a petition protesting against the way the press had handled the case of a mother of eight. This woman had suffered from depression since the birth of her second child, and had just decapitated the two youngest. 'Each of the women poets in the room,' writes Adrienne Rich, 'yes, each of those mothers could identify with her.'[26]

From thought to deed

While some mothers call the baby help line at the first sign of trouble ('He cries so much I could suffocate him. I was about to do it one day, when gripped by panic, I stopped mid-gesture. What do you advise me to do?') others had already acted before asking for help. As for example in the following case:

In reaction to her daughter's rebellious stage, 26-year-old Mrs A threw her to the ground in a fit of rage. This resulted in the child needing three stitches to her forehead. Unable to tell her husband what she had done she picked up the phone and called the help line.

Until her daughter was 4 years and 4 months old, she called twenty-eight times to complain that the child was unbearably rebellious. Instead of putting her toys away she would constantly throw them on the floor. She had practically forced a neighbour into giving her a cake but would spit out whatever she had in her mouth, only ever eating what she liked.[27] She was a cheeky, wild and dishonest child who bullied her friends – she was tempted to keep her locked up at home – or she would complain that since the child had started going to playschool she had become unruly and argued with her father, who settled any conflict by clouting her repeatedly. She did admit that she scolded her for a trifle, that she could not bear it when five or six of her little friends came round to play, but more especially – and worst of all – that she did not find her 'lovable'.

This woman's attitude expresses her general exasperation and impatience at seeing her daughter take charge of herself, a phenomenon which is usually referred to as *matenai ikuji*, which could be described as an 'urgent' type of childcare.

Feeling herself to be rejected by her mother, the little girl seems to take devious pleasure in provoking her, who is quite obviously under a lot of strain. The tension rises, the father becomes involved and has no hesitation in resorting to corporal punishment. Aggressive at home, the child behaves in the same way with other children and rapidly becomes anti-social and incapable of adapting to group life.

The cry from the heart comes at the end of the phone call when the mother at last removes her mask when she says: 'I want to be cosseted too!', an admission which precedes a plea loaded with significance: 'I would so much like my husband to cosset me!'[28] This desperate appeal exposes the feeling of moral abandon with which these women struggle, made all the more lonely since they are not supported by their cold and distant husbands.

Baby or husband help line?

The baby help line receives numerous calls which relate to the indifference of husbands. For example:

As a musician my husband is never home. I am always alone with my child. It is the nights he cries that I dread the most. Once, in an excess of rage, I beat my child. That day, no matter how much I begged my husband to stay, telling him I was at the end of my tether, he still went fishing. I was on the verge of despair.

Every Sunday my husband goes off and plays tennis. He has the gall to tell me that as I never read and have no interest in sport, we have no more to say to one another. As I am always too exhausted to get up in the morning I went to the doctor who gave me something to take. My husband threw the medicines in the bin saying that it was not good to become dependent on drugs.

My husband is no sooner home at half past six than he throws himself into his studies. I'm fed up with looking after two children and doing all the housework. My only consolation is to stuff my face with cakes. The children are draining me. I want to die.

What is so obvious in all these cases is what Christiane Olivier calls 'the drama of never having been cosseted'.[29] On top of this is the desire to have a more meaningful husband–wife relationship. Concerning the latter, it seems that women have evolved more quickly than men who, culturally speaking, still do not consider it 'virile' to display any affection for their wife once they are married, *a fortiori* once they have had their children.[30] And so the 'kind husband' rapidly reverts to his former behaviour pattern by becoming the *breadwinner* and by taking refuge behind a certain indifference or coldness at a time when wives, unlike their uncomplaining mothers, are becoming less predisposed to doing everything themselves – without ever a word of acknowledgement or encouragement from their husbands.

Golf widows (abandoned by their husbands who go off for a round of golf every Sunday with friends or colleagues) have replaced what could be called tennis or fishing widows. There is also the national scourge created by *tanshinfuninsha*, and those who, though physically present, are absorbed by studies, newspapers or television, which makes them just as inaccessible to those around them.[31] Their physical or mental absence means that they are often far from realizing the drama their wives are going through at home until a crisis point is reached. Here is an example, reported in *Asahi* on 10 February 1991, which could be entitled 'The more I feel like beating my husband the more I beat my kids':

Mrs B, 29-year-old a mother of three, of whom the oldest is 5, met her husband at work.[32] Even though they went out together a lot before they got married, she suddenly found that she had to assume absolute and sole responsibility for everything. Her husband, whose philosophy was that once you'd caught the fish there was no point in feeding it, never took her out again. By temperament a stout-hearted and ambitious woman, she was not the sort of person to become depressed. She was more the hysterical type.

The domestic rows soon intensified, with her husband telling her repeatedly that she should shut up and just get on and 'enjoy herself' with her children while he 'slaved away' to ensure they had enough to live on. She would reply that she was perfectly capable of working and would be more than happy to change places with him.

Her husband became progressively more egotistical, never thinking twice about playing mah-jong or drinking into the early hours. His Sundays were gradually taken over either in playing golf or going on trips in the car with colleagues. Young women even began to phone him at home. Mrs B was growing impatient. Unable to take it out on her husband who was drinking heavily to escape their domestic problems, she got into the habit of unloading her frustration on the children. That was how she ended up injuring the oldest with a ruler and how the youngest of eighteen months suffered a fractured leg as a result of being thrown to the ground. It was the neighbours who finally alerted the police. A specialist diagnosed that she had had a nervous breakdown which had degenerated into hysteria because, unable to take her aggression out on her husband, she had turned on the children. During therapy sessions it emerged that, in order to punish him, she had even considered taking her own life and that of her husband's favourite daughter.[33]

This particular drama is sadly typical of the indifference of men, too often partisans of *self-help* and over-preoccupied with their own personal well-being to offer their wives the support they need.

Women are no longer willing to tolerate such selfish behaviour which consists of wanting a wife and children while deliberately refusing to help out. Women are dissatisfied with being told that they enjoy a comfortable life with 'three meals a day and an afternoon nap'.[34] However, this situation is unlikely to be resolved: 37.4 per cent of fathers interviewed replied that they had no regular daily contact with their children.[35]

A survey carried out by the baby help line revealed that the most vulnerable women were not only those who felt bitter towards their husbands but also those were considered to be 'nervous', perfectionists or unable to keep housework to a minimum (see pp. 19–24). However, it showed that women not upset by their children crying or who did the minimum of housework were those best equipped to deal 'calmly' with the situation.

Please teach me to love him

Women do admit the inadmissible, namely that they do not find their children lovable – a euphemism to express their difficulty to grow attached to them. In a study on the history of childhood since 1600,[36] the anthropologists Hara Hiroko and Minagawa Meiko observed behaviour patterns which they had come across in those mothers who sometimes admitted to finding their children unlovable.[37]

Here is an extreme example of a 34-year-old mother of four (three girls aged 8, 4 and 2 and a boy of 6) recorded during a call to the battered child help line:

> Although I have four children, however hard I try, I find it impossible to love the third one. The other three are adorable, but this one is wilful, idle and has given me nothing but grief. She is a fussy eater, which has the effect of exasperating me, and I cannot help but beat or kick her. She is covered in bumps and bruises and I have several times had to take her to the hospital with fractures. As I am in the habit of telling the doctor that she has had a fall, he commented one day how it was unusual for a child of her age to have so many falls. Once, when I asked my sister to look after her, she realized just how awful she was and understood why I couldn't bear her. At this moment in time, she is glued to the television from where she keeps giving me dirty looks. She always looks at me like that. I know she hates me. I can't stand her any more! Hurry up and do something![38]

This mother's inability to love her daughter would no doubt be regarded by specialists as symptomatic of a premature birth where the mother did not have the opportunity to bond with her hospitalized child immediately after delivery. Doubtless this mother (who was herself beaten by her mother) is also caught in the trap of subconsciously repeating a pattern which has thrust her into a vicious circle from which she is unable to escape without help. The problem is aggravated by the fact that her husband – who would actually be the best person to help her – admits that he does not know how to handle the child either and that he does not find her lovable. Rejected by both her parents, the child ends up becoming her brother and sisters' favourite scapegoat.

Here is another example of a mother who wonders whether her daughter could be a battered child.

> My child is such a dawdler that I am always scolding her. When I beat her she cries and then I ask her to forgive me. And yet I cannot stop myself from starting again. I just don't find her lovable.
>
> If anyone knew what I did they wouldn't believe it. I take everything I do very seriously and have been elected to the chair of the Parent–Teacher Association (PTA) of her school. Mothers even come to ask my advice on childrearing matters. I always iron my daughter's uniform myself; she goes to a private school. Although she is old enough to do things for herself I can't hold back from hitting her when I see her idling instead of getting changed.
>
> When I confided in my husband that I found her clumsy and difficult to love, he replied that he loved her as she was and that she was 'a good little girl'. Am I being nasty? Am I abusing her? I am always calm and collected when I am out but back home I get carried away and beat her. Am I a child batterer?

This case is reminiscent of the woman obsessed with tidiness (see pp. 19–20). The fact that she is well educated (and had read several childcare books) and her daughter is privately educated, from primary level up, places her in a privileged social class. Always impeccable, she is searching for the approval of others and lives in fear of being criticized for the way her daughter is being educated. This example illustrates the psychiatrist Saito Satoru's theory when he said, during a symposium in January 1993, that although the battering of children was nowhere near as bad as in the United States, Japan was different from other countries inasmuch as abuse took place in respectable households that were thought to be beyond reproach (see Chapter 8, n. 12).

When this mother admitted her inability to find her daughter lovable, she was told that no child was perfect and that it was quite normal for parents to feel they would like to hit their children. Nevertheless she was advised to accept her daughter as she was: after all it is quite normal for a child of her age to dawdle. She was also told that since there was no miracle formula for bringing up children, she could start by no longer examining her daughter under the microscope, for if she continued to do this, she would always find something to criticize. It would be better if she trained herself to shut her eyes to certain things.

She was also advised to try and accept her daughter's rhythm without trying to force her, for even though some children are not able to dress themselves from an early age, they all get there in the end. 'Go on! You mustn't jeopardize your child's future over a trifle and you must also allow yourself the right not to be perfect', we threw in as a final piece of advice.

The *kyôku mama* is exhausted[39]

In this climate of rigid conformity and extreme competitiveness, it should come as no surprise that mothers have lost their way. Here is the case of a 29-year-old mother with a 4-year-old son and a 2-year-old daughter, who despairs of ever teaching her oldest the *hiragana* 'he's so slow and always has his head in the clouds'.[40] When she heard that the primary school curriculum was quite demanding, she felt obliged to enrol him in pre-school classes.

'Only yesterday,' she explained over the telephone,

I was endeavouring to teach him to read the *hiragana*, but he just wasn't interested. Thinking about it again this morning, I was so cross I slapped his face. While he was crying, I asked him if he would prefer to go to playschool. He replied that he would. He must be happier there than here with me.

This woman is homing in on the differences she observes between her son and his little friends. She reproaches him among other things for not being boisterous enough, and finds it convenient to blame the institutions – playschools or crèches – which encourage competition in a place she is excluded from, by bombarding mothers with conflicting information. For this playgroup, having warned mothers against 'comparing' their child to others, pins up in the hall the height and weight of each child, relating it to what it should be at a particular age. 'I had never realized how small Satoko was,' sighed a mother who would not otherwise have worried.

This last example shows that the mother found her child 'lovable' until she enrolled him at playschool and that this would once more be the case if she decided to keep him at home.

Victims of the maternal instinct myth

A survey carried out in 1980 in the town of Osaka discovered the frustration felt by the mothers interviewed. The study covered a period of six years, that is until the children started primary school. During this period 10–19 per cent of them replied seven times in succession that the years they found the most frustrating were those six years covered by the study. 'Those were the women the most likely to suffer from childrearing neurosis', Harada Masafumi, who headed the inquiry, explained.

In an interview in the economic journal *Nikkei* (14 May 1991), the director of Tokyo's Centre for the Welfare of Children stated that the number of mothers who admit they do not love their children is not as small as might be supposed.

They belong in fact to a generation of women who were promised a more important role in society. And so quite naturally they claim the right to live their lives. The time spent looking after their children is regarded these days as a hindrance. All they see is the negative aspects of the task which is why there is a growing number of them who say that they are unable to love them.

In the opinion of psychologist Misawa Naoko this is the price that has been paid for having been spoilt and never thwarted. 'How could young women not feel frustrated when from one day to the next they find themselves caught in a situation where they have to sacrifice themselves totally to their child?' she adds.

The report in question reveals that 40 per cent of mothers interviewed had never looked after a child before their own, 16 per cent had never even touched one in their lives.

Naitô Kazumi, associate professor at the University of Shôwa, accuses society of being responsible for the fact that women find it difficult to love their children; they are, she says, victims of the maternal love myth according to which all normal women should 'spontaneously' feel love for their children and take pleasure in looking after them.[41] Those who do not feel love are therefore quick to accuse themselves of being abnormal, in other words they ultimately feel guilty of infamy.

Harada Masafumi, Head of the Public Health Department, explains:

And yet maternal love is not an instinct, it is something which gradually develops as you bring up your children. And in a way, a mother who has never had the opportunity to look after small children should realize that it is quite normal not to experience this love she expects to feel.

The director of the Centre for the Welfare of Children reiterates that the husband is best placed to help his wife out of this deadlock. She adds: 'All it takes, sometimes, is something very small, like going shopping with her. It is so important for her not to feel trapped by her role as a mother and not to find the experience hell on earth.'

Although society continues to value a child's upbringing, it is undeniable that an increasing number of women regard the time they spend bringing them up as completely wasted. The law recently passed on maternity leave is proof of the importance placed on a child's education by country and industry, and if women who say they cannot love their children are generally considered to be freakish and/or abnormal, it is essential not to overlook the social and family distortions reflected in this attitude.

THE MISERY OF A BROKEN CAREER

Mrs A, after four years of study, spent five years working in publicity and then was excluded from professional circles when she became pregnant. She told the baby help line that her husband opposed her continuing to work because she had reached the right age (about 27 or 28) to have a child. Filled with regret at having to break her career and feeling herself to be the victim of her husband's decision, she did not find her child 'lovable'. Childcare was an overwhelming experience and the fact that she never had a minute to herself to read a book or the newspaper was positively frustrating. She found the task irksome and exasperating and whenever the child refused his feed she admitted to feeling tempted to throw the bottle to the ground.

She would like to return to work but finding a place in a neighbourhood crèche is no easy task. As a minimum, she is impatient to enrol in one of the courses arranged by the local authority which has child-minding facilities.

Society, her family, her husband and even her employer (who had previously given her the impression that she was indispensable) joined forces to coerce this woman into the only role suitable for someone who has reached the right age to become a mother. Furthermore they told her that whatever she had done before, now her real job was beginning.

Ah! If only I'd known!

The sensation of entrapment is so succinctly expressed by Yûichi's mother when she describes being reprimanded in no uncertain terms by her father for being outside leaning on the balcony while her son is screaming his head off in his playpen:

> My father said that since I had nothing else to do it would be an idea if I took better care of my son. . . . That was precisely my major error . . . I opened my mouth to tell him so but decided to

keep quiet as I knew he wouldn't understand. Yes, my great mistake had been to give up my job for now my job amounted to looking after my child. There are no doubt many women who find this kind of life satisfying but I should have realized that others are able to cope with their children only because they can recharge their batteries at work.[42]

This grandfather, who (like so many others) thinks that it is not worth having children if you are going to leave them in a crèche, is by far the most difficult to convince that a child 'dumped' in a crèche is not going to end up like a child brought up in a children's home.

Nevertheless the social stigma attached to 'crèche-children' remains very real: they are children to be pitied because their mothers have abandoned them in order to satisfy their personal and selfish ambitions. Economic reasons are not seriously taken into consideration because, with a bit of good will and organization, there is always some way of coping.

This is also why crèche-children but not children who go to nursery school are stigmatized, for the latter are sent there with the (praise-worthy) aim of being socialized. It is significant that nursery schools come under the Ministry of Education whereas crèches are the responsibility of the Ministry of Health.

If some women are horrified by the restrictions this archaic vision evokes, the majority force themselves to adapt to what is on offer, and, having got over the initial feelings of depression, resign themselves to applying the very Japanese principle according to which you will be rewarded as long as you apply yourself wholeheartedly, as the section which follows the preceding account shows:

Fortunately, however nerve-racking the initial stages of raising children might be, they do grow up and however tiresome they might seem it doesn't last forever. As the months go by, it gradually becomes easier and you begin to find your child endearing. I was always so busy and exhausted those first two months that the time just flew by but as soon as I began to have some time to myself I was at last able to find him 'lovable'. I suddenly couldn't get over how sweet he was. . . . Little things, like seeing him yawn or drink a lot of milk was enough to make me feel fulfilled.[43]

Though this account is confirmation to all women that their labours will bear fruit, many swear that they would not want to go through it again which no doubt explains why 'bellies go on strike' when it comes to having the second child. Government pleas to do so, fall on deaf ears.

BULIMIA AND ANOREXIA

Distressed at being deprived of their jobs and at having the decision to have a child foisted on them, some women develop eating disorders when food is seen to be as effective a recompense as a cry for help.

I never dared raise my hand against my children as my mother-in-law had warned me that if I did they could end up brain damaged. The oldest (aged 6) was just about bearable but the youngest of 4 annoys me. I refrain from hitting him for fear that he'll go and tell his grandmother but when they're in bed at night I get into such a state when I think about it that I end up emptying the fridge by way of comfort. When I think that before I had them I weighed 50 kilos but that now I weigh 70 kilos. Sometimes I think I'll end up bursting.[44]

Mrs K, a 24-year-old university graduate, had already suffered from bouts of depression before she got married. She would often call the baby help line to say that she could not cope with her 8-month-old son and to admit at the same time that she could not be bothered to eat. She would force herself to cook dinner but could not find the strength to eat any of it. There was nothing she fancied eating and the thought of inflicting this on her child distressed her. Although the help line strongly advised her to seek specialized medical help she called back ten days later to ask how she should wean her child and to say that she felt better. A month later she called again to say that she had stopped eating altogether. The help line endeavoured to put her in touch with a woman who had had a similar experience.

She suffers from mood swings . . . and calls again when her second child is seven months old to report that her appetite is back. She does admit however to getting very depressed, and that when she hits rock bottom she cannot even find the strength to dial the number, just as, the first time she called, she did not have the strength to speak.[45]

Although bulimia is the most immediate form of oral gratification there is, it is both dangerous and demoralizing through its pathological nature as well as through later repercussions. The second caller's eating block seems to have been further aggravated by her refusal to seek medical advice.

The existence of anorexia and bulimia since the mid-1970s inspired Dr Saitô Satoru to set up therapy groups.[46] The therapy offered to bulimics was inspired by 'Compulsive Eaters Anonymous' developed in the United States, where this disorder is taken as seriously as alcoholism and anorexia.

The price of a friendly ear

An article in the magazine *Como* (September 1991) describes the isolation in which mothers of young children find themselves drives them to turn to baby-sitting agencies in search of a lady's companion. Mrs Katô (aged 43) who works for a baby-sitting agency described the situation thus:

> Couples used to call upon our services so that either they could go out or their children would find it easier when they went to the crèche. These days an increasing number of housebound women invite us to go round to listen to them or to help them solve their problems. At a hourly rate of 1,200 yen (minimum three hours) they don't get much change out of 5,000 yen once you have added the cost of transport and the other extras which depend on the number of children, the time of day (the rate goes up after 5 p.m.), and so on.
>
> The terms are that the woman should not be absent for longer than one hour out of the three – if that – and that when she returns she should bring cakes and then lay them out on a plate. Sometimes she will share something that she bought because it was on offer. 'What do you think of these towels? Not bad for the price, are they? I got two for 500 yen! Here, let me give you one as a present!

As a result of her husband being transferred, one of Mrs Katô's clients, a 29-year-old woman with a child of 3, had recently been precipitated into a *shataku* (accommodation provided by the husband's company). She knew no one and had no contact with the neighbours, not even her mother-in-law who happened to live in the same town. Twice a month she called upon the services of a *regular* (a baby-sitter who comes on a set date). 'During the three hours I am there, she seldom goes out, not even for an hour. The rest of the time, we chat. Last time I was there, she even asked me to stay another hour, just to continue'.

'The role of the baby-sitter', explains Mrs Katô, 'is above all to remain a yes man. Whatever the faults of the woman employing you, the golden rule is never to say anything that is likely to upset her, even if and especially if she is obviously bringing up her child the wrong way'.

When she visits some of the families, Mrs Katô is sometimes surprised to see the grandmother living there, like the young woman whose mother-in-law lives on the ground floor and yet who calls upon the services of a baby-sitter so that she can supposedly tidy the cupboards.

A perfectionist in everything she does, all she achieves in three hours is to make *o-nigiri* in the microwave and lay out the washing.[47] She doesn't even touch the famous cupboards, any more than she puts her nose outside, claiming that her 2-year-old daughter would be upset if she saw her mother going out. Since she doesn't leave her for so much as a single minute, I have to admit that I sometimes wonder what I'm doing there. However this doesn't prevent her from calling upon my services another five times in succession!

Her husband, a *salaryman* in the prime of life, is never there, he is either away on a business trip or working overtime. He therefore relies on her to take absolute responsibility for their daughter and the housework. It is not that she does not get on with her mother-in-law but the baby-sitter would class her as a 'timid mother' which she defines thus:

Aged between 20 and 29 they usually have just the one child aged between 2 and 3. The husband is a busy man and always away, so he is never home for dinner. They have very few friends in the neighbourhood and very little contact with other mothers all the time that their child is not old enough to go to playschool. They hardly ever see their mothers-in-law and no one ever phones them. They shun eye contact and questions the sitter might ask. Any replies are brief and they seldom speak, since they obviously have no desire to get involved in a conversation. They go in and out without warning, sometimes without even ringing at the door. Rather than go to the trouble of finding friends in the neighbourhood they prefer to pay someone to come, who will sustain them with their presence or listen to them in their *kakekomi dera*.[48] Is solitude the price that the wives of salaried men have to pay for this newly acquired economic prosperity?

2 Why have children?

LATER AND LATER MARRIAGES

Some say that social pressure to get married is less strong than it used to be and that celibacy is now a much more acceptable state. Pejorative terms such as 'old maid' and 'on the shelf' have been replaced by more neutral terms such as 'unmarried'[1] or 'anti-marriage'.[2]

In a country which probably holds the world record for marriages (95 per cent), these statements need to be put into perspective.[3] Although the ideal age to get married has been deferred, society is suspicious if men or women are not married by the time they reach the age considered to be propitious: 28 for a man, 25 for a woman. The reasons for this can be found in the importance accorded this institution since marriage is thought to make a man stable and well balanced and bring happiness to women.[4] Half the young women interviewed by the Recruit Centre replied that they wished to marry between the age of 25 and 27, while 16.4 per cent said they would prefer to put it off until they were between 30 and 34, which proves that the trend for later marriages (*bankonka*) is far from being general.

Without rejecting it out of hand, it can be ascertained that there are those who wish to defer getting married (for as long as possible). As for the parents, they would appear to be in no hurry to see their children leave home.

With free board, lodging and laundry service all the time they are still at home; wealthy, as they can do what they like with their salary; the *office ladies* (OLs), also referred to as the 'unmarried aristocrats', are moreover not willing to sacrifice these privileges immediately (see Figure 2.1). Their salary is regarded as pocket money and is targeted by the manufacturers of luxury items, such as perfume, furs, jewellery and accessories, as well as catering, tourist and service industries. The

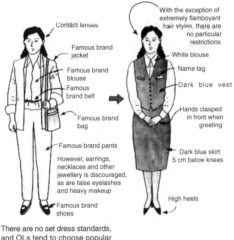

'OL' is a term coined in Japan referring to all ladies employed in office situations. OL are generally hired between the ages of 18 and 22 and leave the company five to six years later to marry. Veteran female employees who go on to management positions are distinguished from OL as 'career women.'

Contact lenses

Famous brand jacket

Famous brand blouse

Famous brand belt

Famous brand bag

Famous brand pants

However, earrings, necklaces and other jewellery is discouraged, as are false eyelashes and heavy makeup

Famous brand shoes

With the exception of extremely flamboyant hair styles, there are no particular restrictions

White blouse

Name tag

Dark blue vest

Hands clasped in front when greeting

Dark blue skirt 5 cm below knees

High heels

There are no set dress standards, and OLs tend to choose popular fashions. However, wearing the same clothing two days in a row is taboo because it suggests staying out overnight.

Uniforms vary widely by the type and personality of the company. Some mass media and apparel firms have no set uniforms.

Figure 2.1 OL (Office Lady)
Source: Japan Travel Bureau, *Nihon e tokijiten* ('Salaryman in Japan'), Tokyo, 1986, p. 13

enthusiasm displayed by OLs – even while they are still studying – to travel abroad is proof that this golden era is a stage which must be lived to the full. It is the philosophy of 'take full advantage of it now' or 'it's now or never', a realistic attitude given that their honeymoon is usually the last time they go on a luxury trip.

Later marriages but marriages all the same

The term *bankonka* reflects the unattractiveness of marriage. Demographers have found that, of all the young people of the industrialized nations, the Japanese are those who are the least enthusiastic about getting married.

A 29-year-old woman interviewed in *Seikatsu Shimbun* stated: 'Thanks to advances in medical science, it is now possible to have your first child at 35. I don't want to end up resentful because I had to sacrifice my young lifestyle for a bunch of kids. I want to enjoy my youth before I start a family!'[5] This view is echoed by many young people who want to put off getting married for as long as possible (see pp. 146–7 and 165).

And yet, bearing in mind that by the age of 40, 95 per cent of Japanese are married, it is highly unlikely that the demographers' fears that these 'unmarried aristocrats' will become 'mature aristocrats' are justified.

Free love is a long way from being accepted into Japanese mores and is still fairly rare. Tsushima Yûko is the daughter of the well-known writer Dazai Osamu; her autobiography portrays, with poignant realism, the drama of a single mother and reveals the general lack of tolerance of behaviour still considered to be 'deviant' in the mid-1990s.[6]

As Tanaka Kimiko writes, the physiognomy of marriage has come a long way in recent years, for with more than half of young women now marrying for love, they are no more prepared to live with the in-laws than they are prepared to heed a cantankerous mother-in-law and, if they do share the same roof, it is now the old who make themselves scarce so as not to disturb the young.[7] 'If the famous demands of young women in the 1960s: "A car, a house but not the old girl!", have become obsolete,' she adds, 'it's because they have come true.'[8]

And yet, if it is the trend for young women to put off the evil day for as long as possible, this 'moratorium' cannot go beyond the age of 30, an age which still represents, in the collective consciousness, the cut-off point after which it is still regarded as abnormal to have a child. If the new generation feigns a certain tolerance towards childless couples,[9] it must be recognized that in Japan marriage is still strongly synonymous with procreation.[10] Japanese women in the mid-1990s have their first child a little later than in the mid-1980s, but it will not be delayed for long: in 71.3 per cent of cases the first child is born within less than two years.[11] Although the majority of young Japanese women are keen to have a child, it is difficult to know whether motherhood is the result of a deliberate choice or whether it is the result of outside pressure – from society or from the family.[12]

Weary of having to justify each *mada*? ('not yet?') from members of the family or the neighbours, a young woman often ends up, intentionally or not, becoming ensnared. As for the 'kind husband' who has become weary of playing this role, he is often happy to see, without too many regrets, a more traditional pattern of behaviour being established. He will now be able to throw himself into his work for the right reason, without ever again having to pretend to be involved in jobs he did not regard as his true vocation.

Whether it is planned or not, the arrival of the child terminates the young woman's career for she vanishes discreetly from the workforce. The relief can be reciprocal, as the young woman has had her fill of the 'joys' of Japanese working life and employers need to 'turnover' their staff. However, the following account is indicative of the state of mind in which many young women enter motherhood.

Never had I cried so much as when I was told of my 'gratifying' condition

Yûki Misae writes that one of her friends told her one day that she had never cried so much as on the day the doctor confirmed her fears.

I began to shed all the tears I possessed. Mistaking them for tears of joy, the gynaecologist beamed at me, he didn't realize that they were tears of vexation! I felt as though I had no future, that my life had stopped once and for all. I was so desperate, so angry that I couldn't stop crying. You at least can understand how I felt.[13]

THE MEANING OF PROCREATION

A study carried out in 1981 by the prime minister's office, on why people have children reveals just how much traditional values were inherent in the act of giving life. The replies fall equally into two categories: that of social responsibility ('in order to contribute to the future of society') and that of family ('to strengthen family bonds'). Though Thailand or Korea might appear to be more traditional, Japan is not exempt, and it is interesting to note that while in France the primary motivation for having a child these days is 'just to enjoy childrearing', in Japan it is out of a sense of duty to society or the family rather than a pleasure in its own right.

A no-profit investment

To put it bluntly, children have become a high-priced commodity. Not only are they expensive to bring into the world and to bring up, but the cost of educating them obliges parents to limit their number of offspring to two. Competition is such that it is practically impossible to raise properly more than two children on the average Japanese budget. In fact the cost is so high (it has been calculated to be between 27.9 million and 35.7 million yen per child depending on whether the child attends public or private schools) that it is advisable to start putting money aside from the moment of conception.[14]

Although most parents consider that their investment in their children's education could be regarded as a distribution of the family's inheritance prior to their death, they have no guarantee that their children will look after them in their old age. Although it is fashionable to say that one wants to cope without having to depend on anyone else, surveys have shown that expectations remain high and that the desire to live with one's children tends to increase with age.

An international study carried out by the Japanese in six countries (United States, Great Britain, France, Thailand, Korea and Japan) showed that Japanese parents do not want to be dependent on their children, but they nevertheless hope to live with them one day.[15] This applies particularly after the death of the grandfather (whose life expectancy has gone up to 75.9 years of age); his wife will on average survive by six years.[16]

Another study has shown that while 6.6 per cent of women questioned anticipated financial assistance from their children, 62.1 per cent of them hoped that their daughter, daughter-in-law or son would look after them.[17] The expectations to be looked after in old age (a duty which traditionally fell on the elder son and/or his wife) have switched to the daughter among the 20–40 age group. The recent trend to have a daughter rather than a son, particularly in the case of an only child, also indirectly confirms this, 'for a daughter will never let you down'.[18] Though these might never be expressed, it would seem that expectations with regard to one's children, or rather one's daughters, are as strong as ever – the apparent detachment unsuccessfully conceals the anxiety that parents feel with regard to these expectations.

Though the reality of a £10,000 a year fully comprehensive old-age pension can no longer be guaranteed, the '3Ks' on the other hand can! This is a specially 'designed' label which defines children as being *kitsui* (tiresome), *kitanai* (filthy) and *kiken* (dangerous), thus implying that the investment of both time and money has become a risky business.[19]

In their best-selling autobiographies, which were made into a film in 1990, Itoh Hiromi and Nishi Masahiko frankly confirm that they are indeed tiresome and filthy.[20] Apart from the material considerations, it is also the responsibilities attached to the status of mother which make more than one woman hesitate before taking that important step.[21] In addition to being obliged to make of them 'someone worthwhile' – this will be judged by how prestigious the school, university and company they enter are – there is also the compulsion to raise them to be well-balanced and happy individuals otherwise the mother will never be forgiven.

The syndrome of the 'good child'

In an interview given to the journal *Croissant* (August 1990), Professor Shiomi Toshiyuki blames the falling birthrate on the competitiveness of modern society, conspicuous from the time they go to playgroup, since the majority of Japanese children can read from around the age of 3 or 4, a phenomenon unique in the world. He deplores the fact that parents are more interested in their children's achievements than their intelligence as such and goes on to say that the parents' obsession with their children's success can hamper their happiness.

A comparative study he carried out in collaboration with American academics reveals that Japanese parents want their children to be docile, well brought up and emotionally mature, which boils down to their being patient, tolerant and persevering. American parents on the other hand hope that their children will display qualities of *leadership* or that they will develop personal opinions. 'To a Japanese parent,' Shiomi proceeds, 'a *yoïko* is an obedient child who agrees to being dropped into the adult world but what American parents want is for their child to be independent and autonomous.[22] Reliant on their good relationship with their children, Japanese parents are also extremely vulnerable. Should the relationship change they will suffer a lot more than their American counterparts,' he adds, striving to explain how difficult it is for them to have more children.[23] 'Load any more stress onto them and the parents would die in harness.' The reason for the drop in the birthrate is essentially psychological but it creates a vicious circle because 'the fewer children they have the greater the expectations of the parents, and the greater their expectations the less equipped they are to take on more'.

A survey carried out by another educationist reveals that Japanese children are the hardest working and achieve the best marks, but that proportionally few children study because they are interested in their studies or 'for the pleasure of studying'. Questioned as to their motivation, half replied 'to get good marks so that I can go to a good school' and the other half replied 'because my parents compelled me to study' and/or 'to please my parents', all reasons which contrast sharply with those put forward by American or European children, for whom studying is a way of getting trained or of becoming better educated.

Although on both sides the long-term objective is the same (to succeed in life), and although in the United States the number of young people abandoning their studies is the source of great concern, the proportions are different, as Shiomi Toshiyuki quite rightly underlines, in that Japanese children are programmed to work in order to please (especially their mothers) rather than because they are personally motivated to do so. By the time they finish they are completely dependent on other people's assessment of them and this becomes synonymous with how they see themselves.[24] 'Our children spend their lives waiting for others to express their appreciation of them,' he explains, 'if they are not congratulated or if they do badly, they despise themselves and feel exceedingly isolated. Since the Japanese are extremely sensitive to the approval of others, it is particularly difficult for children to preserve a positive image of themselves disregarding the opinion of others.'[25] 'All in all', concludes Shiomi, 'Japanese children lack self-confidence and they are always anxious. And because they are hypersensitive, they run the risk of becoming neurotic. School phobia is often the first sign'.[26]

STUDY AND WORK

Another factor frequently put forward to explain the critical drop in the birthrate is that women are now seriously interested in studying. As an office supervisor solemnly explained in the course of an interview:

> The parents of young women used to think it wasn't necessary for their daughters to continue into higher education, and those who did graduate from university viewed their jobs as essentially short-term, that is to say until they got married.[27] It's a very different story today, for the better her education, the better her job prospects. Once they are financially independent they are not so keen to relinquish the reins unless they meet someone worthy of the sacrifice.[28]

This conviction which barely conceals its nostalgia for the past, has also been voiced by certain politicians, notably the Prime Minister, Hashimoto Ryûtarô, who could not hold back (in August 1990) from publicly expressing his regret at the 'huge volume' of women entering higher education which was deterring them from their principal function in life (that of procreation).

Although this assertion was castigated by feminists, there is nothing surprising about it. More recently a teacher, desperate to confide, complained that his two daughters of 34 and 38 were still unmarried. 'They are too intent on their studies'. He was genuinely distressed at having passed on to them his passion for study, and believed that he had failed to bring them up properly.

To force girls to study contains the risk that they might develop a taste for it, thus greatly reducing their chances of finding a suitable match. A professor at the University of Ochanomizu observed during a lecture he was giving at the Maison Franco-Japonaise, that admission to Tokyo University, by far the most prestigious of all, was catastrophic for the parents of one young woman, for she was limited to marrying a young man from the same university (although this is no longer the case, as numerous examples illustrate).[29]

Educating young women is not the same as educating young men

Nevertheless the average parent is still a long way from believing that their daughters need to pursue their studies as far as their sons do, for, contrary to popular opinion, fewer young women undergo a four-year degree course; 22.2 per cent of these spend two years studying in one of the 593 *tanki daigaku* (junior colleges), which are more like professional schools than universities.[30] They then find jobs such as *office ladies*, or those traditionally regarded as women's professions: childcare, nursing, midwifery and childminding. Comparing this figure to the 15.2 per cent of female students who take a four-year degree course shows how different it is for young men, 33.4 per cent of whom take a degree course while barely 1.7 per cent of them go to university for the two-year vocational course.

Japanese mothers questioned on their professional expectations for their daughters, replied that they hoped they would become home-makers, which confirms quite clearly that motherhood is considered to be a profession, if not coveted, then at least respectable and incompatible with having a career.[31] This also explains why 17.5 per cent of parents interviewed as to why they wished their daughters to study replied that it was an indispensable asset to making a good marriage.[32]

The feminist, Higuchi Keiko, challenges the myth which attributes the drop in the birthrate to women's access to higher education and to the enormous number entering the workforce. She explains: 'The real reason is that because of the way life is these days, raising children is no longer done for pleasure, and as long as the politicians deliberately persist in ignoring this essential aspect of the problem the remedy will continue to elude them.'[33]

Although working women tend to have more children than do housewives, the working day is so long that it is virtually impossible to reconcile a full-time job with motherhood.[34]

Maternity leave

In the public sector mothers working in those professions tradition-ally associated with women, such as nursing, childcare and teaching, were in 1975, thanks to pressure from their unions, granted the right to take special unpaid leave for up to a year.[35]

A new law, which came into effect on 1 April 1992, gives parents the right in theory, to claim up to a year's unpaid leave in order to care for their children.[36] Although this law is progressive as far as the personal lives of employees are concerned, one can foresee a certain laxity in its application: women already find it difficult to have the maternity leave to which they are entitled, which at present is fixed at six weeks before and eight weeks after the birth.[37] A survey carried out by the Ministry of Labour also found that barely 17.5 per cent of women who had the right to a year's maternity leave dared take it all, which shows how strong the pressure is on women not to take full advantage of their hard-won rights with complete peace of mind.[38]

Where childcare assistants who work in private crèches have no claim to these same advantages, special arrangements can always be made with their manager.[39] Although women employed by crèches managed by local government are entitled to this rare privilege, their spacing of children is markedly longer than the national aver-age. This can no doubt be attributed to the fact that they do not wish to inconvenience colleagues; the tradition of sexual discrimination continues to be rife even in all-female establishments.

Passed in 1985 to come into effect in 1986, the Equal Employment Opportunity Law (EEOL) which was supposed to give men and women equal rights in the workplace when it came to employment and promotion has not had much impact in counteracting sexual discrimination, women still have the same problems to deal with as soon as they have a child.[40] Higuchi Keiko challenges the law itself, pointing out that as long as men continue to be the sole decision makers when it comes to women's working conditions, it is absurd to expect them to work the same hours as men while they are bringing up children.

It is indeed the case that the hours which the happy few must work do not make any allowances for motherhood or for that matter married life. One of the pioneers I had the privilege of interviewing disclosed that she did up to 110 hours of overtime a month, which meant she got home between 11 p.m. and midnight, without having had any dinner.[41] It is not surprising therefore that when she got married three years later she gave in her notice.

Women who rise to positions of responsibility must also agree to being transferred as do the men, thus this law had a lukewarm reception.[42] As a former student confided: 'It's all very well to say that you agree to being transferred within Japan or abroad, it's not a difficult promise to make if you are the only one you are committing.'

Moreover it is interesting to see that being virtually compelled to give up work when women get married (officially denied by the Ministry of Labour, on account of its being illegal) has also found its way into the so-called 'non-specialized' posts, for a married couple does not have the right by law to work for the same establishment.[43] How can we speak of equality of opportunity between men and women when in this situation it is the woman and not the man who is expected to hand in her notice?

The law on equal opportunities in the workplace in fact turned out to be a pretty deception, for the pace required is such, that it cannot be sustained when you have a home to run.[44] So how could it even be contemplated if there are children involved?

Although these days Japanese women give up work with the birth of their first child rather than when they get married, marriage still remains the principal reason why young women break their careers.[45] This is partly because of the *shanai kekkon* (marriage between employees of the same company) which results in the female employee leaving the company, irrespective of her status (Figure 2.2). They are no doubt nicely thrown out without even being asked, or for that matter without even being given the chance to decide for themselves whether or not they want a career (see Chapter 1).

How I became a housewife

Here is Yûki Misae's story which is typical of the state of mind with which many young Japanese women face the prospect of motherhood (see Chapter 1, n. 7).

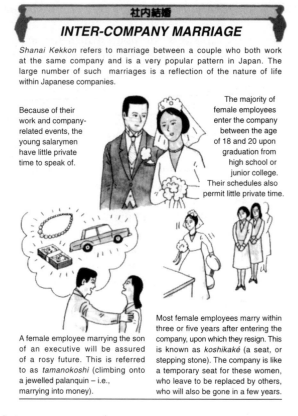

社内結婚

INTER-COMPANY MARRIAGE

Shanai Kekkon refers to marriage between a couple who both work at the same company and is a very popular pattern in Japan. The large number of such marriages is a reflection of the nature of life within Japanese companies.

Because of their work and company-related events, the young salarymen have little private time to speak of.

The majority of female employees enter the company between the age of 18 and 20 upon graduation from high school or junior college. Their schedules also permit little private time.

A female employee marrying the son of an executive will be assured of a rosy future. This is referred to as *tamanokoshi* (climbing onto a jewelled palanquin – i.e., marrying into money).

Most female employees marry within three or five years after entering the company, upon which they resign. This is known as *koshikaké* (a seat, or stepping stone). The company is like a temporary seat for these women, who leave to be replaced by others, who will also be gone in a few years.

Figure 2.2 Inter-company marriage
Source: Japan Travel Bureau, *Nihon e tokijiten* ('Salaryman in Japan'), Tokyo, 1986, p. 108

How did I choose to become a housewife? Actually it wasn't all that difficult to leave a job I had very little interest in. I was quite happy after I left, doing minor jobs that came my way which allowed me, now and then, to go to the cinema or to an introductory course on dyeing textiles.[46] Under the circumstances why not have a child a bit earlier than others do? And that is how, without having properly thought out the actual consequences of my actions, I found myself at one and the same time a mother and a housewife.

Not once did I ever entertain the idea of having a job while I was bringing up my children. Following in my mother's footsteps, I had always been of the opinion that women owed it to their children to bring them up themselves.

Superwoman? Not me! If a woman goes out to work it means that after a day at the office she then has to go home and look after the children until the following day. When you think of the skill and dexterity needed to combine the two (not to mention working twice as hard as anyone else) it was something I could never have contemplated doing.

Somewhat nonchalant by nature and determined that my life would be more cool than the national average, I decided that the best solution was to stay at home without having to rely on any one except myself.

Personally I still think that if you have very young children it is extremely hard to hold down a job. No salary could compensate for the amount of energy you would need to expend. Not to mention the problems presented by unforeseen illnesses or accidents when taking any time off is quite out of the question. As to finding anyone to help out, forget it. And I am sure that I am a long way from being able to imagine the dreadful reality of being part of a *tomokasegi* (working couple).

A public opinion survey carried out by the Prime Minister's Office found that barely 18 per cent of young women questioned wished to continue working once they had children, which would indicate that to young Japanese women, having children and looking after them are still highly commendable. Regardless of the level of education, this trend has barely fluctuated. These responses which contrast radically with those collected in five other countries, reveal that women still adhere very much to the concept of *seiyakuwari bungyôkan*, or the division of labour between the sexes where the man is the *breadwinner* and the woman is the guardian of the home.

Resigning after marriage or the birth of the first child

Although in the 1990s women might appear to work for much longer than they used to, it is probably the rapidity with which they return to work after the birth or births of their child or children which creates this impression rather than any actual increase in the number of those who choose not to give up their careers. If working women represent 37.9 per cent of the total workforce, around 60 per cent of them return to work once they reach the age of 35 which coincides with the time their second child begins primary school;[47] in the absence of a second child they are expected to re-join the workforce much earlier.

As soon as they leave their first job they lose all the benefits to which they were entitled and have no choice but to go back part-time (*pâto*), to be paid an hourly rate of 700 yen.[48]

As women have, in theory at least, had the choice since 1986 of taking the royal road (as it is called) or jobs classed as 'general', to choose the second is an unquestionable admission that the family will take priority over work.[49]

Since they work on average for between three and seven years, depending on when they leave secondary education (at 18), the two-year degree course (at 20) or the four-year one (at 22), employers consider that there is very little point in investing in their training. The tasks they are entrusted with are not seen as contributing to an increase in productivity or for that matter to an improvement in quality, and any increase in salary to which they should in theory be entitled based on length of service is not, in the employer's eyes, justified; since it would cost less to have a younger and just as efficient workforce carrying out these tasks (Figure 2.3). There is the tacit understanding on the part of employers that their female workers will leave of their own accord either when they marry or when they are expecting their first child which means they can never be accused of discrimination against women as theirs is a policy de facto based on age.

Young women usually leave their jobs when they are supposed to. However, there can be a problem if they remain unmarried for too long or if they are 'tempted', as some women are, to stay on anyway. It is common practice to apply (politely) for permission to 'borrow the names' of those who show no sign of getting married and then it is not long before these appear on the list of leavers. Few argue as this might result in intolerable sexist pressure being brought to bear.[50] Some employers justify this by pointing out that as women are not as strong or as intelligent as men, the housework they are obliged to do once they are married would waste the energy they are expected to display in the workplace.[51] Neither are they reluctant to challenge a law which compels them to give their female employees maternity leave and other benefits when they become pregnant, since these are extra costs difficult to justify because a corresponding drop in their efficiency is to be expected.

Those who have dared challenge the law

Cook and Hayashi have collected information on five legal cases brought by women who were forced to resign because they had got

OL の仕事
OL'S DUTIES

Whereas OL were once involved primarily in serving tea and making copies, the times are changing. With the passage of equal opportunity legislation in Japan, the number of women in pursuit of specialized jobs (and not general office work) is on the rise. There are more female managers than ever before, and this trend is certainly expected to continue.

Newly hired female employees are put in charge of serving tea and coffee (*ochakumi*). However, with more and more companies installing automatic coffeemakers, there is less and less need for such *ochakumi*.

Copy-making is another job once assigned solely to OL. But the advance in office automation has enabled anyone to make large volumes of copies in a flash. As a result, this monotonous chore is no longer assigned exclusively to OL.

Some OL only enter a company to kill time until they marry and will resign as soon as they find their man. This trend is also changing, however, and many OL stay on the job even after taking their nuptial vows.

Many women devote themselves to professional careers. To them, maintaining harmony between home and office can be a major burden.

OLs perform many roles within the office as well

OL are fond of gossiping in the kitchen area. These exchanges often reveal extremely accurate views of the work attitudes of co-workers and relations with superiors, providing an important source of in-house information.

Experienced OL are able to size up a visitor's importance immediately and know whether or not to serve tea. New employees can learn much about customers from observing such women in action.

OL can also teach new recruits much about how to generate fluid human relations and other fundamentals in becoming an accomplished salaryman.

OL who marry salarymen serve to further cement the bonds between the company and its employees.

Figure 2.3 OL's duties
Source: Japan Travel Bureau, *Nihon e tokijiten* ('Salaryman in Japan'), Tokyo, 1986, pp. 82–3

married or had a baby, where the temporary workforce was dismissed or they were dismissed at the age of 30 or a different age on the grounds of gender.[52]

Suzuki Setsuko is quoted by Cook and Hayashi as one of the first to have had the courage to bring a case against her employer, Sumitomo Cement, by accusing the company of forcing her to give up her job when she got married. When first employed by Sumitomo Cement in July 1960, she had been required to sign an agreement that she would leave the company by the time she was 35 at the latest, for it was company policy that all members of the female workforce should be automatically dismissed once they were married. She married in December 1963 and should have resigned in March of the following year, the official line being that this was 'for economic reasons', although the condition had appeared in her contract of employment.

In October 1964, she took her employer to court for unfair dismissal, under the rules of the Constitution. Pointing out that marriage did not amount to grounds for dismissal, she asked that this practice be abolished for it was, moreover, an attack on a person's individual liberty. Sumitomo Cement's response was that in 1958 the decision was taken, with a view to assisting the male workforce, to employ a temporary (until marriage) female workforce to take charge of serving tea, photocopying, shopping and possibly the cleaning of the offices.

The Court recognized that forcing a woman to leave her job when she got married was tantamount to sexual discrimination forbidden by articles 14 and 24 of the Constitution. Although the Working Code does not explicitly forbid this form of discrimination and allows that a 'reasonable' distinction be made in working conditions according to gender: the basic principles of the legislation which exists to safeguard workers' rights, however, forbade any form of sexual discrimination.

The argument according to which a woman's efficiency decreases once she is married was also contested. The affair came to an abrupt end, with Suzuki agreeing to leave the company after the birth of her second child. The system remained unaffected by the case.[53] However, a precedent had been set and OLs began to appear in the press and even on television with reports of the contracts they had been forced to sign. Other cases followed and the courts had to recognize that to force a woman to give up her job when she got married was contrary to article 90 of the Civil Code which was opposed to the undermining of social order.[54]

Cook and Hayashi quite rightly stressed the vulnerability of women dismissed when they got married. They quoted the case brought against the Furukawa Mining Company by six female employees settled in 1977, where the Court returned the unsatisfactory verdict that 'there was no evidence that these women had been dismissed as a result of their change of status'.

As to Suenami Kazumi, employed by the Mitsui Naval Construction Company, as her maternity leave was drawing to a close, she received a letter from her employers requesting that she hand in her notice. When she refused, her employer pointed out that he was quite within his rights to terminate her contract after the birth of her first child, in view of the agreement concluded with the entire female workforce which 'committed them to leave after marriage'. A 'special clause' allowed those who applied, to remain on a contractual basis (renewable each year) until the birth of the first child.

Braving her employers, Suenami returned to work and was then dismissed. Mitsui underlined the ancillary nature of the tasks given the female workforce (filing documents, answering the telephone), which warranted a different treatment. But it was generally recognized that 'it was a well-known fact' that the efficiency of the said employees degenerated once they were married. The Osaka Magistrate Court merely ruled that this was no more than an infringement of the Working Code.

Although it is generally believed that in Japan the lifetime employment system prevails this principle is in no way guaranteed, especially for women involved in ancillary jobs, who have always been regarded as temporary workers whose contracts are either renewed or not, without any need for further explanation.[55]

PRIORITIES NEVER DISCUSSED

All the female students I questioned saw their calm assurance weaken the moment the subject of children was brought up. A survey carried out by the Recruit Center found that the desire to look after their children personally remained extremely strong (88.5 per cent and 96.8 per cent respectively depending on whether they had completed a further four or two years of study) and that the only alternative which would leave them relatively free of guilt would be to entrust them to a member of the family, preferably their mothers. They seemed to share the generally held view that it is 'absolutely' or 'fairly' essential for the mother to devote herself to the education of her children while they are still very young (the view of 85.3 per cent of women questioned from across the age range).[56]

A mother heavily involved in her job is the favourite theme of television soaps where the classic scenario is as follows: a mother decides to work part-time but she gradually becomes more engrossed in her job. Her mother-in-law grows tired and begins to complain of the burden of the extra work and responsibility. The husband becomes touchy and the children start developing problems (they become nervous, violent, anorexic, neglect their studies or run away). The woman is very successful in her job which takes up more and more of her time. The tension increases and erupts. The husband becomes violent or unfaithful and soon begins to drown his sorrows in alcohol, finding solace in the company of sympathetic young colleagues or bar hostesses who cosset him. The couple's relationship is in a bad way and the mother-in-law only makes matters worse by siding with her son against her daughter-in-law or by trying to turn her grandchildren against their mother. The heroine finds she has to choose between her job and her family. The 'choice' is made. Contrite, she returns home and takes over. It is the return of the prodigal daughter. All's well that ends well.

Problems experienced by working women

Research into the pros and cons of being a working mother revealed that those questioned (whether or not they had children) listed the main advantages as 'a change of scene', 'friends' and 'a purpose in life', while 52 per cent of Japanese men considered that a job 'inconvenienced' the rest of the family.[57] The most frequent disadvantages were: not enough time to do the housework properly (31 per cent), the mother's physical and nervous exhaustion (23 per cent) and inadequate care of the children (20 per cent) whose educational failures are still regarded as being the result of having a working mother. As to the children, they complained that their mothers were always exhausted, that they ate dinner too late (traditionally dinner is eaten around 6 p.m.), that they were 'forced' to do household chores, that there was never enough time to communicate or that they were bored when she was not there (even though they appreciate as they get older the added autonomy and independence).[58]

An international study examining the problems experienced by working mothers, found that it was much worse for the Japanese due to the shortage of domestic help.[59] This is proof indeed of the lack of progress made when it comes to changing the attitude, even of those concerned, that housework and childcare is a woman's prerogative. The study shows that they can expect no help from their husbands.[60]

A correct presumption: Japanese husbands in fact hold – as do their children moreover – the prize for non-participation.[61]

As for the small percentage of women who persisted in reconciling full-time work with motherhood, only 5.3 per cent said they intended to continue work even if it meant using the services of an outsider; of the female students questioned, 16.1 per cent still saw the only possible solution to be to call upon 'another member of the family'.[62] The option of outside assistance is only ever considered once the child has reached the age of 3 which shows the extent of the impact of the slogan: *Sansai made, haha no tede!* ('In mother's hands up to the age of three!' – see Chapter 4), a slogan which echoes the old adage: *Mitsugo no tamashii, hyaku made* (literally: 'The soul of a child of 3 will remain constant for life', in other words: 'What is not achieved by the age of 3 never will be').

The chief problem which full-time working mothers continue to face is lack of flexibility of most crèches. Although in theory the majority of crèches open at 7.30 a.m., childcarers rarely begin before 8.45 a.m. because they themselves are often mothers with small children. They are therefore reliant on other crèches where they have to drop their children off first. Though crèches close at 6 p.m. the rule is that children must be collected between 4 p.m. and 4.30 p.m. depending on the circumstances, the remaining time is seen as being ninety minutes' (or two hours') grace, which parents can take if they have special permission to do so. This is vindicated if their respective working hours are incompatible; a privilege not available however to the very young (aged 6 to 24 months) whose mothers are obliged to collect them by 4.30 p.m. at the latest. Anyone familiar with the length of time it takes to travel in Japan from the workplace to home (in Tokyo 180 minutes is the average return journey but it is the same story in many large towns) not to mention the ritual of overtime, will understand that it is virtually impossible for a mother to aspire to dealing with a full-time career as well, unless grandmother is at home or nearby and willing, without making too much fuss (which is becoming extremely rare), to collect the child from the crèche and provide care until the parents return.

If a career woman's success used to be attributed to the fact that there was a grandmother at home, a growing number of them are now leaving the professions.

At the beginning of the 1980s if a woman wanted to secure a place for her child in a crèche, she had to prove that there was a valid reason (for example the grandfather being in hospital) why the grandmother could not come to the house to look after her grandchildren.

Nowadays it is the grandmothers who take the children to the crèche. They have been heard to complain bitterly that they find this very restricting. Having at last got rid of their own children, they want to enjoy their new-found freedom – some would like to knit, others to do calligraphy or aikido, while others would like time to go swimming (one was learning to swim at the age of 70). And, if they cannot go on world tours, they all dream of a short break in a thermal resort with friends of their own age. The importance of gateball (a Japanese version of croquet) in the lives of elderly people is also a factor: play begins at 7.30 every morning, so it would be difficult to find the time to take the children to the crèche.

To see this lack of enthusiasm on the part of grandmothers is to wonder whether they have any right to expect their children to look after them in their old age. And yet it would seem that the expectation exists. But the question prevails and it will be interesting to see what happens. Be that as it may, there is a lot of talk these days about *kodomo no pettoka*, the way parents look upon their child as they would a domestic pet. This might be more appropriately applied to grandparents who want to enjoy their grandchildren but not too much (and when they want to) and who carefully avoid taking any responsibility for them.

This archetypal mother-in-law can be found in the famous cartoon *Akkochan*: she is too absorbed in the calligraphy of poems to take care of her two grandchildren even though she lives under the same roof as her daughter-in-law and takes full advantage of all her 'labour'.

The cost of childcare

In the report on the falling birthrate I came across the case of a woman who worked full-time in a foreign advertising agency who declared that over ten years the cost of childcare for her two children had come to 10 million yen (excluding food, clothes and schooling). In view of this it is understandable that many women question the real benefits of a double income.

> My mother looked after the oldest. Up at five on a Monday morning she just had the time to jump on the train and arrive in time for me to leave for work at half past seven. She would stay until Friday and then go home for the weekend. She did this for nine months. The tenth month she broke down.

So she enrolled her child in a crèche. She placed an advertisement in the paper to find a minder to look after her child between 5 and

7.30 in the evening, offering to pay 700 yen an hour when the average rate at the time was between 400 and 450 yen. She wanted a regular minder who lived nearby. However, this was met with very little enthusiasm on the part of the applicants who preferred to look after children in their homes.[63]

'Very soon there were only three or four left. I chose the one who promised that whatever happened she would never let me down!' Despite paying 50,000 yen a month she still had to prepare the evening meal the day before so that her employee could give the children her undivided attention.[64]

> Frankly I was exhausted, both my two children cried a lot at night and until the second was a year old, I suffered from chronic sleep deprivation. I sometimes wonder how I ever managed. However, physically and financially speaking, the most difficult period was the one prior to the second at last being able to go to a crèche when he was 1.[65] I put an advert in the paper to find a childminder, but as this involved working more than twelve hours at a stretch I didn't get more than five or six replies. I chose the person who lived the nearest to us. However as she lived in the opposite direction from the crèche the oldest attended, I was obliged to do a three way journey by taxi morning and evening between the childminder, crèche and home. I ended up spending 2,000 yen a day on taxis, which added 20,000 to 40,000 yen a month to the cost of childcare. I don't have to tell you that that was most of my salary gone! Over a period of ten years the cost of having my children looked after came to 10 million yen. Consequently, the prospect of paying school fees no longer fills me with dread!

Which is just as well for there are still some hard times ahead. The *Asahi* newspaper estimated (3 March 1995) that the cost was between 27.9 million and 35.7 million yen, depending on whether the child attended public or private schools, until university graduation at age 22.

The above account is not unusual, thus the majority of women break their careers when their first child is born. What is the point of insisting on paying a minder, they sigh, who won't do the job as well. This is confirmed by the two great dips in the statistical curve (which has remained fairly constant over the years) which illustrate the pattern of female employment in Japan; the only noticeable evolution is the point at which they return to work: nowadays mothers do not wait until the youngest goes to school before returning to paid employment, which no doubt explains their impatience to see their child become more independent. Although polls indicate that women's intentions are to re-enter the workforce at 35 at the most, few women have the patience to wait that long.[66]

What if I work part-time?[67]

The economy is supported by a part-time workforce which is coming back onto the market and which is all the more advantageous since it is inexpensive. How much the government colludes in this is unclear because women who earn 120,000 yen a month are exempt from paying tax and do not pay national insurance since they are covered by their husbands' contributions.

The main advantages of part-time work are that women can do the housework while they are looking after the children, that they can adjust their hours to suit, and that they are not in positions of responsibility which gives them peace of mind. However, in a country where a full-time job often implies that the employees work over forty hours a week, part-time work very often corresponds to what would be considered as full-time in France. An intermediary stage exists, referred to as *full pâto*,[68] which denotes full-time work on part-time pay.

And what about the father in all this?

While the majority of fathers agree that their wives can work as long as it does not affect their personal comfort, society generally ridicules the 'kind' or 'accommodating' man who helps his wife. Men who collect their children from the crèche run the risk of being thought idle (how many normal men could spare the time for this kind of contingency?). But if society (in a country where some salarymen face the prospect of dying from overwork) is inclined to deem a man who is supportive as not a man, it should be recognized that their working conditions rarely allow them to help their wives (Figure 2.4). Competition and the exploitation of the workforce means that an over-evident father is in fact running the risk of being penalized in the race for promotion (*shusse banare*),[69] or of actually finding that he has been shunted into the sidings with the *madogiwazoku* (employees excluded from the group are symbolically placed 'near the windows').[70]

Apart from the fact that employers are unwilling to bend the rules, it should be recognized that men much more than women still cling to the principle that husband and wife should have 'clearly' defined

サラリーマンの休日
A SALARYMAN'S HOLIDAYS

While Japanese salarymen are indeed hard workers, they naturally do have holidays. Nevertheless, they often find it very difficult to use this free time for private pursuits

Work
Holidays are often considered one phase of work. An extremely common example is golf with company superiors or clients.

Home
Because salarymen have little chance for daily contact with their families, they often feel compelled to go to amusement parks or the zoo on holidays. This is known as 'family service' (*kazoku sabisu*) in Japan.

Recuperation
Exhausted by their work, many salarymen use holidays to catch up on sleep. Such holidays will consist largely of napping, television and meals.

Figuring eight days off per month, a common pattern might be:

The first Saturday of the month: Play golf with superior.

The first Sunday: Exhausted from golf, sleep all day.

The second Saturday: Report to the company for holiday work.

The Second Sunday: Take family to the local zoo.

The third Saturday: Day trip with co-workers.

The third Sunday: Company baseball tournament.

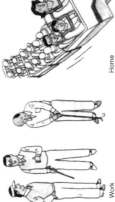

The fourth Saturday: Attend a co-worker's wedding.

The fourth Sunday: Entertain client during a round of golf.

Figure 2.4 A salaryman's holidays
Source: Japan Travel Bureau, *Nihon e tokijiten* ('Salaryman in Japan'), Tokyo, 1986, pp. 112–13

roles. If studies have revealed that a man's contribution to the house-work is not necessarily in proportion to the number of hours his wife works, when it come to caring for the children, the tasks he is willing to do are those which are the most satisfying: giving them a bath, or rather sharing a bath with them,[71] playing games, and so on.[72] As we have seen, working conditions being what they are, very few women expect any more from their spouses.

The few calls for the greater involvement of fathers in their children's education which appeared in the mid-1970s have had very little success. For example a campaign in Yokohama granted fathers special 'childcare hours' to give them the opportunity to be with their children; in the town of Koganeï an organization suggested that if fathers participated in the education of their children this would result in the 'transformation of men through childcare'.

If these movements have all more or less miscarried, this is because their aims reflected the wishes of women rather than those of men, as can be seen in the literature which was produced within the frame-work of the *danseiron boom* (the boom in men's studies).[73] Another initiative which came to nothing was that of the Tanashi Town Hall which gave fathers permission to take an hour off work so that they could be more involved in caring for their children. So far no father has taken up this offer.

Though some fathers have exceeded the adoption of the law on parental leave (see Chapter 8), it is questionable what its overall influence on men's behaviour will be.

3 Fathers

My father is a *salaryman*
Who spends his life in crowded trains
With his head bowed down, and
His toes trampled on
Oh! How busy he is!
At the weekend he does as he pleases . . .
My daddy is N⁰ 1 in Japan!
(Song accompanying credits of
Osomatsu-kun's cartoons)

DO JAPANESE FATHERS LOVE THEIR CHILDREN?

A detailed examination of a government survey carried out on Japanese fathers provokes this disturbing question: 'Do Japanese fathers love their children?'[1]

Without hesitating, Itoh Hiromi's husband Nishi Masahiko,[2] replies: 'No, the majority of Japanese men do not love their children.'

Some will say that they love them in their own way, which cannot be denied. But be that as it may, the findings of this survey are very worrying when we take into account that 37.4 per cent of fathers questioned admitted that they had no contact at all with their children during the working week (see Chapter 1), any contact they had being around thirty-six minutes a day. A lack of oral communication (54.4 per cent of fathers communicate daily with their children),[3] and a general lack of interest in their children's lives and pursuits,[4] are reflected in the admission that they do not make good companions because they do not have the time or because they must devote themselves to their jobs (Figures 3.1 and 3.2).[5]

Japanese fathers have very little time to converse with their children on a daily basis; indeed 16.1 per cent of them have no contact

Coined in Japan, the term 'salaryman' refers to all male office employees, white-collar workers and those who hold administrative posts in private companies.

70 per cent of university graduates become *salarymen*

Shirt: white or single colour

Newspaper: sport and finance

Short hair, side parting: *shichi-san* style ($\frac{3}{10}$ on one side and $\frac{7}{10}$ on the other side)

Tie: an indispensable part of the uniform

Briefcase containing essential tools of the trade: notebook and electronic calculator

Average annual salary in 1984: approx. 5 million yen

Pocket money around 50,000 yen a month (to include cost of week-day lunches in restaurant)

Figure 3.1 Mr Average Salaryman
Source: Japan Travel Bureau, *Regard sur le Japon* ('A look at Japan'), Tokyo, 1985, p. 118

at all with them on public holidays. Even at the weekend there is no desire to make up for lost time. One hour and thirty-two minutes per week, including Sunday, seems to be all they can offer their children.[6] Japanese fathers do not appear to have any great desire to communicate with their children.

The way they fill their leisure time suggests that they avoid rather than look for contact with their children. Although the answers indicate that they spend their days off with the family, it is interesting to see how important their outside interests are in their lives (54.7 per cent) compared to hobbies centred on the home (35.9 per cent), though with the latter the father might just as well not be there for the hobbies do not involve the other members of the household (38.3 per cent). The majority of Japanese men have the extraordinary ability of living as though nobody else was there.

サラリーマンの外観

THE SALARYMAN'S APPEARANCE

'Salaryman' is a word coined in Japan, used to refer to all white-collar workers who receive a salary. In a very real sense, salarymen are the driving force behind Japan's phenomenal postwar economic growth.

Metal frame, square-rimmed glasses.

Short hair parted at the side in the 'seven-three' style.

Dark red necktie with diagonal stripes.

White or light blue cutter shirt.

In the coat pocket: Address/schedule book, wallet, name card case, commuter train pass, etc

Dark blue or grey suit.

Black leather shoes.

Figure 3.2 The salaryman's appearance
Source: Japan Travel Bureau, *Nihon e tokijiten* ('Salaryman in Japan'), Tokyo, 1986, p. 10

The family 'service'

One Japanese journalist was amazed when reviewing the findings of a survey carried out on German fathers in which these had replied without hesitation that their favourite hobby was their family. When a Japanese father does spend time with his family, it is in effect referred as a 'service', as in the expression *kazoku sâbisu* (the family service). Consequently, if he accompanies his family to the restaurant, it is a favour he occasionally grants and certainly not a prerogative.

The use of the term *pettoka* (the regarding of a child as a domestic pet) is very relevant when it comes to fathers. However, it does not prevent them from having a guilty conscience, for 80 per cent of them replied that they thought about their children 'a lot'.[7]

FATHERS WERE NOT ALWAYS LIKE THIS

The anthropologist Hara Hiroko has explained that Japanese fathers used to help out a lot when it came to looking after the children.[8] They would change their nappies, put them to bed and let them stroke their chests, to make them think it was their mother's breast.[9] Moreover, the childcare manuals written in the Edo period (1603–1867) were actually addressed to men. They described for example how the husband should give the baby milk if the mother was in short supply. Hara Hiroko concludes:

> In exchange for this, their wives probably toiled like slaves. However this does not diminish the fact that they did behave like this, even if it was the prerogative of the farming communities. And so you can see that the grandfathers of today's students were far more involved in the raising of their own children than their sons have ever been in theirs.

Conversely the children of the *bushi* (Samurai) were the mother's responsibility until it was the father's turn to take charge of the boys' moral upbringing, introducing them to literature and the martial arts.

It was in the Meiji period that the doctrine of *ryôsaikembô* first appeared (the paragon of the good wife and wise mother) establishing clearly defined husband–wife roles.[10] When the industrialization of Japan saw the emergence of a new middle class determined to mould itself on the *bushi*, the husband–wife role models were established, confirming the man as the *breadwinner* and the woman as the guardian of the home (Figure 3.3). And this is why fathers these days have virtually nothing to do with their children's education.[11]

Hara Hiroko states that it is probably because childcare has become the exclusive domain of the mother that no significant or properly documented study on fathers has ever been done. It is perhaps significant therefore that the folklorist Yanagita Kunio, who spoke at length on the subject of mothers in *Imo no chikara*, has never written anything on the subject of fathers, and that the few studies that do exist deal mostly with their absence.[12]

Neither do Hara and Wagatsuma fail to notice that Miyamoto Tsuneichi, one of the few ethnologists to have written on fathers, did no more than acknowledge that the bond uniting them to their children was weak.[13] Even when the father is there, his children never seem to develop the kind of nostalgia for him that they have for their mother.[14]

As in many countries, communication traditionally took place

サラリーマンの妻
A SALARYMAN'S WIFE

When there are no children, or the children are grown and out on their own, the lifestyle of a salaryman's wife is extremely monotonous. She will encounter many dangers and temptations as a result.

6:30 a.m.
The wife begins to fix her husband breakfast.

Midnight
The tired hubby arrives home, and she lays out his bedding.

During the day, she sits frozen before the TV.

When there are no children in the home, the wife's work consists of these two basic chores. Between these jobs, she has little to do and spends much of her time alone, inside the home.

She will take many approaches to break the monotony.

One of the most common solutions is to join housewives with the same dilemma for shopping or for gab sessions over tea.

Outgoing wives play tennis, golf or other active sports. Such behavior was rarely seen up to just a few years ago.

One of the wife's duties is to shuttle the kids back and forth to school by car or on foot.

When the husband is rarely at home, the wife and children take off to amusement parks or movies together.

Figure 3.3 A salaryman's wife
Source: Japan Travel Bureau, *Nihon e tokijiten* ('Salaryman in Japan'), Tokyo, 1986, pp. 110–11

when the father passed on a craft or technical knowledge to the son, with the addition of advice of an ethical nature (the attitude a man should adopt in relation to work, and so on). The need to abandon the family business in favour of going to work in an office or factory robbed the father of his former sources of prestige and authority, thus depriving him of the ability to communicate with his children.[15]

A society without fathers

Borrowing an expression from Paul Federn (a disciple of Freud's) Doi Takeo states that a characteristic of modern society is that it has become a fatherless society.[16] The famous psychiatrist says: 'Although historical circumstances have been quite different, it could be said that Japan has become a fatherless society since the Meiji Restoration (1868).'

Moreover the famous psychoanalyst Kawaï Hayao stresses that not only is Japan a fatherless society but also, because the father has been eliminated from the family, Japan has become the country of the 'great mother'.[17] Higuchi Keiko adds that at home the father does not exist.[18] 'And not only does he no longer exist,' she continues, 'but he no longer has a space to call his own which means that he has become a veritable intruder in his own home.'

DO YOU LOVE YOUR FATHER?

The response to this disconcerting question is somewhat neutral when compared to that of the other two countries surveyed (the United States and Germany). Only 68.6 per cent of children questioned believed that their father loved them.[19] Barely 60.1 per cent of these felt that their fathers understood them (as opposed to 90.5 per cent in the United States and 90.4 per cent in Germany) while 62.7 per cent felt that they could count on him whatever happened (as opposed to 87.3 per cent and 80 per cent respectively).[20]

Despite the lack of enthusiasm, the desire to communicate more,[21] not to worry him (91 per cent as opposed to 58.6 per cent and 87.1 per cent) as well as a wish to look after him later in life,[22] all indicate the existence of a sense of duty as well as a notion of filial piety.

In response to the question 'Would you want to be like him when you grow up?' 54.6 per cent of boys questioned (as opposed to 68.2 per cent in the United States and 51.8 per cent in Germany) replied in the affirmative, which shows that the father continues to be a model to half of them. Less than 30 per cent of girls questioned replied that they wished to marry someone like their father,[23] which suggests that they would prefer to share their lives with someone more helpful or gentle than him. The reaction of a former student illustrates this: 'My father never says a word or even stretches out his hand when we're at table, he merely points to what he wants.'

'These days fathers appear at their worst when they are at home. What kind of model do they make when they lie dozing in front of the television all day?' asks the sociologist Yamamura Yoshiaki.[24]

However imaginary the father's place might be – television is thought to be more influential than him – he does remain a symbol; although he acknowledges that his children no longer respect him, 77.5 per cent of fathers questioned nevertheless profess they are in control.[25] Similarly, while 47 per cent of children might regard their mothers as being more strict (as opposed to 23.2 per cent who said it was the father and 21.7 per cent who said both were) or more demanding (58.6 per cent as opposed to 12.3 per cent),[26] without hesitation they reply that the family revolved around the father (62.4 per cent as opposed to 10.3 per cent).[27] He is without question the one they most fear.

It is above all in his work that the father is projected as a role model. But if the amount of power the father has in the decision-making process casts a shadow on his importance, it is undeniable that he owes his continued prestige and place in the family to his economic role. Hara and Wagatsuma also say that although the father is there for only a few hours a week, he nevertheless fulfils his function of role model.[28]

In a study on the family background of delinquent children from Tokyo's working-class areas, De Vos and Wagatsuma underline the correlation which exists between the image the child has of his father (as projected by his mother) and his deviant behaviour. Whatever the father might be like, the fact that he is given his proper place in the family and that his prestige and position of authority are recognized; this would seem to be a determining factor in the behaviour of adolescents. This study also shows that even if it is the woman who wears the trousers, as long as she grants the father his place in the family when he comes home, he fulfils his function as a role model. If she criticizes him openly in front of the children, especially the son, the latter is likely to look elsewhere for a male role model, a young *yakuza* liable to lead him astray.[29]

FATHERS: ABSENTEE OR OSTRACIZED?

It is difficult to tell whether it is the men who have excluded themselves from the family or whether it is the wives who have alienated them. The answer no doubt lies halfway between the two, men finding it more practical to be elsewhere while the women have created a *modus vivendi* for themselves to offset this absence. Although the media are full of analyses of the mother–child(ren) relationship, there is no mention of the father–child(ren) relationship. This has provoked a reaction from certain groups who have challenged the exclusion of the father from the dyad and demanded in particular that he be incorporated on the health record. As a general rule, fathers usually ignore initiatives which have strong feminist undertones.

Though some do venture along to PTA meetings,[30] they unfortunately run the risk of being classed as failures of the system (can a man who takes time off work really be taken seriously?). To continue taking this minor step requires great courage. Japanese society is not one that views meetings where the sexes mix with a favourable eye and this inevitably leads to the increased discomfort of those who are otherwise motivated to do so.

During a symposium an American woman pointed out that school sports days do not even bother to address the fathers who are present.[31] 'Why do you ignore them when they do you the honour of turning up?' she protested before accusing the school of sexual discrimination against men. It is highly likely too that more than one father will hesitate before collecting his children from the crèche for fear of being thought a failure. Finding themselves in a woman's world, men certainly feel uncomfortable.[32]

As for the women, there are many who dream of a crèche where they could 'park' their husbands when they retire; given a few drinks, some will talk for hours describing what they plan to do once they have buried their husbands.[33]

As Hara and Wagatsuma emphasize, the ideal husband should have a strong constitution, never be at home but remain sympathetic to his wife and children.

Whether they like it or not, fathers have gradually become excluded from the family cocoon. As Higuchi Keiko observes, a father no longer has a corner at home which he can call his own: he is more like an intruder,[34] seen by his family as 'Giant Garbage' or, after retirement, as a 'wet dead leaf, difficult to peel off the ground'.[35] There is an expression for pensioners who are idle and demanding:

washi zoku (for *washi mo iku*, meaning 'I'll go with you'), implying that they are now a burden to their wives whom they follow around everywhere.

The recent phenomenon of the *kitaku kyôfu*, that is to say men allergic to their own homes.[36] is no doubt due to the lukewarm welcome they get from their families. The economic journal *Nikkei* (25 January 1992) describes the case of a 46-year-old businessman: brilliant, swiftly climbing the ladder of promotion, already the owner of his house, always willing to undertake foreign business trips, never objecting to being transferred alone so that his children's education would not be disrupted, this man's unwavering self-confidence crumbled the day his wife reproached him for being irresponsible, accusing him of being the cause of their 14 year old's – in his second year at secondary school – school phobia:[37] 'Sir is always too busy doing something else, unless Sir is too tired of course! It's all your fault that your son has suddenly developed a school refusal syndrome, that he is now aggressive towards me!'[38]

This came as a great shock. It is indeed true that he has been more tired of late but he put this down to age. He is forced to admit that his workload has increased. But it was for a good cause. And now he is being accused of being irresponsible and told that he is an unworthy father.

An unworthy father? He is mortified. Yes, he is always away but he has fulfilled his role as the head of household perfectly. As someone whose principle has always been that growing children should never catch anything more than a glimpse of their father's back, he cannot admit that his son has developed a school refusal syndrome.[39] His calm assurance, his self-confidence suddenly vanish. He now wonders what life is all about.

He loses interest in his job but this does not prevent him from coming home later and later. In vain he tries to make himself see reason but the moment he is near the house, he breaks into a cold sweat and suffers from palpitations. Instead he goes to a hotel, for the thought of his family gives rise to feelings of rejection. However, he realizes he cannot continue to avoid the situation forever.

All Japanese fathers run the risk of going through an identity crisis. They become so engrossed in their work that to hear themselves accused of not assuming a role for which they were not prepared, leaves them confused. The wife of the workaholic cited by *Nikkei* is no doubt right when she says he is partly to blame for their son's problem but more worrying still is the husband's employer's responsibility in all this.

The scourge of transfers

The father's absence is further aggravated by another phenomenon, transfers, which are frequent among employees aged 40–50 of the larger companies (Figure 3.4).[40] Although in theory men have the right to turn down a transfer, to implement this is to acquiesce to being shunted into the sidings.[41] In effect it is compulsory, for the company will not take personal circumstances into consideration.[42] Either the whole family moves or the father sets off alone leaving his wife in charge. The company's conscience is clear. After all, is it not prepared to finance the cost of moving the whole household? However, there are three major obstacles to such a move: in order of importance these are the children's education, the family's house (on which there may be a large mortgage) and the problem of elderly parents.

The reason most frequently given is the children's education, particularly if they are at secondary school or college; ironically it is those who have made the most sacrifices for their children who end up having the most problems with them later.[43]

The difficulties encountered by the father's absence will of course depend on the ages of the children. The loss of his company at playtime and the sadness experienced by children of pre-school age because their father is not there are the ones most often quoted. For primary school children, their absent father is unable to keep up with their studies.

But it is college students who are the most unsettled, and their predicament becomes greater depending on how long the father has been away.[44] Consequently, if he has been absent since they began their primary education the problems become extremely serious.

Above all, the parents fear the long-term effects a prolonged absence might have on the child's personality (however much the father might be perceived as being a shadow,[45] he is none the less an important figure); especially since, as a general rule fathers, even when they are present, do not follow their children's education.[46]

These transfers have many more repercussions. As well as the inevitable marital problems,[47] women worry about their husband's health, the economic burden of running two homes and the extra responsibility which falls to them.[48] As for the husbands, they complain about having to do their own housework, cooking and washing. There are several books which aim to initiate them in the art of coping with everyday life, containing recipes which are 'simple and nourishing' and little 'tips' on how to simplify their lives: for

転勤

TRANSFERS

A salaryman employed by a company with many branches will normally be transferred several times as his career advances (*Tenkin*). Where, and to what position he is assigned, is a pivotal career concern.

Promotion

Demotion

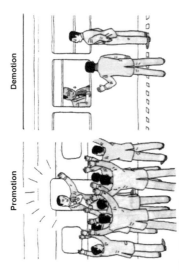

Eiten (Promotion Transfer)
Assignment to a higher position in a branch in a major city is a clear promotion. Co-workers and subordinates gather to congratulate him before he departs for his new assignment. Salarymen are naturally attracted to a superior who may be able to improve their own status in the company

Sasen (Demotion Transfer)
Assignment to a small regional branch, even in a higher position, is considered a strong sign of sasen (demotion). In this case, only a few truly close friends see him off. In principle, however, a change of assignment is considered a promotion.

• Tanshin-Funin (Solo Assignment)

Solo assignment (*tanshin-funin*) is a unique transfer format in which a salaryman is assigned to a branch office away from his family. There are various reasons for living alone, one being the focus on children in Japanese family relations and the concern that a superior education will not be attained in the prefectures. Businessmen who refuse to go on solo assignment are literally discarding their hopes of career advance.

Only on payday does the wife remember that, yes, she is still married.

The husband must do his own cooking and laundry, often a lonely and aggravating experience.

A considerate husband tries to come home on weekends, with most of his own pocket money used to pay the transportation costs.

Less considerate husbands just send home the money, creating an atmosphere which increasingly resembles divorce.

Figure 3.4 Transfers
Source: Japan Travel Bureau, *Nihon e tokijiten* ('Salaryman in Japan'), Tokyo, 1986, pp. 48–9

example they are recommended to buy a dozen sets of underwear to avoid running out.

However much the Ministry of Education reports that absence can sometimes produce a 'new balance', one cannot help but be struck by the extent to which employers encroach upon the private lives of their employees and the extent to which they are responsible for the family or marital problems the employees experiences.[49]

A placid and silent husband

A reader of the revue *Wife* paints a picture of her husband, giving an idea of the crisis threatening married couples in Japan. According to the editor the picture is typical of the average Japanese couple. Here is a slightly condensed version of the original:

> One day, I asked my husband point blank: 'If you had the opportunity, would you go on one of the organized sex tours to the Philippines or Taiwan?'
> – 'I'd be too worried about catching AIDS!'
> I found the candidness of his reply disarming. My husband is an extremely nervous man. He has an excellent reputation. At home he is quiet and considerate. He's clean and tidy and when I ask him he does the housework without making a fuss. He does the washing up and the laundry but he can't cook. He loves puzzles but I find it really exasperating that once he starts on one it's impossible to drag him away from it. I am very careful not to leave them lying around. Actually it's been a long time since I last saw him do one and he's not so keen that he'd go out and buy one. In fact my husband is a *tanshinfuninsha*. He lives alone in a home for single men where breakfast and dinner are provided.
> 'Goodness, you've put on weight again!'
> He is alluding to my fat stomach, but my husband comes home only two or three times a month. They say that when a woman puts on weight, it's because there's something missing in her life. And I am indeed twenty kilos overweight. But I can't help eating anything I can lay my hands on and since I am incapable of sticking to a diet, I do nothing about it.
> My husband comes home late on a Friday evening and stays in until the Sunday evening. He leaves after dinner wearing the suit he arrived in. He always drives back [to the train station] and I go with him. The steering wheel is sweaty from his hands but the silhouette I see in the mirror is that of a stranger. Tokyo is really

far away. I play a cassette. I prefer rock to ballads which make me feel rather melancholic.

When I collect him from the station on a Friday night I don't even put the radio on. He always drives back. 'Be careful, you're not used to driving any more. You haven't been drinking beer, have you?' He brakes hard on purpose. He smiles. Although it's just the two of us in the car, if we do speak he's never the one to start a conversation. Back home, he has a bath and then a drink while he's watching the sport on television and when he's had an *ochazuke* he plays with the cat.[50] He helps himself to another drink and then says: 'I'm bushed, I'm going to bed.'

On the Saturday morning, the children wake up all excited, shouting: 'Daddy's here!' He's still half asleep. They're forever bickering whether he's there or not, in any case he's always glued to the television. I end up shouting hysterically: 'You could at least tell them how to behave while you're here!' It's like banging my head against a brick wall. He can find nothing better to do than play with his daughter or make models with his son.

I would love to be able to talk to my husband

On a Saturday evening I always make lots of tasty dishes which he invariably eats in silence. I can't help asking him if it's good and when he doesn't reply I return to the attack: 'It's nice, isn't it?' He nods his head unable to tear himself away from the television screen. As he's always bad-tempered when he's hungry I prepare everything in advance but it's always the same story. I have to keep telling myself that after all, I am a housewife, and it is my job to do the cooking.

'The amount you drink and smoke, you shouldn't be stressed!'
– 'Right, and you don't stuff yourself silly, no?'

He's always stuck in front of the television. By midnight he's a bit tiddly and says: 'Right, I'm off to bed, then!' His head's hardly touched the *futon* [mattress rolled out on the tatamis] and the sound of his snoring echoes through the house. If I've done everything I have to do, I watch a film on television or read until late. In the end I go to bed around two in the morning. His mouth wide open like an idiot, my husband snores next to me. He's drunk on alcohol and tobacco. I turn my back on him as I hate the smell of his breath. He's so intoxicated he sleeps right through until morning.

I'm not exactly sure when it was but I do remember trying to wake him by slipping into bed with him. He turned away saying:

'Lay off! What's got into you?' I tried again four or five times but I got really upset in the end. He probably didn't even realize. All the hours of overtime he does, the travelling and the time spent away from us exhaust him. He works hard to feed his family. It's a wicked thing to say but I feel so neglected by this workaholic. I'd love to be able to communicate with him! I seldom have the opportunity to meet anyone as I'm at home all the time. In fact I wonder how I could be unfaithful to him, even supposing the opportunity were to present itself I could never cheat on them, him and the children. And yet I can't take any more, an uncommunicative husband is something I can't stand! . . .

When you've been a housewife all your life you lose interest in everything. And because I feel that my life is going nowhere, I just carry on eating anything I can lay my hands on. Housework is a never-ending chore and as the children become more independent the daily routine becomes dead boring.

What with school fees and the cost of running two homes we live from hand to mouth. Maybe I should go back to work but I'm not sure I'd be able to cope. As I've already had one major operation, I'm frightened of becoming ill again if I push myself too hard physically. Even if I don't go back to work in the foreseeable future I have to get out of this crippling daily humdrum. I'd like to get on better with my husband who finds his job and being away from us so exhausting.

The other evening when he'd just come home, I suddenly asked him: 'You never talk to me. All you ever think about is getting drunk. You just ignore me completely.' He couldn't believe it. 'So why are we together then? What's the point of being married? Yes, why the hell did you marry me? – Isn't it great to have children, no? Children . . . ', he repeated without conviction.

I'm fed up to the back teeth with the children! When I think how they have always been my sole reason for living, how I have dedicated myself body and soul to them, washing mountains of clothes, forever cooking tasty dishes. And now my husband is working himself to death so that he can feed, clothe and educate them. He who always wanted to have children no doubt feels he has fulfilled his obligations to them. Actually I think he's a good father, he really does adore them.

He doesn't play around, doesn't cheat on me and never complains about how much I spend. . . . So why am I constantly dissatisfied? I would like him to speak to me more. I would so much like him to acknowledge my existence!

'Do you by hate me?'

– 'Please, at your age . . . '

I don't think he does hate me and I don't hate him either.[51] . . . Given the fact that we chose to journey through life together, and that we shall all be called away by death some day, I'd like to be able to share my thoughts with him while we're still on this earth. . . .

When the children were still small he'd come home in the middle of the night completely drunk without ever having phoned. One day when I was berating him, he said that rather than moaning I should go out and work instead of him. The expression on his face was terrible. He made me realize how precarious my position was for I don't have a penny to call my own.

His leitmotif is: 'I'm relying on you for the children!' But whereas as I am beginning to stand up to him, he is retreating into silence.

'I'm starving, there's nothing to eat,' says my son.

– 'I thought you had cookery lessons at school? Couldn't you sometimes show me what you've learned to do?'

– 'Come off it! That's your job isn't it?'

– 'What d'you mean that's my job?'

– 'Stop twittering and get me something to eat quickly!'

To think that he used to be so sweet! These days he's positively odious. He's grown up in an atmosphere where there were 'clearly defined husband–wife roles', I'd like him to be different but it's difficult when I'm only a housewife myself. I do realize however, that if he is going to change then it's up to me. At the moment I am putting a lot of thought into how I can take myself in hand. Seriously, if this stony silence of my husband's is going to continue then I have no choice but to change myself![52]

While reading this you cannot help but remember that these days parents can expect to spend another twenty to thirty years together once the children have left home. That is why the art of getting on together as husband and wife has become a favourite topic at conferences.

'Women devote their entire lives to their children,' states the writer Okifuji Noriko in the newspaper *Nikkei* (28 January 1992), 'when husband and wife suddenly find themselves alone they soon realize they no longer have anything in common, that they have nothing left to say to one another and that each bores the other to death. The women begin to wonder at that point whether there's any advantage in staying with such a partner.'

Okifuji knows what she is talking about from having gone through a crisis in her own life when her children left home. The prospect of having to spend the rest of her life with her husband drove her to a nervous breakdown.

A government survey found that what women considered as important in old age were, first, health (51 per cent), second, good relations with their partner (19 per cent), third, better family relationships (11 per cent).[53] It is interesting to see how the various responses were influenced according to gender. While women in their thirties (21 per cent) emphasized the importance of 'good relations with their partner', by the time they were in their sixties the importance drops to 10 per cent. Men value the relationship more once they are over 30, their appreciation growing from 19 per cent to 26 per cent between the age of 30 and 60.

'Having lost all their illusions by then, women realize they need to rely on their health more than on their husbands,' Okifuji declares, wondering at the same time how these gentlemen would react if they knew that their wives regarded going on a trip with them as being more of a chore than a pleasure. More than one woman confided: 'When I do travel for example, I would at least like to be able to divest myself of my role as a wife, however if I have to go with him, I end up on my knees.'

This situation can be linked to the increased number of divorces among pensioners: women generally put up with the situation until the last child is married so as to avoid damaging their prospects. Others wait until their husbands are on a pension before they disappear so that they can claim half for loyal and reliable service.[54] This situation has been the subject of many television serials; *Fûfû* in 1978 was one of the first and most popular of these: the heroine cannot stand being alone with her husband any longer and blackmails one of her sons, by threatening to commit suicide, into taking her into his home. Then for a while she moves in with her sister who is already looking after their mother. She eventually comes to the conclusion that cohabitation is not always the best solution. In the end she decides she will try to understand the man she regards as a stranger whom she finds again on a pilgrimage to the battlefields he had formerly fought in as a *kamikaze*.

4 The ten commandments of the good mother

The various theories fostered by paediatricians are presented in the form of this oppressive Decalogue, with a view to illustrating more effectively their part in the Japanese reluctance to have children.

THOU SHALT BOND WITH THY FOETUS (TAIKYÔ)

Originating in China with the earliest signs of its existence going back over two thousand years, *taikyô* was a collection of maxims advocating that a pregnant woman should endeavour to avoid all stress. For example she should never watch a house-fire for fear that her child would be born with a strawberry birthmark.

Kobayashi Noboru, Thomas Verny and Brazelton's translator, is without a doubt the paediatrician who, at the present time, is the most often associated with *taikyô*.[1] He owes his following to the television programme where he 'proved' with the help of an ultrasound scan that the stress experienced by the mother who comes to request an abortion causes foetal distress. He did this by drawing the viewers' attention to the immobility of the foetus, 'curled up, as if terrified', and then went on to show how after the woman had changed her mind the foetus relaxed and began to move around 'happily' again. The impact of the programme was such that Kobayashi Noboru was hailed grand master of *taikyô*. According to him, the 'programme' of preparing for motherhood begins at the start of the pregnancy: the hormone of love secreted by the pregnant woman will bring out her feelings of maternal love and subsequently help her find her child 'lovable' once he or she is born.

Because the umbilical cord is a steady communicator of the mother's emotions, Kobayashi emphasizes that foetuses are particularly vulnerable to the mother's stress which can cause them to sink into depression or even drive them to suicide (*sic*). This explains miscarriages and stillbirths.

While Kobayashi Noboru believes the mother should feel maternal as soon as she is pregnant, Natsuyama Eichi is of the opinion that she must be initiated in *taikyô* the moment she decides to have a child even before she is pregnant.[2] As for Oshima Kiyoshi, he makes this an obligatory rule for any woman who is sexually active. Taking into consideration the fact that a woman is already three months pregnant when she goes for a pregnancy test,[3] he advises all women who are likely to be so, not to expose themselves to unnecessary radiation and not to take any medication, especially headaches and flu remedies.[4]

Oshima Kiyoshi maintains that mothers used to live in symbiosis with their embryo, a *sine qua non* condition to bring a normal pregnancy to term. Like Kobayashi Noboru, he states that the symbiotic link or bonding between mother and child takes place before birth: during the gestation period. The ultrasound scan is a magic moment and all mothers – without exception – weep with joy, an emotion transmitted to the foetus which immediately sets into motion the process of attachment. He declares, moreover, that when the mother weeps for joy, the foetus begins to move in a 'rhythmic' and 'spirited' way, thus concluding that it is the mother's duty to develop the foetus' emotional life by showering him or her with all her love.[5]

In addition to a stress-free existence, it is of course necessary to lead a healthy life and eat a balanced diet; Oshima therefore strongly recommends three highly nutritious foods and forbids three others – eggs, milk and soya – since these are considered to be allergens.[6]

Before tackling the effects of stress on the embryo, the high priests of *taikyô* endeavour to persuade the future mother that 'the foetus is a person' who sucks, swallows, suckles, smells, tastes, sleeps, urinates, listens, registers and who sometimes even has erections. He is hungry, prefers certain positions, cannot tolerate others, experiences cold, fear, the desire to live or die, in other words he has his own private life while remaining dependent on his mother. And when the activities of the latter are not to his liking, he will kick her fairly hard in order to communicate this to her. He might well feel sleepy whereas his mother is wide awake or he might be feeling playful just when she is trying hard to get herself off to the land of dreams.

If stress should be banned, Oshima adds, it is because it causes a rift between the mother and her *in utero* child, thus destroying the symbiotic link which was uniting them. And if by some tragedy the symbiosis is destroyed, this can result in the foetus feeling unwanted, indeed 'expelled' from his mother's womb. This can result in premature delivery, miscarriage or intra-uterine death: disguised suicides, according to Dr Oshima where the umbilical cord is sometimes squashed 'as though to impede the flow of oxygen'.[7]

It is also to spare the foetus that he is opposed to the child's sex being divulged since there is the risk of the mother's disappointment reaching the child.

Apart from *in utero* suicides, Oshima Kiyoshi warns his readers (with the backing of charts) that women who are stressed are more likely to give birth to homosexuals. Based on work done in Germany by Dr Dormer, who links stress brought on by the Second World War to the increase in the number of homosexuals (70 in 100,000 of whom were born between 1944 and 1945 as opposed to 50 in 100,000 born in 1942–3 or 1946–7), Oshima comes to the conclusion that the foetus' 'masculinity' or 'femininity' is determined *in utero*.[8] Oshima advises expectant mothers to lead a 'natural' life until the sixth month of pregnancy if they want to have a baby who is truly masculine, since maternal stress can impede hormonal secretions.

Not only is the foetus exposed to the mother's emotions but also stress can have a particularly damaging effect on the development of the brain, not to mention physical development, especially after the first three months.

THOU SHALT LOVINGLY DEVELOP THY FOETUS' IQ

'Tell me what you're thinking and how you live and I will tell you what your foetus' IQ is.' This could be the message from Kobayashi Noboru or Oshima Kiyoshi since they highlight the 'unlimited' power of these together with the mother's contribution to the successful development of his synapsis. Oshima explains,

> Every day the foetus produces 50 to 60 million brain cells which are not renewed once the child is born.[9] Bearing in mind that the brain is formed during the foetal period, it is our duty to encourage the production of cells, indeed to stimulate it.

As the development of the brain is determined by stimuli received, anything not done during this decisive period is irreversible.[10] Its uniform development is therefore one of the commandments of the *taikyô*, since the essential will be done *in utero*.[11] Oshima then goes on to say that it is the mother who moulds her child's IQ and that the sound cerebral development of the foetus is, according to him, directly linked to emotions experienced by the mother. The recipe is simple: all the latter has to do is lead a pleasant and harmonious life, contemplate beautiful objects, listen to lovely music or speak to the child in her womb in a 'melodious' voice which remains the principal bearer of her tenderness.[12]

There are innumerable books dealing with the development of the brain in children,[13] but Ibuka Masaru, chairman of Sony and founder of the Early Development Association, is certainly accepted as a leading authority. The author of a number of books on this subject,[14] he carried out, in collaboration with a team of medical experts, a series of experiments which consisted of making the foetuses 'listen to' *haïkus*,[15] for up to six minutes three times a day. Another programme consisted of reading newborn babies poetry and fairy tales in French over a period of six months in order to see if that would give them perfect pronunciation in that language later in life. Although, as the master himself even admitted, the results are not conclusive, babies who had 'listened' to *haïkus* in their mother's womb 'did show a reaction' after birth, as revealed by their heartbeat.[16]

Even more intensive than the Sony method is the Ishii-Doman method which states quite openly (while remaining indifferent to the racist overtones of the treatise) that a Japanese child has an average IQ of 111, whereas a white child will have one of 100 and a black child 90.[17] This high score is attributed to having to learn Chinese characters, which are said to stimulate the synapsis. Although there is no reference to this in the method, based on this logic Chinese children should have an astronomical IQ if it is to be measured against the number of characters used.

Having observed the difficulty that first year infants have to assimilate the 80 characters on the programme, Ishii regrets that the first few years of a child's life are not put to better use with the child beginning to learn early. In fact he believes that a baby is capable of assimilating up to 600 characters during the first six months of life, with the so-called genius period being somewhere between 0 and 2 years of age. On the assumption that a 5 year old is capable of assimilating 2,000 characters, Ishii's method, over a five-year period, covers the first nine years of the school curriculum, in other words, what is generally attained by the end of secondary school around the age of 15.

The appeal of the method is understandable given the impressive number of characters which need to be memorized, for an Ishii-Doman baby who keeps up the pace will have achieved the same standard as a school leaver by the time he or she enters the first year infants. The only disadvantage of this miraculous method; which also claims to develop the child's artistic sensitivity through the memorizing of *haïkus*, is that it costs a mere 240,000 yen (1987 rate) a sum which covers the cards used in the first stage of the learning process and the equipment needed to use them and to record other languages.

Sixteen times more expensive than the Sony method, its advantage is that it teaches a total of 2,000 characters (as opposed to Sony's 60 cards) presented as a 'deliberated' progression, the early learning of English being a highly recommended option. The only thing the method does not explain is how to motivate such young children on a daily basis, without alienating them.[18]

If listening to soothing music opens up the foetus' brain it is because the foetus is a music lover. Domestic rows are therefore prohibited for fear of producing an anxious child, for the mother's hysterical voice could raise his blood pressure, and even go so far as to make him anaemic.[19] Also the author of a work on *taikyô* through music, Oshima Kiyoshi strongly recommends Mozart and Vivaldi.[20]

Kobayashi Noboru has no hesitation in mentioning in passing, that Menuhin and Rubinstein remembered melodies heard *in utero*.[21] He also recommends Suzuki's famous method which offers a boxed collection of ten cassettes to 'develop the foetus' genius'[22]. As for Oshima, who illustrates the cover of his CD with a close-up of Kobayashi Noboru's book, he begins by presenting pieces by Mozart, Saint-Saëns, and so on. The second phase is devoted to the soothing sound of water while the last claims to plug the foetus' brain into alpha waves. Oshima also recommends a cassette entitled *Taikyô – akachan to no sutekina communication* ('Education *in utero* – invaluable communication with your baby', Walkman Books) which includes pieces by Bach, Handel, Debussy, Saint-Saëns and Chopin, as well as a CD which is a compilation of pieces by Mozart and Saint-Saëns, entitled *Maternity Classics*.

There are countless numbers of cassettes and CDs destined to stimulate the foetus.[23] It is difficult to know how to chose from the twenty lullabies from around the world (destined to be memorized *in utero*),[24] a symphony of birds or insects with orchestral accompaniment,[25] instrumental music cleverly superimposed onto *in utero* sounds,[26] or melodies which promise to give him beautiful dreams,[27] or to wake him gently,[28] to soothe him,[29] or to plug his brain into alpha waves.[30]

THOU SHALT GIVE BIRTH IN PAIN

In Japan the most difficult path is always the most favourable and labour is no exception to this rule. Mothers are therefore not spared from being told of all the risks they would be exposing their unborn child to if they requested an epidural (which very few hospitals in fact administer), it being understood that pain has a value *per se*, inasmuch as it is supposed to create the bonding between mother and child. This is also the basis of Kobayashi Noboru's philosophy: he considers that a woman who has suffered to bring her child into the world cannot avoid 'finding him lovable'.[31] This was also the response I was given when, after having given birth (in pain of course), I asked a nurse why acupuncture as an analgesic was not automatically practised in Japan.

During a symposium a woman said that she had no regrets at having suffered so much when she was in labour because it was from this ordeal that she had drawn the necessary strength and love to give her (7-year-old) child the seat she was being offered on a train (*sic*).[32]

Also a partisan of 'natural' childbirth, Oshima Kiyoshi justifies his position because it is essential not to damage the newly born child's brain. He insists that a normal delivery encourages the stimuli which help the baby adapt to the new life outside the womb; a Caesarean or, worse still, an epidural would deprive the body of this experience. Violently opposed to epidurals, he explains that baby monkeys born in this way had shown themselves to be incapable of holding onto their mothers after birth, their brains having received insufficient oxygen.

Though Oshima acknowledges that bonding does not begin at childbirth (this should be established from the onset of pregnancy),[33] he regards it nevertheless as having a significant role to play in the successful consolidation of the mother–child relationship because of the impregnation which 'normally' ensues from it. However, having observed that pain does not always automatically create a bond, he puts forward a complementary method of impregnation, founded on a permanent oneness.

Kobayashi Noboru insists that it is necessary to give emotional support to a woman in labour in order to assist her during the delivery. He uses research undertaken in the United States to demonstrate that an assisted labour is twice as quick, that Caesareans are much rarer and that complications generally associated with a difficult birth (expulsion of colostrum in the amniotic fluid, an apparently stillborn child, the need for forceps, and so on) are extremely rare.[34]

Kobayashi Noboru also recommends that the infant be put straight into his mother's arms the moment he is born so that she can greet him with a message of love by putting him to the breast, a procedure destined to provoke a feeling of wholeness in the mother which will in turn trigger off her love programme.[35] This *fureai*, this epidermic interaction, is the magic process which will establish the symbiotic bond between mother and child.

Oshima Kiyoshi goes on to say that if mother and child do not have this interaction immediately after the birth the maternal instinct will have difficulty surfacing and the bonding will have problems establishing itself.[36]

The best way to establish this famous bond is through *skinship*, Hiraï proclaims. He uses this term (which he is proud to have introduced into the Japanese language)[37] to include: taking the child in one's arms, stroking him, being cheek to cheek with him, carrying him on one's back, cuddling him, gazing at him, speaking to him, singing him a lullaby, playing 'Peek-a-boo!', suckling him, changing his nappy, doing *takaï, takaï*,[38] or playing with him.[39]

This is why Oshima and Hiraï both condemn the custom, current in almost all Japanese hospitals, of leaving newborn babies in the nursery, bringing them to their mothers only when it is feeding time. They recommend that, on the contrary, the baby must be left in a cradle in the new mother's room. Hiraï Nobuyoshi even advocates home deliveries,[40] which, he says, are now being practised again in the West,[41] where they are trying to rekindle maternal love.

THOU SHALT STRIVE FOR ONENESS WITH THY BABY, NIGHT AND DAY

To reinforce his arguments, Kobayashi Noboru does not hesitate to brandish the horror of the *gyakutai* by emphasizing the link between the absence of *skinship* and the way that children are treated badly later on in life. He quotes research undertaken by Dr Marshall Klaus (at present director of the Children's Hospital at Berkeley) and classifies the mother–child relationship depending on whether the child was put into her arms immediately after birth, twelve hours after, thirty-six hours later, etc., right up to the child who was never put into the mother's arms. In Marshall Klaus' study, mothers were scored according to the quality of the interaction which took place with the child; the highest marks were obtained by those who had had their baby in their arms as soon as the child was born. The year-long monitoring of the four categories of children confirmed how important it was for mothers to have held their babies immediately so as to be able to 'feel' them and therefore be able to understand why they cried. The longer the delay in giving the baby to the mother, the more likely she was of being 'indifferent', indeed 'completely indifferent' to the baby's cries. Kobayashi implies that a high proportion of babies born prematurely become battered children; this also explains why mothers are encouraged to put their hand in the incubator in order to stroke their (premature) babies.[42]

Not content with encouraging mothers to aspire to a oneness with their child (a not unreasonable suggestion), Hiraï, like Kobayashi, recommends the ancient practice of sleeping with the child (*soïne*). Hiraï reminds mothers how, traditionally, Japanese women slept with their babies at the breast so that children could suckle whenever they felt the need.[43] This was a blessing which went on until the birth of the second child, for it meant that the infant did not wake up the rest of the household. Around 1950–5, to avoid accidents (particularly suffocation) Japanese mothers were discouraged from sleeping with their babies. That is why, with some help from the West, babies were gradually relegated to special beds and 'abandoned' in their own 'cold' room. Hiraï portrayed the unnatural western mother, reading a book while she rocked her child with her foot, or leaving him in his playpen, taking him for a walk on reins and going out in the evening with her husband, 'abandoning' him without the slightest feeling of remorse.[44] Hiraï Nobuyoshi adds:

> Since Japanese children have had their own rooms and sleep alone, a deterioration in the mother–child relationship has been observed, for a child who sleeps alone is deprived of *skinship*.

Kobayashi Noboru, who boasts of having put pressure on the Ministry of Health for this advice to feature on a mother's health record,[45] recommends: 'It is very important that you sleep with your child.'

It was towards the end of the 1960s and the beginning of the 1970s that this failing began to appear in the form of post-puberty nervous disorders.[46] Noticing these 'dysfunctions', an alarmed Kyûtoku Shigemori said: 'A baby left alone in his bed is incapable of being bright and breezy.' He traces the source of the problem back to 1955, a period when the economy was booming and which coincided moreover with mothers losing their child-rearing instincts.[47] The consequence of this was that babies were subsequently insufficiently stimulated and displayed symptoms verging on hospitalization.

The most vulnerable children were those who had been classified as easy who were virtually ignored, under the pretext that they were growing up by themselves. This lack of love engendered retarded development and sometimes autism.

Starting from the principle that children can suffer from *skinship* deprivation, Hiraï Nobuyoshi cannot entreat parents enough to return to the good old methods. 'In the old days Japanese women would attend to their many chores with the baby strapped to their backs, and the child became *iki iki* (alive) to his mother's rhythm', he reminds us, deploring the gradual disappearance of this custom.[48]

THOU SHALT BREAST-FEED THY CHILD DAY AND NIGHT FOR A WHOLE YEAR

In 1955, 70–80 per cent of Japanese women breast-fed their children. Hiraï Nobuyoshi blames the evil influence of the West for the fact that this custom suddenly became unfashionable with the recommendation in the 1960s that babies should always be breast-fed at fixed times. Because bottle-feeding made this task easier, only 20 per cent opted to breast-feed. Noting however that by the second or third month they had run out of milk, Kyûtoku Shigemori concluded that Japanese women had developed a 'disease of civilization'. Having drawn a parallel between the increased number of roads and the escalating production of powdered milk and having emphasized the impact of rapid economic growth on the precariousness of the good old traditions, he denounced society for being in some way responsible for the decline or disappearance of this mother instinct.[49]

Aware of the deterioration in the mother–child relationship, experts (Hiraï Nobuyoshi, Kobayashi Noboru and the Ministry of Health among others) felt compelled to strongly advise women to put their babies back to the breast immediately. These exhortations coincided with the publication of findings by Spitz, Bowlby, Harlow, Klaus, Kennel and others, which upheld the importance of bonding, by brandishing the spectre of institutionalization or the syndrome of the unwanted child with its chain of possible consequences including child-battering.

The crusade of these experts, together with the Ministry of Health's campaign to promote a return to breast-feeding, was followed by a sharp rise in the number of women breast-feeding their babies – 50 per cent of women did so fully or partially (41 per cent), of which 64 per cent considered it to be fairly or very important (30 per cent).[50] One of the questions asked before a child is admitted to a crèche relates directly to the subject of breast-feeding, almost certainly with a view to gauging the mother's 'maternalness'.

Kobayashi Noboru led the crusade instigated by the Ministry of Health to bring mothers back to the nurturing instinct. Author of a book on breast-feeding,[51] and translator of Dana Raphaël's book,[52] he stated that nature had endowed women with the best possible 'tool' with which to 'imprint' her child.

'Is there anything more intimate in a relationship than that which is created the moment the breast comes into contact with the child's lips? Epidermal contact between the mother's replete breast and the child's soft lips creates a bond which is theirs alone and which unites them one to the other.' Added to this is the connection made through the ideal position for eye contact, which allows the child to 'fuse spiritually with his mother.'[53] Kobayashi emphasizes that breast-feeding simultaneously stimulates the baby's five senses for not only does he 'drink her with his eyes', but also the baby absorbs her smell, the taste of her milk and the *skinship* which is associated with it.

In addition to the fact that an infant's cries trigger the mother's automatic lactation reflex,[54] Kobayashi stresses that its production, which stabilizes after around day five, will vary according to the number of babies she has had to feed.[55] Moreover he notes that the quality and taste of her milk fluctuate while she is breast-feeding, stimulating or slowing down the baby's appetite and thereby 'regulating' it.[56] He also reiterates the immunizing properties of the mother's milk which protect the child from the possibility of outside infections.

Another argument to convince even the most recalcitrant: mother's milk makes the baby intelligent. Simplistic though this might be, Kobayashi's assertion is backed up by the composition of human milk, which is different from that of other mammals: it contains more sugar and less protein thus allowing humans to think, reason and build up their brains, at the expense of the more highly developed motive power needed by other mammals.[57]

Finally, breast-fed babies are far more placid than those fed on artificial milk. With a view to proving this, Kobayashi observed how two groups of babies reacted when their mothers left the room: only those who were bottle-fed started to cry. He concluded that only those who were breast-fed felt instinctively that their mothers would return.

Never mentioning the physical pleasure a woman can experience when she is breast-feeding,[58] Koboyashi Noboru stresses the 'technical' advantages of the action of suckling: the uterus contracts thus allowing it to get back to normal, it protects against breast cancer, it controls the mother's weight and it is an excellent form of contraception.

As to Kyûtoku Shigemori, he deplores the fact that Japanese women no longer know how to breast-feed, that they do not enjoy it, that they are in too much of a hurry to get it over with and that they are even the cause of an allergy to powdered milk, known as *milk girai* (a phenomenon he traces back to 1953–5) which is, according to him, the expression of the infant's confusion at having been deprived of love and who could become neurasthenic.[59] The fact that their milk dries up after two to three months is, in his opinion, further proof that mothers are getting worse.

If it is no longer vital for newborn babies to be given mother's milk, it is essential that they receive her love, explains Hiraï Nobuyoshi, who maintains that breast-feeding on demand is essential, for the infant's physical and psychological development, an option which has the merit of putting the baby at the centre of the mother's world.

The drop in infant mortality encouraged mothers to opt for bottle-feeding for it gave them a much appreciated new freedom. 'And yet,' he stresses, 'numerous studies confirm that children who have not been breast-fed actually develop short- or long-term personality problems',[60] Hiraï adds,

If all those books on childcare encourage mothers to breast-feed, it is so that they may communicate their love without which they run the risk of ending up with a problem child. I'm not saying that maternal love surfaces automatically, nor am I speaking of the sexual pleasure mothers experience through contact with the infant's lips,[61] but it is absolutely essential to understand the deep-seated reasons as to why European and American women have been detracted from their duty.[62] Their reasons unsuccessfully mask their egocentricity, for their sole concern is to remain attractive to their partners and to be rid of any responsibility to a third party.

In conclusion, all women who choose for personal reasons to bottle-feed rather than breast-feed are thereby expressing an egoism which is bound to attract relational difficulties later on. That is why childcare books carry the message that maternal love is passed on through the milk, a declaration, Hiraï emphasizes which, though not scientific, is no less full of common sense.

To Hiraï, the campaign launched in 1965 by the Ministry of Health favouring a return to breast-feeding because of the antibodies found in human milk, had no other objective than to reinforce the psychological link between mother and child at a time when barely 20 per cent of mothers were choosing to breast-feed.[63]

The Oketani school of breast-feeding[64]

Although this school is not championed by any of the experts quoted, in a way it is the culmination of their theories. Its founder, Oketani Sotomi, claims that all women can breast-feed as long as they follow the few simple rules behind her ingenious method (essentially this is a series of massages destined to stimulate the production of milk, avoid any initial engorgement of the breasts and regulate the flow over a year).

A former midwife during the Manchurian War, Oketani Sotomi recalls how the baby of a young woman who had died in childbirth was given to a wet-nurse who had her own to breast-feed. She was anxious at having an extra burden in time of famine and she accepted unwillingly. This reluctance was inevitably passed onto the infant who 'chose' to die soon after.

According to Oketani Sotomi, the moral of this story is that a breast given without love loses its nutritional properties. The other lesson she draws from her experience is that, even in a time of famine, massages not only stimulate but also improve the quality of the mother's milk.

Oketani, who claims she is able to tell at first glance whether or not a baby is being breast- or bottle-fed, declares that a baby breast-fed for a year has a perfectly developed personality.

It is possible to recognize a baby reared on his mother's milk because 'his face (thanks to the action of his chin) is round but healthily so. His complexion is clear, his skin supple and his eyes bright'. On the other hand, a baby reared on artificial milk is fleshy and apathetic and interested only in sleeping. One of Oketani's disciples who agreed to see me added that the baby will be 'fat but without weight'. Covered in this bad fat, and with an overlarge head, he will fall over more easily due to the fragility of his joints.

That mother's milk makes a child more intelligent is obvious to Oketani; besides, breast-feeding stimulates the mother's instinct for she experiences a sense of achievement and feels naturally attached to her child. Oketani writes: 'Although this is the ideal food not only for the child's but also the mother's physical well-being, it is essentially the love which flows from the mother's heart, automatically imprinting the child, which constitutes the basis of his well-being.'

By making the mother responsible in this way, the method aims to put her under her child's control. Not only must she breast-feed him every three hours night and day for a year, but also she must be extremely careful what she eats so that he gets only the best, for the child's emotional well-being depends on the quality of her milk. Oketani writes: 'When the quality of the mother's milk changes, the baby changes too.' Consequently, the mother must live in complete symbiosis with her child for a year and suffer for him in order to create or maintain this famous bonding so dear to Kobayashi Noboru.

Oketani advises those who find it difficult to get up at night, to set the alarm. She writes: 'If your baby is fast asleep do not hesitate to wake him for your milk production will be affected if you do not feed him at night.' She also warns that babies who have not been fed during the night are more likely to cry a lot between the age of 6 and 9 months and that they tend to become difficult children.[65]

The very idea of the mother having a job is of course quite out of the question (how could she?), but the message is subtle rather than forbidding; the regime inflicted on her makes working an impossible option.

For those who might not understand, Oketani Sotomi reiterates: a baby cries not to demand money but only to be given 'his mother's delicious milk'.[66] Moreover, mothers should not worry about the cost (in March 1996 this was an enrolment fee of 5,660 yen, a payment of 3,600 yen for a weekly massage lasting thirty minutes plus the cost of transport, since many women travel in from the outlying suburbs of Tokyo): 'It is the most beautiful gift you could give your child. It is cheaper than a piano and it is an investment for life'.

A working women is 'tolerated' only as long as she continues to breast-feed her child every three hours. Oketani quotes the example of a teacher who managed this feat.[67] What better nightly rapprochement could there be to compensate for the mother's day-time absence? 'Oketani *Sensei* [Master] says that with a life expectancy of 80, it is not too much to ask that you sacrifice a year of your life to your child', the follower interjected when I expressed concern over the mother getting tired. And I hung my head in shame like a naughty child. 'Anyway,' she added, 'what might appear difficult in the first month becomes easier in the second and natural in the third.' What is vital is that the mother perseveres for the first hundred days.

Breast-feeding is also a wonderful opportunity to eat healthily and there are many women who continue to do so afterwards because they feel so well, the repercussions of this should also be of benefit to men. When I asked whether men did not in fact feel excluded from this dyad, I was told that they had to understand and should accept it for the sake of their child's well-being.[68]

Half an hour later I was still having problems trying to decide whether I was dealing with a new religious cult or a school of traditional art. We might also question whether the women who come regularly to have their breasts massaged,[69] do not do so to ease the solitude and break the monotony of their existences,[70] or at least to seek out much needed encouragement and motivation.

Since the end justifies the means, Oketani advises women whose babies cannot suckle properly to have the frenum of the tongue cut. This radical method is somewhat extreme and leaves one feeling decidedly uncomfortable. Why must babies be mutilated? 'In order to help them,' was the instant reply, 'in any case, it will prevent them from developing a lisp.'

Oketani Sotomi is extremely critical when it comes to speaking of those doctors who, at the beginning of the Shôwa period (post-1926), propagated the idea that powdered milk was no worse than breast milk for in doing so, they helped turn women away from their 'instinct'. Furthermore, they misled mothers by advising them to wean too early, around ten months, when twelve months would have been better – or even not until the child could walk since 'being weaned is an important step towards independence'.

Oketani's method of weaning is extremely radical:[71] she advises the mother to draw a face on each breast and to lift her blouse each time the child demands his due by saying: 'All gone!' 'Some babies are surprised, others cry, but they have to be made to understand that it is like the final curtain of a play! In any case,' she promises, 'they never come back.'

THOU SHALT PREPARE THY CHILD'S FOOD LOVINGLY

Of Japanese mothers questioned, 75.5 per cent replied that when the time came to move their child onto solids they prepared the meals themselves; barely 1.4 per cent resorted to commercial baby food.[72] This does not prevent Hiraï Nobuyoshi from recalling with nostalgia that in the old days a mother would focus all her energy on the move to solid food.

> These days there's a range of little powders on the market and all you have to do is mix them with boiling water in order to make the baby's cereal. They cater for all tastes and ages (from the first to the third) and come in a variety of consistences. You can also get small jars of fruit, vegetables or even mixtures of meat and vegetables. All the mother has to do is buy them and open them. These require the minimum of energy on her part – a quarter turn

and they're open. The child's meal is prepared in no time at all. All she has to do is get him to eat it. The same goes for the rest of the family's three daily meals. All the mother has to do is choose an instant or pre-cooked product whether it be meat or the accompaniment. Even ham is sold ready sliced, cut to within a millimetre with an electrical appliance. She doesn't even have to go to the trouble of cutting it herself. All she has to do is lay the slices on a plate without ever having to use her initiative.

Before these gadgets existed the mother had to slice the bread or meat herself thus investing a part of herself in the task. Slices cut by a mother whose mind is not on the job were irregular and while a generous hand cut generous slices, a parsimonious one produced very thin ones. Be that as it may, the mother had the opportunity of expressing herself and when the children put the food in their mouths it was as though they were tasting their mother.

Hiraï goes on to say: 'The same can be said of flavour and taste. In my native Tôhoku, I recall how, unless a daughter-in-law could produce *tsukemono* (pickled vegetables) herself she was not regarded as being an accomplished housewife for her mission was to give her family flavour and variety.'[73]

On this nostalgic note, Hiraï Nobuyoshi launches into a criticism of industrialization which he holds responsible for the collapse of the family and the standardization of people's life style – pre-fabrication being a prime example – not to mention meals which are now insipid and uniform.

'We live in a time which is incapable of keeping children at home,' he deplores. 'And that is why "mother's touch" is disappearing. In fact, while we're about it, why not manufacture a robot that would take over feeding and changing the children!'

This extract is significant because it urges women to resist the advances of modern science and to return to that same hard life their mothers had. Commercial baby food is rejected not only because it is too easy an option but more especially because it prevents the mother from 'imprinting' the food she prepares. In this we find expressed the whole ideology of the *kokoro-o kometa tezukuri ryôri* (the 'hand-made' magnetized by mother's love).[74] It is probably for this reason that many schools prefer not to be equipped with a canteen for it gives mothers the opportunity to continue to express their love for their child. This often leads to competition between mothers – known as *obentô kyôso*[75] – to find out who makes the best cold meal, whose is the best presented, the most copious, appetizing, etc. And for the majority of playschools to 'release' the children just after – rather than before – the consumption of the famous *aijô bentô* (or *bentô* of love) is linked with this ideology. Even those crèches which are equipped with a canteen have their '*bentô* days'. Several times a year (in some crèches once a month) mothers provide cold meals which are judged and so to speak marked by the childcarers. In the crèche my daughters attended, they even displayed a photo of the children with their *bentô* boxes open on their knees. How could anyone not compete?

In an article entitled 'The women of today are lazy', a reader aimed this criticism at her fellow women: 'These days they do not even make their children's *onigiri* themselves, and whenever there is a school outing they just go out and buy them ready made' (see Chapter 1, n.47). This was followed by a nostalgic description of her mother who always used to say that food prepared by a mother could never harm her children because she had made it with her heart.

Indeed, some of our students who were over the age of 20 were still bringing into university the cold meals their mothers had lovingly prepared for them.

THOU SHALT WASH THY BABY'S NAPPIES THYSELF

'Do you wash your baby's nappies?' is a question which often crops up for this is one of the tasks which, like breast-feeding, means you are a good mother. In an article in the journal *Aera* (February 1992), O-Kiko san, the wife of the crown prince's brother, was praised not only for always feeding her daughter herself (this was accomplished with the help of those plastic bags which enable women to freeze their own milk) but also for ecological reasons – she had never resorted to using disposable nappies.

Disposable nappies, on sale everywhere, are considered (through choice) to be a demonstration of laziness or wastefulness. The study undertaken by the Franco-Japanese Centre for Documentation on Women confirms this trend, for 93 per cent of Japanese women interviewed in 1986 replied that they used terry nappies which they washed themselves (barely 1.4 per cent used disposable ones and 4.9 per cent hired them), because 'it was normal' (51 per cent), 'better for the baby's health' (34 per cent), through 'guilt' (20 per cent) or for economic reasons (19 per cent). Clearly, resorting to the products of modern technology is to run the risk of being classed as lazy or a spendthrift.

Doctors and experts of all descriptions will explain that the baby's health is at stake and that the discomfort of wet terry towelling nappies will make the child easier to potty-train, an instinct that disposable nappies destroys.[76] The majority of women nevertheless opt to use both, reserving disposable nappies for nights and outings.

In the crèche, terry towelling nappies (twenty a day) are very much the symbol of a mother's love as they give her the chance to atone (partially) for her desertion.

With a view to persuading the most obstinate, an enlightened educational expert Taniguchi Yûji, produced two books whose titles are most revealing: *Mama kami omutsu-o tsukawanaïde* ('I beg you, never use disposable nappies!', 1986) and *Yamete yokatta kami omutsu* ('What a good thing I stopped using disposable nappies!', 1989).[77] The subtitles of the first work: 'I was in danger of losing my brain', 'The baby's future is determined by its nappies' explained where he stood. Taniguchi tells his followers to try disposable nappies so that they can judge for themselves. He unashamedly illustrates his book with a photo of himself wrapped in a disposable nappy: out of a sense of duty, this man stoically endured the discomfort of the thing (for six months) and said that each time it became 100 per cent saturated the first time he urinated. It is not surprising that his team of fifteen researchers gave up the experiment after two days because 'their buttocks were so sore'. Taniguchi soberly concluded that if the manufacturers were to experience for themselves how 'hellish' the nappies they produced were, they would not be able to recommend them to their clients. And he quotes, to support his case against what he calls 'petroleum nappies', the account of a 63-year-old grand-mother who, having been in hospital for an operation vowed that her grandchildren would never have to go through the ordeal she underwent when she had to wear them. He also quotes a reader from Sapporo who wrote, after she had tried both kinds of nappies, that she grew so hot she became 'irritable' and 'could think of nothing else'.

The 'expert' states that when a baby cries, is agitated or fractious, it is solely because of the unbearable dampness. But what is really devastating here is that the mother who insists, for reasons of personal convenience, on using disposable nappies, is destroying her child's confidence in her and unconsciously encouraging the child to become inert, rebellious, indeed naughty. And that is not all – nappies actually hinder the proper functioning of the brain and put off the day of the child being toilet trained.

In the face of such adversity, Taniguchi remains dispassionate and recommends a type of nappy which goes under the gentle name of *baby nenne* (literally 'baby bye-byes'), which is both absorbent and more 'natural' – the baby should be naked.[78] He recalls how in the old days, mothers were not troubled by their baby's leaks. They merely put a cotton nappy on them and a 30 centimetre square cushion in place of an undersheet.[79] 'These days,' he deplores, 'mothers cannot bear their baby's undergarments or mattress getting soiled. Why, don't they want to wash them? Don't they want to put the mattress out to dry? What's the point of being parents then?'

The controversy over disposable nappies has given rise to Taniguchi's educational theory. This is how he sums it up:

In the old days, disposable nappies were never used. Anyone resorting to them would have been accused of being slapdash. And yet these days it has become the fashion. However, the mother who does use them is not so much bringing up her child as resorting to 'mechanical rearing'. Now that she doesn't change her child she no longer has the chance to observe him properly, and she is in such a hurry to get rid of the nappy that she doesn't even take the trouble to check the contents or their consistency. . . .

If we take into consideration that by the age of 3 the brain has already achieved 80 per cent of its development, we can understand the impact the child's education will have on him as well as the repercussions it will have on his character or developments later in his life.

Taniguchi cites a crime which received widespread media coverage and explains in passing that if the assassins had had their full quota of love during their infancy such things would probably not have happened. And he infers that present day problems (such as suicide, domestic violence, shoplifting, etc.) are striking evidence of the moral wilderness in which children find themselves and that it is the family which is to blame rather than the educational system.

But this invective against women does not stop here: is it not blatantly obvious that they have better things to do than go to work? Taniguchi declares:

Why put your 'darling' child in a crèche entrusting him to a stranger? To have another 100,000 or 150,00 yen a month? A child needs love not money – he needs his mother's love. If he doesn't get his full quota, he will not be pure of heart but cold and he will be argumentative and cruel by nature. All these are distortions aroused by that sense of loss the child experiences are translated into an inability to be away from his parents before the age of 12.

He concludes that when a woman has a child, it is her duty to devote herself to him for the first ten years of his life (minimum five years if she is absolutely determined to return to work).

Indeed Taniguchi is lobbying the Japanese government for mothers to be granted a minimum maternity leave of three years during which time they should receive a monthly allowance of 50,000 ycn, to represent a kind of housewife's salary.

The impact of the message is fairly significant: by condemning it as slapdash upbringing, he is endeavouring to 'sell' mothers the idea that they must grit their teeth and make sacrifices, an injunction often expressed in *Hahaoya, gambare-ron!* ('Have courage mothers!')[80] It is a question of convincing mothers that by washing nappies themselves they are being given a unique opportunity to express their love; and as an authority on psychology writes in Taniguchi's book:

> When a mother changes her child's nappy ten times a day, she is being offered three hundred opportunities a month to be in close contact with him. If we add to this a monthly total of 210 feeds – an average of seven a day – we have a total of 510 interactions destined to give the child the feeling of being loved. The reason why disposable nappies (which only need to be changed four times a day) should be banned, is that not only do they encourage the child to forget himself but more importantly they limit the opportunities for skin contact between mother and child.[81]

Terry-towelling nappies are the symbol of maternal love!

When the mother has seventeen interactions a day with her child, it is impossible for her to do anything else, which is unquestionably the point of the exercise. Her place is very much with her child: on that, Taniguchi is absolutely clear; and because the bond uniting mother and child is established during the first year, any mother who is the slightest bit concerned for the physical and emotional well-being of her child will always strive to make herself available for a whole year. 'I should like mothers to bring their children up themselves for how could any woman have the heart to leave her child in a crèche?' he is fond of repeating.[82]

In any case the point is quite acceptable to his readers. This woman from Toyama for example admits to having realized just how 'reckless' she had been, the day her child returned from the crèche with seventeen bite marks. 'This deplorable incident prompted me to give up my job,' she laments, 'for I was the cause of my child's suffering. Had I continued to work, he would have spent a third of his early childhood in the crèche. As a mother I was blind. These days, I cuddle him, sing to him, read him books, play with him as much as possible and every day I pray that the scars on his heart will heal.'[83]

While it is interesting that she blames the other children's aggression onto the fact that they wore disposable nappies (only her child used the famous *baby nenne*), the account of this prodigal mother who saw reason (alas, too late!) is particularly striking because of the remorse she expresses. Mission accomplished, we could say, since the aim of Taniguchi's conferences is precisely to make 'reckless' mothers feel guilty.

A haematologist (Okazaki Toshiaki), whom Taniguchi allows to speak in his second book, goes even further. It used to be said that the earlier you took a nappy off a child the more intelligent the child would be:[84] starting from this principle, he believes that one can 'create a genial and healthy child'.

> The better the baby's circulation is, the more intelligent and healthy the child will be. On the other hand, a foetus who floats around in bad environment will be stupid and delicate. It comes as no surprise to learn therefore, that the singer Matsuda Seiko, who suffers from bad circulation, went into premature labour and had to be delivered by Caesarean section.

And so a mother is responsible for the state of her health. Not only does she get the baby she deserves but also it is her fault if she needs a Caesarean to bring the child into the world. To take this reasoning to its logical conclusion, a woman who has an abnormal child has only herself to blame;[85] she must shoulder the responsibility and spend the rest of her life atoning. Not only does this haematologist's plea for a 'genial and in every way perfect foetus' contain more than a hint of eugenics which is most disturbing, but also it is, not surprisingly, an indictment against women. Guilty because they are no longer interested in having children, they are also, when they do have them, responsible for their intelligence: 'tell me what your child is like and what his IQ is, and I will tell you what kind of mother you are.'

Guilty because they no longer know how to bring their children up, women are also guilty if they love them too much or too little. Should they develop school refusal syndrome (see Chapter 3, n.37) or later on in life, company or home phobia, it is the mother and always the mother who will get the blame.

Taniguchi's programme of culpability is most effective, as can be seen in the following account:

> I am a 20 year old housewife. My husband is 25. One of my friends lent me your book *Mama kami omutsu-o tsukawanaide!* ('I beg

you, never use disposable nappies!') I had no idea that disposable nappies were so harmful. The hospital where I gave birth recommended me to use them and I thought they were a good thing, not to mention the powdered milk for no one had shown me how to breast-feed. It was my mother who showed me what to do when I came out of hospital but I had no milk for over a week, whereas my breasts had been bursting with milk immediately after the delivery. It's really strange.

After having read your book, I realized how harmful disposable nappies were and that it was my baby's future that was at stake! From now on I am going to take my courage in both hands. The thought that I might already have done my daughter untold damage is extremely distressing. In the evening she's inclined to be grizzly but the moment I pick her up she stops crying. As this had prevented me from getting on with the dinner I had been in the habit of leaving her to cry. However I now realize that that was the last thing I should have done and understand your point of view completely. I was also taken aback to read your statement that a mother who doesn't respond to her baby's cries is creating a gulf between them, destroying her child's confidence in her and creating a dark and deep wound in his heart. I was an unworthy mother! I am very repentant, for it was for the sake of convenience that I used disposable nappies and that I propped her up whenever I gave her her bottle. Looking after a baby should not be a hurried affair, even though it can be more trying than the delivery itself. Never again will I touch a disposable nappy. Your book has really made me think. I was so lucky that it came into my hands.[86]

The eighty letters which form the skeleton of his second book confirm the impact his ideas have had and the breadth of reactions it provoked. Taniguchi boasts that he has travelled the country and given two thousand lectures in nursing colleges, the public health services, schools, universities, research groups headed by professors, gynaecology units and even department stores on staff training days. Letters from nurses and the reactions of school pupils carry the same message: 'Thank you for having brought us the good news and for having saved us from committing the irreparable, for more than anything else I want above all to be a good mother and a wise wife.'

Although these statements are not without their contradictions,[87] the average reader will have understood that terry-towelling nappies make a child intelligent whereas 'petroleum nappies' are a veritable torture, and that consequently any mother worthy of that name would never touch them again.

This is no doubt why you can still see terry nappies hanging up to dry in the windows of flats, being blessed and sterilized by the sun's gentle rays.[88]

THOU SHALT SHOWER THY CHILD WITH BOUNDLESS SELFLESSNESS

One single word sums everything up for Hiraï Nobuyoshi: mothers used to be the living proof of selflessness. Used to obeying their father, their father-in-law and then their husband, they learned to put their personal interests second to those of the household. Furthermore, since marriage depended on obedience rather than love, women had to endure their fate 'without a word, without a sigh'.

Compared to this model, Hiraï Nobuyoshi states that modern women have become immature and egoistic. 'Is it any surprise,' he emphasizes, 'that their children have become temperamental, egotistical and solitary social misfits?'[89] A concept fundamental to his theories is the disappearance of women's selflessness, their 'maternalness', which is one of the factors behind the fact that emotional deprivation inevitably produces social misfits.

And so, since women have been programmed by nature to be mothers, those who refuse to have children are by definition egoists. The study of maternal scruples, which he refers to as *omoiyari* (the faculty to think of others, a quality which the next generation will lack), had led him to observe the relationship between the desire to have children and the pleasure that women take in looking after them. Now, the personal histories of the women who come to seek his advice, reveal that their desire to have children was never channelled when they were very young and consequently never blossomed.

If we are to believe Hiraï Nobuyoshi, family planning is to blame for the deviant behaviour of today's mothers. He recalls how in the old days, children were regarded as a 'a gift from the gods'; however, he omits to say that the gift was sometimes 'returned' (see pp. 116–22). They were born 'naturally' and were not the result of judicious planning. While he acknowledges that destitute families were in the habit of selling their daughters (see Chapter 5), he does not miss the opportunity of nostalgically recalling that the poorer people were, the more children they had.[90] 'These days parents worry about the financial and moral cost of having children, not to mention the amount of time they have to invest. And the more egotistical a mother is the more difficult she finds it to give her child what he needs and the less she is able to display any *omoiyari*'. Hiraï adds:

To some parents, a child is hardly more than an 'accessory', regarded solely as a segment of the panoply it is necessary to have after a few years of marriage.[91] To appreciate this all you have to do is look at the dreams of those women who cannot have them, who picture themselves taking a child for a walk (hence the choice of the word 'accessory'). If he's lucky his parents will be delighted with him, but when the narcissistic wound (that is to say the gulf that exists between fantasy and reality) is too great, then the mother is wont to detest him, and then he ends up maladjusted – aggression being the most common symptom of this. . . . There are mothers who by freely admitting that they could do without such a detestable child are revealing their innermost feelings.[92]

Research carried out by the author found that 25–33 per cent of young, unmarried women did not like children; and 50–60 per cent of the same group had never had any contact with small children. According to him, 30–40 per cent of women polled said they did not want children; but 75 per cent of these were 'overjoyed' when given the news that they were pregnant.[93] Since he considers gestation to be 'the most auspicious time to foster the maternal feeling', he finds it distressing to discover that 20 per cent of women questioned said that right up to the moment of delivery they had 'experienced nothing special'.

Although 90 per cent of husbands were delighted when they heard the good news, it would appear that one-third of women were worried about how their husbands would react.[94] And finally, while 60 per cent admitted they found caring for their child tedious, 5–15 per cent considered that their lives had been turned upside down, 40–55 per cent went so far as to admit that they wished they could be relieved of their burden.

According to Hiraï, women who are not very maternal are more likely to have suffered from emotional deprivation during their early childhood. A woman who has not had her full quota of *amae* will have a tendency to deprive her child of it.[95] Hiraï does not hesitate to write: 'It is these women who abuse their children the moment they are thwarted'; he then cites the case of a 5-year-old child who had convulsions as a result of being left in his bath for too long as a punishment for not having counted correctly to one hundred.[96]

Banned during the Meiji period (1868–1912) and the Second World War, when the militarist slogan 'Be fruitful and multiply' was prevalent, abortion became legal in Japan only after 1948; abortion is supposed to have had the effect of delaying the phenomenon known in the West as the unwanted child. The term was coined in Europe and the United States during the 1960s and originally referred to children who were 'accidents', born out of wedlock and hence immediately sent to an institution. The correlation which exists between the rise in the number of unwanted children and those who are battered is of great concern to Hiraï especially since he can see emerging in Japan – some twenty years later – a similar new 'breed' of mother who is 'cold and not very maternal'. This is how he describes them:

> Barely attached to their husbands emotionally, they seldom talk about him, sullen and recalcitrant they have no sense of humour and however hard we try to encourage them to have more physical contact with their child they cannot. Through a sense of obligation, they perform their duties mechanically, and their child ends up in a state akin to hospitalism[97] – which can be identified by the following physical symptoms: retarded or arrested growth (dwarfism), excessive thinness and loss of appetite (anorexia), difficulty sleeping, unhealthy complexion, extreme vulnerability to complications accompanying certain illnesses and eczema; or the following emotional symptoms: an inert, cold or remote manner, sluggish and taciturn by nature, unresponsive to external stimuli, late talker or slow learner.

Hiraï repeats the observations made by Spitz that the psychiatric problems which children develop as a result of being deprived of maternal love during their first year of life, are 'irreversible'.[98]

He credits the phenomenon of *kyôiku mama* (literally: 'a mother-education' which applies intolerable pressure on the child) to the triumph of this egalitarian discourse which promises success to anyone willing to follow the rules of the game (these rules are the same for everyone) and capable of unstinting effort.[99] Capable of appreciating nothing beyond their children's grades, these 'ambitious' and 'vain' mothers are responsible for the egoism they have fostered. And Hiraï believes that their educational zeal is to blame for social deviancy, school refusal (see p. 69) and violence in the home – of which they are of course the prime target.

'Willing to do anything, as long as their child studies,' he writes, 'they spoil them rotten and through having over-protected them, turn them into impetuous, fainthearted egoists.' And while he accuses mothers of being responsible for the banes of which they complain, he warns them that any child who is not sufficiently independent and who becomes temperamental, will become a social misfit. 'Destined to mope around on his own, he will never have any friends and will make a mess of his marriage by remaining impassive for the rest of his life.'

THOU SHALT TIRELESSLY SEEK TO ROUSE THY MATERNAL INSTINCT

Kyûtoku Shigemori paints an even bleaker picture. He deplores the fact that at the present time, over 60 per cent of children suffer from psychosomatic ailments, 'diseases of civilization', the root cause of which is 'poor consolidation of the mother–child relationship'. And in his book which bears the provocative title: *Bogenbyô* (which could be said to mean 'Illness caused by Mother') he quite openly accuses mothers of making their children ill.[100]

'Whilst it may not be unusual to catch two or three colds a year,' Kyûtoku writes, 'it is not at all normal to have a permanently runny nose.' And, although colds are usually viral or infectious, the modern day predisposition of which we speak, can be none other than a 'cold of civilization',[101] which usually manifests itself only in the morning and the evening. They cough all night and before long the so-called cold develops into chronic asthma. There are now four hundred times more cases of this new form of asthma (said to be an allergic or psychosomatic reaction) that there were twenty years ago. What is more, asthma, which is normally easier to treat in a child than an adult, no longer responds to treatment because it is psychosomatic, and as a consequence of this 1 per cent of cases are fatal.

'The most vulnerable children are those who are apathetic, spoilt, temperamental and surly,' Kyûtoku goes on to explain, adding that most of the time it is a sickness of the soul – due to an educational error committed by the mother.[102]

> What is worse, [he says] is that my colleagues are quite blind to the fact that these children are the victims of a profound evil. They insist on treating the symptoms as though the child were really suffering from bronchitis. They prescribe all kinds of drugs and tell the mother not to give them a bath but to keep them in the warm – treatments which do no more than aggravate the situation.[103]

His private practice,[104] originally an ear, nose and throat (ENT) clinic, no longer restricts itself to dealing with asthma and chronic colds, it also treats autism, school refusal (with its classic symptoms of abdominal pains in the morning or when it is time to go to school or even playschool), anorexia and in a more general way, all behavioural problems (children who are emotionally disturbed, apathetic, quick tempered, difficult, and so on).

The root of all these evils is the fact that young mothers are devoid of any maternal instinct. Unlike a mother duck with her ducklings (a process described by the ethologist Konrad Lorenz) the mother did not 'imprint' her children before they were 3 years old and this has produced fertile soil for all kinds of psychosomatic illnesses: in other words the mother is the source of the evil, as the term *bogenbyô*, used by Kyûtoku to describe these illnesses, implies so well.

He blames this loss of a mother's educational instinct on childcare books, since nowadays common sense and intuition have been replaced by a knowledge of books. He writes:

> Parents these days, only know how many hours their child should sleep, how many calories he should consume or how many characters he should know before he starts school. If the child weighs 200 grammes less than the neighbour's there's a crisis, and although this might be important when it comes to cattle what significance can it possibly have to a human being?

'Childcare books cannot give anyone moral or physical strength', he goes on to explain, adding that these days children enter school with 'an as yet unstructured personality.' He concludes:

> Our educational system is heavily reliant on the assimilation of knowledge and produces children who have a head full of facts but no physical resistance and empty souls. On a human level, they are incomplete beings like robots, which explains why towns are overrun with colourless human beings.[105]

Behind this spiritual collapse of the family, Kyûtoku Shigemori also perceives the contemporary Japanese mother's inability to create a nostalgic image for herself the way her mother did.

Kyûtoku deplores the fact that today these vehicles of ancestral wisdom and common-sense proverbs are no longer around. 'A child of the wind' urged mothers not to cover their children too much, and, while they were at it, not to over protect them unnecessarily.[106] Needless to say he also quotes an expression mentioned earlier, according to which a child's soul is formed for life by the age of 3.

Kyûtoku is of the same opinion as the psychoanalyst Kawaï Hayao who states that by wanting to eradicate the last vestiges of feudalism the very foundations of Japan's patriarchal society have been destroyed and fathers have at the same time been divested of their authority.[107] Like Neumann, this psychoanalyst believes that this is why Japan became the country of the *great mother*. According to Kawaï all the evils of which society suffers spring from his compatriots' inability to carry out the symbolic act of killing the mother, because through regressive fantasies Japanese men are constantly striving to recapture the original symbiosis.

Kyûtoku is also of the opinion that Japanese society is being impeded by its 'maternal' nature. 'In a society dominated by the father,' he explains, 'the extended family is the principal model, it encourages cooperation and support, work and economy. On the other hand a society dominated by the mother encourages relaxation, ease and the quest for pleasure. That squandering of money follows saving and conflict and rebellion follow mutual aid. Therefore, in his eyes 'matriarchy' breeds anarchy whereas 'patriarchy' engenders nationalism. Moreover he blames the collapse of the extended family and the ensuing moral collapse of the nuclear family onto the fact that the bonds of solidarity have been weakened. He deplores the fact that: 'in this matriarchic world, now that the mother no longer has any financial worries, she has tended to home in on her children and dominate her husband.' He goes on to say that while some have been contaminated by educational fever, it is his opinion that others have become indolent, irresponsible, telly-addicts, followers of the *laissez-faire*, and the most dangerous of all are those who call themselves working mothers.

THOU SHALT ABANDON ALL PROFESSIONAL ACTIVITY FOR (AT LEAST) FIVE YEARS

Work as an 'alibi' or the work of mothers on trial

Hiraï also condemns the fact that mothers – irresponsible and spoilt, with their labour-saving electrical appliances[108] – nowadays throw themselves into a job of their choosing and make crèches totally responsible for their child's upbringing. He might just about tolerate part-time work but he deplores the growing calls from those 'obsessed with work'[109] who go so far as to demand that the opening hours of crèches be extended,[110] when they are not demanding a special minder for sick children, or even a night minder.[111]

Crèches were no doubt originally intended to relieve women in farming communities during the harvest[112] – at that time the survival of the poorer families depended so much on women's work – or even to allow women to work for the nation during the Second World War, but Hiraï believes that their proliferation has had an adverse effect.[113] For many women having a job has meant they have been able to get away from their mothers-in-law. The sharp rise in the number of working women – particularly high around 1955 – has led to a relaxation of the entry requirements to the crèche, which has in turn encouraged the development of women's egos.

'Women who have any sense of duty at all break their careers to bring their children up themselves',[114] Hiraï writes, stating that a working woman who puts her child in a crèche is displaying a serious lack of selflessness.[115] 'Anyway,' he concludes 'only a woman who is capable of selflessness should be allowed to become a mother'.

If Hiraï's ideal is a country where there is no place for welfare it is because the systematization of the protection of childhood has, according to him, precipitated the loss of women's 'maternalness', for by parking their children in a crèche, they have too often ignored the repercussions this might have on the symbiotic bond which is supposed to unite them to their children.[116] He blames the disintegration of the family onto the Welfare State.[117]

To Hiraï the fundamental problem of placing children in a crèche is a relational problem which manifests itself in the poor consolidation of the mother–child relationship when it is not through the pure and simple absence of this relationship.[118]

At the end of the 1950s when he was adviser to the association of working mothers, he was able to observe for himself the effects on children of having a working mother: children looked neglected or gave the impression that they were suffering from emotionally deprivation, or lack of *skinship*; so much so that they clung unnaturally to their mothers. He particularly remembers one child who at 8 years old was still demanding to be cuddled. He recalls one visit he made where he was able to study the pathological behaviour of children who 'clung systematically to adults' and describes how he detected, among such symptoms as hospitalism and expressionless faces, a lack of drive and the regrettable habit of bullying the weakest which can eventually result in 'perverse' behaviour towards a handicapped child.[119]

According to him, children with personality disorders – signs of emotional deprivation – can also have learning difficulties, which is a clear indication that they are indeed retarded.[120]

While childcarers complain about 'irresponsible mothers', who bring their children to the crèche 'wearing dirty clothes',[121] Hiraï accuses them of not being loving and of no longer knowing how to fulfil their roles as proxy mothers. They have, in other words, lost their vocation.

We would be wrong to believe that Hiraï is out of date or alone in holding these opinions: this determination to bring mothers back into the home so that they can devote themselves full-time, or at least part-time, to their children is a general trend. Simply reading the articles which intimate that crèche children are being abused gives some idea of the disapproval incurred by a mother who leaves her child in one.[122]

In a similar vein we find in the psychiatrist Kawaï Hiroshi's book, the case of a mother who comes in search of advice: she has put her child in a crèche after having devoted a whole year to him, during which time she breast-fed him and showered him with *skinship*. She slept and played with him and went to the trouble of finding him friends in the neighbourhood. A 'good mother' then, until the day, that is, that she tried to leave him at the crèche. He reacted very badly: tantrums, endless tears, refusing to eat or sleep. When his mother collected him in the evening, his face was 'ravaged with tears'. The alarm bell sounded when he started ignoring her, giving her only 'black' looks, unworthy of their mother–child relationship. That night he had a high temperature and gastric flu which meant that he missed his first ten days at the crèche.

> My in-laws who live in the neighbourhood told me that I was inflicting undue suffering on him and that they felt sorry for him. They repeatedly told me I shouldn't insist on leaving him at the crèche and that they would rather look after him themselves. He was indeed deteriorating before our very eyes. He had stopped walking and hardly ever said a word. It was as though he had suddenly stopped developing. I can't tell you how worried we were.

The episode had a fairly happy ending inasmuch as a simple change of crèche allowed the child to adjust to being separated. However the letter reveals just how guilty this mother felt when she asks the psychiatrist if the experience is likely to leave him permanently scarred. Here is the reply:

> What we have here is a typical case of grief caused by separation. The child's initial reaction is to cry, a prelude to anorexia likely to degenerate into a state of depression or indeed a nervous break-down.
>
> The diagnosis falls like a cleaver.
>
> Blessed with a mother excellent on all counts, fastidious and a perfectionist, this child would have grown up into a good little

child. While she was perfect, everything was fine, apart from the sadness this child experienced in the very depths of his being which he has concealed from her, for this child obviously lacks independence and self-confidence and the after effects can be long term.

Finally, the psychiatrist suggests that the child's need for *skinship* be gratified as soon as possible, otherwise there was the risk that he would remain dependent during the period referred to as the 'second weaning'.

This reply is fairly typical of those to be found in manuals and magazines on childcare where, having diagnosed the problem, the paediatrician consulted then advances two extreme examples which leave the mother with no alternative. Ingrained with the important ideology he has happily passed on, he relinquishes all responsibility which encourages the mother even more.

5 The nostalgia for yesterday's mothers

If Hiraï blames all social ills onto the birth of the nuclear family, it is because the wisdom of the ancients no longer has a voice. And that is why mothers these days are immature and egoistical, a previously unknown phenomenon.

THE OSHIN SYNDROME

Oshin is the name of the heroine of a television drama that went out twice a day for a year, whose viewing figures broke all previous records (98 per cent). Oshin is much more than the epitome of the good wife and wise mother, she is courageous, hard-working and persevering. Born in 1901, and sent away at the age of 7 to be a nurse-maid (see pp. 125–6) and general dog's body, she slaves away without respite until the day she marries a farmer and then, persecuted by her cantankerous mother-in-law, slaves away at his side, a baby strapped to her back. Every conceivable tragedy befalls her, including, as a child, seeing her mother plunge into the icy waters of a river to abort her foetus.

Oshin's second baby is stillborn, her eldest son is killed in the war and her husband commits suicide. Despite these tragic events she is imperturbable and goes through life ready to face whatever happens next. The success of this drama lies in the fact that Oshin embodies an ideal which conforms to the nostalgic image of the 'Meiji Mama' which Hiraï Nobuyoshi describes as follows:

> In the old days (that is until the end of the Second World War) society was feudal and/or hierarchical and relied absolutely on patriarchy and the superiority of man over woman.... The father's authority reigned supreme over the whole household. To oppose this authority would have been a sign of ingratitude, endorsed by the removal of the rebel....

Marriages were arranged without prior consultation with the interested parties and . . . the couple often did not meet until their wedding day. If the parents were opposed to the youngsters' choice, there was no question of standing up to them. If the case arose, all they could do was run away, an act which would result in being instantly disinherited.

The daughter-in-law's only role was to minister to the household and domestic science classes went as far as to teach young girls how to massage elderly people's necks.

The mother-in-law took charge of training her daughter-in-law and the latter had to comply absolutely with her instructions. Completely deprived of her freedom, the more dependent she was, the more her docility was appreciated, a characteristic moreover that her family had taken care to cultivate. . . . If her mother-in-law was not satisfied with her she would be thrown out for not being able to adapt to the family's tradition, an argument which even her husband could not challenge.

Should she dare return to her family she would not be made welcome for she carried the stigma of rejection. To avoid this kind of disgrace, her parents were careful to advise her on her wedding day never to cross their doorstep again, which meant that she had to endure her fate however inhuman that might be. . . .

In the main there must certainly have been mothers-in-law who treated their daughters-in-law well but there were many who repeated the vicious cycle of the cruel training they had been subjected to, and it was not unusual to see a young wife crying in a corner of the kitchen. . . . The first to get up in the morning and the last to go to bed, farmers' wives were no better than beasts of burden. . . . Hence the term in Tôhoku *Tsuno no nai ushi* (oxen without horns).

Love was supposed to come after the marriage and some of the couples did get on well, but as this was not to keep mother-in-law happy, husband and wife had very few opportunities to be alone together. Seldom loved by their husbands, women were considered to be nothing more than 'baby-machines'. And if they were sterile they were thrown out, hence the expression *konaki wa saru* ('farewell to the barren').[1]

When a woman could not give her husband children, if he was wealthy he could take a mistress whose children would appear in the family records. To the outside world, the number of mistresses a man had was a sign of wealth; his legitimate wife was told to keep her mouth shut.[2]

The remarkable thing which emerges from this account is the idealization of what mothers used to be like: this beast of burden, this belly to be inseminated,[3] already a mother before she was 20, became the very symbol of self-denial, sacrifice and selflessness. It was taken for granted that her children were her sole reason for living.

In a highly evocative book on the theme of the Meiji mother, around fifty famous people described their mothers with the same tearful nostalgia.[4]

The nurturing and protective mother

'The moment she was up in the morning, she went down to the well to wash the children's clothes which she spent her nights repairing. She was busy from morning to night; her hands were never idle. She was indeed in service to her family.' Takuma Taketoshi maintains,

> No-one of my generation ever saw his mother asleep. By the time I got up in the morning, mine had already been up for some time, busy preparing my breakfast and packing lunch for school. At night, while I was sleeping, mother would be darning socks or busy doing something else. I have no idea when she went to bed. As far as we were concerned that was how things should be.[5]
>
> Everything a child ate had been prepared by his mother. Of course that means the child was breast-fed but she also made her own soya paste which was the basic ingredient of the soup we had with every meal; and pickled vegetables.

As a result of this children developed a taste for their mother's cooking and it is with nostalgia that they remember it for the rest of their lives.

'Hand-made' included clothes for she made them all herself and repaired them (preferably at night), not to mention mattresses which again she stuffed with cotton. 'In the old days, mothers fed us on their milk, and all the food we ate was prepared by her,' Takaishi Kunio, former vice Minister of Education goes on to add[6] 'She made the special feast days dishes, sweets, cakes, everything was made at home. She made our clothes including our Sunday best. We didn't even have to go to the barber's because she was the one who shaved our heads.'

The child is always described as being 'stuck' to his mother. Asleep at the breast, snuggled up against her all night until the next child came along, he spent his days on her lap or her back, so that he could 'top himself up' whenever he wanted to without preventing his mother from attending to the many jobs she had to do. 'Aged 84 when she died, never did I see her without a needle in her hand. She just couldn't help it. You could even say she died working.'[7]

This devotion was even reflected in their physique, for these house-keepers were generally so thin that it was considered a compliment if anyone told them they had put on weight.[8]

Women were no less busy in the better off commercial circles. Shiroyama Saburô, whose parents ran a business in Nagoya, remembers that they were always sixteen at the table (the four brothers and sisters, their parents and ten employees) and that his mother, even with the help of one or two servants, never had a moment's rest.[9]

'Pelican mothers'

Only a mother could understand, trust and love her children. When it came to supporting them, she was afraid of nothing, not even her husband's opposition or wrath. Ready to pay for their studies with the sweat of her brow, she would go so far as to give them her savings in secret, so that they could buy whatever they wanted or whatever it was their father had said they could not have. And if the oldest son did not want to take over his father's business, it fell to her to back him up and help him follow his chosen path in life.

Here for example is an account by Tezuka Osamu (1926–89), famous designer and 'father' of the character *Tetsuwan Atomu* ('Astro-Boy'):

> When I was at school, I used to keep my drawings a secret from my father, but when he found me drawing in the notebooks my mother had bought me, he would confiscate them immediately. There were times when he even threw me out. And while I was outside crying, mother would steal out and tell me to come in because she had apologized on my behalf. . . . When I told my mother of my plans to become a comic strip artist, she said I had to do what I wanted and that she would not stand in my way. Without her, Tezuka Osamu would never have been.[10]

And there is another account from the cinema critic, Yodogawa Nagaharu, born in 1909:

> When I told my mother I had no intention of pursuing my studies – not even at school – because I intended to devote myself entirely to the cinema, all she said was: 'Oh, right', but I knew she was apprehensive despite her assent. My father was against the idea, but she won him over. When I was of marriageable age, I told my

mother I wanted to remain single for the rest of my life so that I could apply myself to my passion with single-minded devotion. She looked troubled but never said a word. Not once did she stand in my way. Everything I have today I owe to her. She trusted me 99 per cent and I have to say she did everything she could to make me happy. She was kind. She was gentle. I do not remember her ever getting hysterical. If I have always felt good about myself, confident and self-possessed, if I have been able to dedicate my whole life to the cinema, it is all down to her, and her alone.[11]

The husbands of the Meiji women have often been described as violent, adulterous and frankly obnoxious. However, their offspring have no recollection of ever having heard their mothers criticize their fathers:

My father, who was in the military, was extremely austere. I don't think I ever saw him smile or relax at home with the family. To this day I still wonder how mother put up with someone so unpleasant. And yet they weren't a bad couple, and I don't think I ever heard my mother speak ill of him.[12]

Mother would wake us up (in the middle of the night) shouting: 'Your father's home!' He was fond of the drink and always came home late and drunk. As I was frightened of attracting my father's wrath, I would get up, rub the sleep from my eyes and then kneel in the doorway next to my mother, both hands on the ground and head bowed in welcome. He would refuse to enter if we did not perform this ritual. He was a veritable tyrant. Mother ministered to his needs as best she could; in my view she did far too much for him. And yet, I have no recollection of having witnessed any quarrel between them.[13]

A hand of steel in a velvet glove

Behind their apparent frailty there lurked a hidden strength and dogged fearlessness. Whatever the circumstances, the mother was armed to handle any catastrophe: house fires, earthquakes, epidemics, bedridden and senile old people. Her composure, her capacity to deal with the impossible, made her and still make her the admiration of her children:

My brothers, sisters and I still recall our mother's hidden strength, concealed as it was beneath so much gentleness. It was the famous earthquake in Kantô (1923) which first brought it out. Our father, completely ruined, died of a stroke, and my youngest brother contracted typhoid. Three of us were ill at home and my oldest sister died before the week was out. Despite all these events, each as devastating as the next, my mother weathered the storm by preserving her sang-froid. She was marvellous. She was the very embodiment of courage.[14]

And finally – and this could be what endeared her so much to her children – not only did their mother never scold them, but also she was always there to comfort them:

Although I did some really stupid things when I was young, my mother never lost her temper. I was often in trouble at school because I was quite undisciplined but she never told me off. We are all adults now but my brothers and sisters agree they never saw her get angry either.[15]

Kobayashi Isamu also has no recollection of ever having seen his mother get angry, except the day he took it upon himself to cut his sister's hair.[16]

Takuma Taketoshi writes:

Most mothers before the war brought their last child into the world around the age of 40. At 38 or 39 their fertility had been demonstrated through the production of eight or nine children. Consequently they had another four or five years before they were free of basic tasks. Not until the age of 45 were most of them shot of nappies but by then they only had a few years left to live. Before the war, their lives were completely taken up with looking after children.[17]

In Taishô 9 (1921), eighteen years before the Second World War, a woman probably had her fifth (and last) child around the age of 35, which corresponded to the middle of her life and not the end.

NEITHER SAINT NOR MARTYR

The Meiji mother – human beneath her saintly exterior – found egotistic and emotional ways to compensate for her inferior status. As everything was denied her, she lived through her children and through them found pleasure.

As Tanaka Kimiko writes, at the heart of the Meiji mother's gifts, was more than just a simple response to the wishes of her children; she wanted to give them all that had been denied her. And the men of today, who remember their mother with so much love and nostalgia, do not realize that what they took to be the most objective and purest of loves was in fact a narcissistic one. By doing everything in her power to ensure that they prospered, her children's success was hers.[18]

That is why one of her greatest pleasures – not to say the only one – was to help her oldest son realize his ambitions for and against everyone. Marginalized by her status, she was in a better position to share his point of view even though it was not necessarily that of her husband, nor that of society in general. Her 'theoretical' acceptance of the social system and its values did not prevent her from being avenged, more or less consciously, for the cruelty of her fate. Supporting her oldest son in his refusal to take over from his father was one of the rare means at her disposal. Hiraï writes:

> Although this devotion degenerated into being overprotective, mothers were not castigated since they were the very incarnation of the ideal of the loving mother. This love however was a sham for the sacrifices they made for their children were in fact a form of egotistical compensation for their own misfortunes. Moreover, they were an insurance policy for their old age. However much they appeared to be at their children's beck and call, what was regarded as being a supreme sacrifice on the part of the mother, was in fact an expression of her egocentricity. Even today, a mother using public transport, with a child on her back, clutching bags of shopping who gives her seat to the oldest so that he can admire the view while she remains standing, is the very personification of this. . . . And yet, this same mother will pour out her deepest feelings at the slightest disappointment. And the dreadful treatment she is holding in reserve for her daughter-in-law will be a manifestation of her jealousy indeed her contempt at having been dispossessed of her son.

The touched-up portrait of the 'Meiji Mama'

The ethnologist Ofuji Yuki is no doubt right when he says that mothers had a mountain of work to do which took priority over looking after the children who were left to their own devices and who learned very early on how to fend for themselves. They had to deal with solitude from a very young age and learn to do without their mother while she was working in the fields. All the time that she was breast-feeding the infant she would put him in a basket and take him along with her but the moment the feeds could be spaced out, he would stay with his grandmother, or all alone, waiting for her to return.

'However much the children cried or screamed, there was no one to comfort them and it was not an unknown phenomenon for them to cry until they were completely exhausted', he writes, stressing that this was in no way shocking since one used to say that it was an infant's job to cry.

Ueno Hidénobu echoes this when he describes the lives of the Kyûshû miners whose wives, pregnant or not, would go down the pit with them. Since they continued to go down until the baby was due, there were many who gave birth down there. If they had a miscarriage they would wrap the foetus' body in old rags and then throw it into a corner of the mine. They would endeavour to stem the haemorrhage with straw ripped from their sandals or old newspapers that were lying around, before going back to work as if nothing had happened. Those who gave birth at night would try next morning to get someone at the entrance to the mine to look after the newborn for a small sum. At the risk of a beating if they were discovered, they would sometimes sneak out to feed the baby. Some had no choice but to take the infant down with them in a basket which they would then hang from the coal face so that they could rock it as they worked. They would stop only to put the child to the breast. It was only when they began to crawl that the children really became exposed to all kinds of dangers. However often they put coal in their mouths, though, this did not prevent their mothers from taking them down. When they had to go down to the bottom of the shaft they would protect the child's head with rags.[19]

If children's 'divine' membership (see pp. 115–17) exempted them from being educated up to the age of 6, then once they were 7 they would join the children's cooperative whose task it was to socialize them and initiate them to a harsh discipline.[20]

Around the age of 15, the boys (at the centre of this group of young people) would be given certain responsibilities to shoulder during religious and village festivals which allowed them to be ranked as adult. The young man would learn to get on with the others and to unite his strengths to theirs.[21] He would also learn to conform to the norm by aspiring to nothing more than a quiet and prosaic existence and a job for life, any other vague desires he might have would be received with collective derision.

Young women were taken in hand by their own group to be taught good manners so that they could enter into a good marriage.

The mother's role in bringing up her children as it used to be

Though the status granted a mother was not respected, at least it was respectable.[22] Her role consisted of giving birth painfully, of ensuring the infant's survival by breast-feeding and taking charge of the material side of life which meant working long hours washing the nappies by hand, getting up at night to comfort the baby or carrying the body around on her back so that the rest of the household was not disturbed. 'At night when you cried, I would put you on my back and take you outside. The stars were all misted over because my eyes were filled with tears.'[23]

The child she bore was above all the child of the *ie*;[24] it was the grandparents or father who took charge of his education, *a fortiori* when a boy or oldest son was the sole heir and issue of the line.

Such was the inferiority of the mother's position that in order to be obeyed she was obliged to summon a more powerful and respected third party, the grandmother for example, by saying: 'Well, don't you understand what your grandmother's telling you?'[25] Accidents were not infrequent (children drowned in rivers, or burned alive when they fell into the fireplace dug in the ground); it seems possible that the saying '*Nanasai madewa kami no uchi*' ('The first six years of a child's life are in the hands of the gods [of the Shinto pantheon]') was also meant to put very young children under the protection of the gods in order to ward off dangers that were lying in wait for them.[26]

NOT QUITE A GOD NOR QUITE A MAN

In its traditional interpretation this saying actually implied that the child was a small, unstable, amphibious being, adrift somewhere between the world of gods, spirits and men.[27] It was believed that a child's soul took seven years to be properly 'integrated' into the human world. Entering the child's body at birth to give it life, it could also momentarily leave its physical receptacle (when for example the child was ill). This is why it was imperative that the child play the role of intermediary during the religious festivals where the gods were invoked. And the ceremonies which punctuated a child's early years had no other function than to prevent the child from slipping forever back into the other world.

The first ceremony was the *nazuke iwai*, when the child was given a first name. Then when the child was 1 month old he was presented at the Shinto temple. The hundredth day following his birth marked the beginning of weaning when the baby was given his first taste of solid food and the *hatsu tanjô* celebrated his first birthday. At the age of 3, the ceremony of *obitori* granted the child the right to wear the *obi* (kimono belt); at the age of 4, the young boy donned his first *hakama*;[28] at the age of 6 he became a fully fledged member of the clan.[29] Incorporated in these ceremonies was the *shichi-go-san*, a feast which celebrated little girls reaching the age of 3 and 7, and little boys the age of 5, who on this occasion went to the Shinto temple, usually dressed in a kimono, over which the boys wore the *hakama*.

All these ceremonies were said to soothe their souls. The pomp which still surrounds the ceremony of entering primary school is doubtless a sign that these days it is considered to be a rite of passage between infancy and childhood.

Apart from these other purposes, ceremonies were supposed to placate the *mushi* the child harboured. *Mushi* means insect, worm, flea, larvae, caterpillar or vermin, it also means temperament or irascibility. The expression *kan no mushi* intimates that children are the victims of their *mushi* for it can make them prone to crying fits and night terrors. It used to be said of a nervous child that the *mushi* of the *kan* (nerves) was strong or excited (according to the definition in the *Kôjien*).

When children had a tantrum it was said that their *mushi* had woken up. Victims of the so-called *mushi*, they became the victims of their humours. By definition, however, a child was innocent, but an exorcism could be carried out in the Shinto temple with a view to appeasing the *mushi* in those who were judged to be highly strung, even disturbed. This was known as the *mushi kiri*.[30]

At best the child was seen as a gift from the gods, but there was an unfavourable side to this duality for the newborn was not yet considered to be a human being. Until the soul was fully integrated into the world of the living, it continued to be linked to its former state to which it was still partially attached. The child's existence therefore remained somewhat precarious for there was always the possibility that any 'surplus' would be returned to the gods. Infanticide could therefore be thought of as a kind of 'return to sender'.[31] This is what emerges from the euphemisms used to describe infanticide since all could be rendered by the term 'return'. It was not unusual to hear it said that children who would be difficult to raise were being 'returned'. They were then put into a straw sack and taken to be thrown into the river.[32] The expression *higaeri* ('do the journey in a day') is extremely significant since it meant that the baby would be leaving the day it arrived.[33]

It was considered preferable to prevent newborn children from uttering their first cry as this was the symbol of birth, so that the soul could be 'pulled' from the Animistic pantheon. An infant 'born' dead, therefore stood a better chance of being reintegrated into the Shinto pantheon. The custom of burying the body with the placenta was also supposed to allow a more rapid and favourable reincarnation. The brusqueness of the different expressions in use, depending on the region, suggests that it was an inevitable rather than a tragic occurrence. Hence 'to go in search of crabs', 'to turn him into a mole', 'to serve him up to the frogs', were terms often used to refer to the newborn, who was to be wrapped in straw and thrown into the water, as was *tai no esa*, 'carp food'.[34]

Abortion and contraception

Yanagita Kunio's school suggests that formerly the only known form of contraception was prolonged breast-feeding. In the prefecture of Tochigi, another method consisted of hopping five or six times, of drinking cold water or chilling the abdomen immediately after intercourse. Another technique, borne of superstition, was to try and influence fate by giving the last-born a name which predicted the destiny of those who would follow: Urayoshi (from *yoshi*: that's enough) or Sutejirô (from *suteru*: to throw or abandon) for a boy; Tome (from *tomeru*: to stop), Sute (see Sutejirô), Sue (the last) or Yoshi (see Urayoshi) for a girl.

As far as abortion was concerned the method most commonly practised was to introduce Physalis roots or acupuncture needles into the woman's uterus when she was five months pregnant. In the prefecture of Fukui, women were aborted with needles from the wild mandarin tree, sharpened bramble twigs, Japanese coltsfoot, dwarf bamboo shoots, poisonous plants or burdock roots.

Matsunaga Goichi describes how some women in an attempt to eject the foetus would jump from a great height, burn moxa on their navels or even drink mercury.[35]

The women of Kyûshû who continued to go down the mines up until the last minute could be suspected of secretly hoping that they would miscarry.

In Edo women who could afford them, would get hold of medicinal plants. Besides the Physalis root, the most commonly used were probably convolvulus seeds mixed with water.[36] More frequent in towns than in the country, abortions carried out by gynaecologists or midwives were far beyond the reach of most budgets. Their clientele was mostly made up of servants whose pregnancies were an inconvenience to the families employing them.[37]

Infanticide

If infanticide was considered to be preferable to abortion this was because it protected the mother from the dangers inherent in the techniques used.

Infanticide was never carried out in a casual manner and was resorted to only in cases of extreme poverty, particularly in rural communities where yet another mouth to feed could endanger the rest of the household. Hence the meaning of the term used: *mabiki*, 'to thin out the plants'. It was in fact considered indecent for a poor family to have many children and families would give in to what was more or less conscious group pressure to get rid of the 'surplus', under pain of seeing themselves excluded from the support community. The decision was taken for them.[38] Moreover, women resorted to infanticide rather than become the laughing stock of the village for having a baby at an age judged to be inappropriate (after the age of 40), if not indecent.

The following handball song from the prefecture of Shimane, chanted by children, illustrates the situation well:

> Why has my elder sister lost her appetite?
> She's seven months pregnant . . .
> If it's a boy, he will be instructed in a temple
> If it's a girl, we'll put her in a sack of straw
> We'll tie it up with string
> And let her flow gently down the river,
> The birds in the sky will come and peck her,
> The loach in the river will come and nibble her,
> But where have all these carnivorous birds gone?
> They have migrated to far off lands.[39]

It was also imperative to 'thin out the plants' in the Kyûshû region as well as in other deprived regions of the archipelago. The *kakure Kirishitan* or 'hidden Christians' during the suppression of Christianity in the Tokugawa Period were no exception.[40] To relieve themselves of the weight of guilt associated with infanticide, they had skilfully interpreted Christ's tragic death on the cross as God the Father making his son do penance for the massacre of the Innocents. Viewed from this angle, Christ became a fellow sufferer, sharing with them the burden of innocent lives which had to be sacrificed in order to ensure the survival of the others. The figure of the Virgin and that of Kannon, or more particularly *'kosodate Kannon'* (protector of children) were merged into one. As a mother, the Virgin Mary should have had a better understanding than Christ of the misfortunes of the sacrificed children. It is for this reason that the Catholic writer Endô Shûsaku claims that the *kakure Kirishitan* 'purged' Christianity of its paternal nature in favour of a more maternal one, since the mother – through her compassion – is more capable of understanding misfortune and human misery. The early Christians would have 'humanized' the image of a God regarded as being over strict, by making him take his share of responsibility and by superimposing on him another more sympathetic and maternal figure.[41]

Little girls or newborn babies displaying malformations or abnormalities were the most at risk and there was a general belief that mothers should not have more than three children. For example, infanticide was extremely common in the prefecture of Iwate at the beginning of the Meiji period (1868–1912) and it was not regarded as unnatural for a woman to suffocate a child when she already had three. Hence the real meaning of the expression *ichi hime ni Tarô*, now wrongly interpreted as being 'the king's choice': ideally a girl then a boy as the girl was expected to help her mother raise her brother. The expression actually implied that it was better to have two boys (to secure an heir and a spare) whereas one girl was more than enough. And so, in the prefecture of Kagoshima, custom demanded that one girl and two boys be kept 'and that the rest be killed off (*sic*)'.[42]

In the prefecture of Chiba, south-east of Tokyo, it was apparently not uncommon to say: 'If it's a girl, stamp on her, if it's a boy let him be!', phrases to be found in many Japanese lullabies.[43] In the prefecture of Kagawa, before the Meiji period, it was written that many little girls were killed because only boys were capable of taking over the fishing from their fathers.[44] For this reason husbands and in-laws considered 'girl wombs' to be a veritable calamity.

The one giving birth had very little say in the matter. For example in the prefecture of Akita, just before the baby emerged, the midwife would ask the family: 'Do we keep it or not?' (*oku kâ okânaika*). She sometimes went so far as to ask: 'Do we keep it if it's a boy? Or do we get rid of it whatever the sex?' Apparently the mother had only the right to utter weakly: 'This time at least we could have kept it'.

The birth of twins was a very bad omen for they were considered to be too close to the animal kingdom, hence the terms: 'animal belly' (*chikushô bara*) or 'piglets' (*butago*) a play on words with *futago* (twins) to denote the mother and the fruit of her womb. Also thought to reflect the mother's sexual wantonness, they were even more suspect if they were of different sexes for it was thought that they were the reincarnation of crossed lovers driven to commit suicide. To avoid becoming the laughing stock of the village, custom had it that the second should be kept since it would be the strongest having 'followed' the first.[45]

Infanticide was often carried out by midwives called *toriage bâsan* (from *toriageru*: to give birth) or *onibâsan* (from *oni*: ogress). Some back-street abortionists, cheaper than midwives, specialized in 'thinning out the plants'. They would obstruct the newborn's respiratory tract with damp paper before the child had time to utter a first cry, a method known as *kamihari*.[46] The method would vary depending on the region – babies could be suffocated with the placenta, strangled or drowned in a basin, and so on. In the prefecture of Fukui, midwives would press down very hard on the newborn baby's fontanelle. In the prefecture of Gunma, they earned the depressingly descriptive nicknames of 'child-stabbers' or 'child-crushers'.

The poorest of families who were unable to pay the 'ogress' for her dark services were obliged to do the deed themselves. When a father drowned his child in a tub, it was then said – in the prefecture of Gunma in particular – that he had been made a disciple of *Jizô*.[47] It was sometimes the father who took it upon himself to throw the newborn into the river. The baby was not always dead when he was wrapped in a straw bag, as shown in the following account recorded in the prefecture of Iwate:

> Having placed the child in a sack of straw, the father, who had drunk a fair bit, would set off with the screaming bundle over his shoulder to go and throw it in the river. It was said that he served him up to the frogs.[48]

Another text speaks of a method which consisted of the father holding the newborn under his knees while he obstructed his respiratory tract with rice bran, or a method whereby babies were strangled with a rope or even strung up by their feet.[49]

In the prefecture of Kagoshima, the task often fell to the mother-in-law. She would usually cover the newborn's face with wet paper, suffocate him under a mattress or crush him with her knees.

When the mother had to take the initiative, she usually asphyxiated the child against her own breasts. Sometimes she crushed the child with her knees (prefecture of Aomori) or just sat on him (prefecture of Gunma). Others preferred to give the children a chance of survival by abandoning them in straw sacks in the hope that a charitable soul would take pity on them. In the prefecture of Nagano it was said that the necks of these babies remained bent from having been put in a sack.

The most barbarous method was the one known as *hoshikoroshi*, that is starving babies or rather depriving them of food and drink so that they died of hunger after a month. It was said of these children that they 'died with their mouths open'.

Newborn babies' bodies were usually wrapped in straw and thrown into a river or marsh. In the prefecture of Okayama, it was the custom before throwing them into the river, to place a fan with a boy's body and a ladle, bamboo whistle or scissors with that of a girl, before wrapping it in a straw mat. The 'bundle' was then tied with string in three places so that it looked like straw packaging.

Sometimes the newborn baby would be thrown down the toilet while still alive or was left under the manure to become fertilizer. Babies were often buried under the *engawa* or *doma*, areas everyone walked over and well out of sight of the prying eyes of neighbours who did not always know a baby was expected.[50] Still in Okayama, it is written that a newborn could be thrown away 'just like that. That way they ended up as food for kites, crows or foxes'. In Matsueshi (in the prefecture of Shimane) there was a rumour at the beginning of the Meiji period, of a dog having been seen with a baby's arm in his jaw.

In the prefecture of Kagawa, the newborn was wrapped in a cloth before being hit with a mallet. The body was then taken to the mountains to be buried. It was sometimes wrapped in a mat and attached to a weight so that it would sink to the bottom of the sea.[51] In Okinawa, before drowning the newborn they stuffed rags into the child's mouth and there were also reports of infants being buried alive. These little corpses found floating here and there in the marshes probably fuelled the legend of the *kappa*, who looked like partially formed foetuses – mummified or in the process of decomposing.[52]

Despite the fact that abortion was made illegal with the restoration of the Meiji in 1868 and although it was decreed in 1880 that anyone having an abortion or carrying one out would be regarded as a criminal, infanticide continued to be practised in some regions all through the Taishô period (1913–24) and even into the beginning of the Shôwa period (1924).[53]

In Meiji 2 (1870) a decree outlawing infanticide in the prefecture of Kochi led to all children born that year being nicknamed 'the survivors of the Edict'. Figure 5.1 is a *mabiki-ema*, or painting representing infanticide, on display at Kikusuiji Temple in Chichibu, 33rd station of the Kannon pilgrimage. *Mabiki-ema* or *ukiyo-e*-style painting is a warning against infanticide. On the right side of the

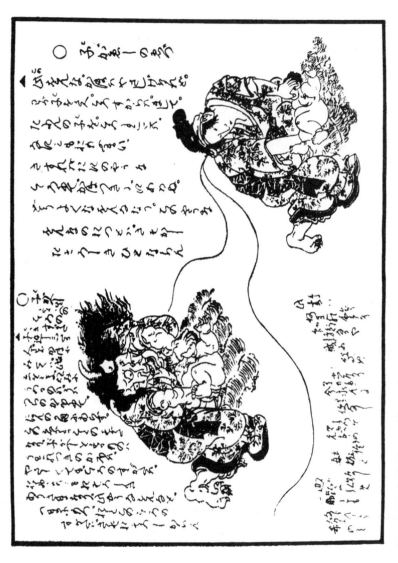

Figure 5.1 Mabiki ema (kogaeshi) or painting representing infanticide, Kikusuiji Temple, Chichibu
Source: Reprinted by kind permission of Kikusuiji Temple, Chichibu, Japan

painting, one can read *kogaeshi*, meaning 'returning a child' (to the Gods). It was believed that the newborn did not yet belong to this woman and could be sent back to the other realms, wishing him better luck for his next reincarnation. The text informs us that this angel-faced woman, who strangles her child, is actually a demon. This is the inscription written on top of the mother and demon:

As this angel-faced woman
is able to kill her own child,
she could kill any other child.
Her heart is that of a demon
and the kindness of her face
conceals her real self
because she is a cruel person.
No doubt this woman's husband
is a horrible person too.

May all those who have sent their child back (to the gods)
 (i.e. committed infanticide)
look at this picture if they want to see their true self.
What is reflected in the mirror
is not their real self,
which is represented in this picture.
Those who have committed infanticide
may harbour kind features.
They are in fact horrible beings
worse than demons.
No doubt this wife's husband's heart is awful too.

The sale of little girls

In some disadvantaged provinces when a girl was born she was raised until the age of 10 to 14 after which she could either be sent to work in the mills (the theme of some cradle songs),[54] or she could be sold as a prostitute for what was a pittance to the average family but a fortune to the destitute.[55] This was referred to as *kuchi berashi*, literally, 'cutting down on the number of mouths to feed'.

Pierre Souyri describes how pimps would scour towns and country-side in search of little girls who, having worked as servants, were forced into prostitution around the age of 14. Money paid by the client went to the establishment and the girls had to reimburse their employers all expenses which had been incurred since they had been separated from their parents.

The mortality rate among the girls of Yoshiwara (a famous red light district in Tokyo), victims of maltreatment, undernourishment and tuberculosis, was quite frightening. Locked up, they were never allowed out unless a rich patron bought their freedom – unfortunately a very unlikely eventuality. When they fell ill, they were left huddled in a dark room until they died of neglect. They were buried near Yoshiwara, in an appropriately named: 'temple where corpses are thrown'.[56] More often than not they suffered from tuberculosis, were under- or mal-nourished, were kept caged-up like animals – sacrificed for the benefit of their family, they were performing the greatest act of filial piety there is, which is why they were sometimes compared to the incarnation of the goddess Kannon.

The Karayukisan

Morisaki Kazue describes a strange 'Yellow Trade' which went on at the end of the nineteenth century and which probably carried on right up to the end of the War in the Pacific; it aimed to supply the western colonial trading posts of South East Asia. The carriers which scoured the South Seas would usually go to stock up in Amakusa in the prefecture of Kumamoto in Kyûshû, where the most destitute families would sell their nubile daughters into prostitution. So as not to alert the whole neighbourhood to the fact that they had a daughter for sale, the parents would discreetly light a fire at night which could be seen from a long way off.[57] These young girls, aged between 14 and 18, were usually abused sexually while still on board ship in lieu of payment for their voyage. They were called the *Karayukisan*, 'those who went abroad'; *Kara* – referring to the China of the Tang Dynasty or to Korea – was a metaphor for abroad. They would end up in the brothels of Siberia, Manchuria, Australia and even Bangkok, Hong Kong, Shanghai, Singapore, Sumatra, Calcutta, Bombay or Africa where their clientele consisted mainly of westerners. The registers of a certain Muraoka confirmed that some 3,222 young girls from the Shimabara region had been transported in this way between 1889 and 1894. Records show that in 1908 there were around 5,000 Japanese prostitutes in Singapore alone. Although history books have been careful to erase these dark memories, we can safely presume that tens of thousands of women would have been shipped off 'for the good of the country'. These young women, having accepted their fate through a sense of filial duty and who sent their parents money, would only return (if they ever did return) around the age of 30.[58]

The unhappy lot of the little nursemaids

Later, in the Meiji period and right up to the end of the war, little girls as young as 6 or 7 were placed in small towns or villages to work as nursemaids. As Mariko Asano Tamanoi says, to their employers they did not represent an external sign of wealth but an economic necessity for they were too tied up in their work to be able to look after their children themselves. They were begrudgingly given board and lodgings but were asked to stay in the temple courtyard or in the street so as not to get in the way of the household. The lullabies and nursery rhymes they sang to cheer themselves up or to get their charges off to sleep, reveals the extent of their distress and despair:

> One, we are all bullied.
> Two, we are all hated.
> Three, we are all forced to talk.
> Four, we are all scolded.
> Five, we are all forced to carry babies who cry a lot.
> Six, we are all fed with terrible food.
> Seven, we are all forced to wash diapers in the cold
>   water of the river.
> Eight, we are all impregnated and shed our tears.
> Nine, we are all persuaded to leave, and finally,
> Ten, we all must leave.

Or:

> This baby cries a lot.
> I want to exchange him with someone else's.
>
> What can we do with a naughty child?
> Let's put him on the drum
> and hit him with green bamboo sticks.
>
> Listen, my master and mistress.
> If you treat me bad,
> I may exert an evil effect on your kid.

While all these 'cradle songs' reflect the frustrations of these young girls who found it so difficult to see themselves as 'little mothers', and whose only option was to work off their frustration on the child entrusted to them; the following reveals instead how despite everything she remained a traumatized little girl:

> I want to go home.
> I want to see my house.

I want to see my mother's face.
Even if I cannot see her, I want to talk to somebody
about my wretched life.[59]

As we have seen, the placing of this Meiji mother on a pedestal needs to be qualified. And what should be said of all those charters which have been landing in Tokyo since the early 1980s, regularly disgorging all the adults who were once children abandoned in Manchuria after the Second World War and that not one mother has returned to find? We should observe moreover that these mothers are not rushing to these reunions either, the official line is that they could not bear to subject themselves to public scrutiny. And who can blame them when we consider what an enormous number of small girls were sold rather than abandoned prior to their mother's departure.[60]

Appearing before the television cameras these 'ghosts' promise their families that all they ask is to be allowed to visit their ancestors' graves so that they can pay their respects. They wish them no harm and will return to China immediately afterwards. How can we begin to understand the despair of those who nobody went to find?

6 Demographic malaise

The anxiety that demographers are experiencing is all the more understandable when we see that the birthrate is dropping in proportion to the rising number of abortions. Even more disconcerting is the fact that 70 per cent of abortions are carried out on married women and that one in two of these has had at least one abortion in her life.[1] Abortion is so high on the list of unavoidable perils that it is often said that a husband and wife who get on well throughout their married life are very lucky if the number of children the wife has, is equal to the number of pregnancies she has had.[2] Official statistics confirm that women between the age of 30 and 39 have the most abortions, peaking between 35 and 39 once they have brought one or two children into the world (see pp. 38–41). In fact the percentage is reversed, for if 72.2 per cent of women between the age of 20 and 29 have not yet had an abortion, 72.8 per cent of women between the age of 40 and 49 admit they have had this unfortunate experience. A study carried out by the group Wife quoted as an extreme example (taken from the 261 women questioned) the case of a woman who had had a total of nine abortions – three before she was married and six afterwards. As the authors themselves point out, if one were to bring to light the problem of abortion (still regarded theoretically as a crime despite the law passed in its favour) the majority of married women could be classed as criminals. What emerges from all this is that abortion is actually considered to be a method of contraception to which women resort when all else fails.

Contraception is still usually left up to the man. In 1986, for example, nearly 80 per cent of couples used condoms. The relatively high failure rate is due to its somewhat haphazard use or because it is used to complement the Ogino or rhythm method.[3]

The embarrassment experienced by young women when it comes to speaking 'about those kinds of things', or making the necessary manoeuvres required to introduce spermicidal sponges, pessaries or caps before sexual intercourse, covers the temperature method, which is also frowned upon.

The study carried out by the group Wife does however reveal that once they have done their duty by producing one or two children, two out of three women (i.e. 67.6 per cent) consider that it is up to them rather than their partner to take the initiative as far as contraception is concerned.

AVAILABLE OPTIONS

Although information is available since 80 per cent (one of the highest percentages in the world) of women questioned practise or have practised some form of contraception, the failure rate reveals the empiricism of methods described by Fujita Shin'ichi as 'underdeveloped',[4] for the pill is still regarded as a treatment rather than a contraceptive.

Do you want to keep it?

This is apparently a routine question asked by gynaecologists when, in their view, the patient is not up to coping with the responsibilities of motherhood. This is the question that women can expect if they are too young, too old (nearly 40), overweight, single or just simply that they already have two children. I heard it asked of a young woman in the cubicle adjacent to mine in one of the biggest state hospitals in Tokyo. Caught unawares, the aforementioned patient, who was barely 20, started to stammer. Given the lack of privacy this was hardly surprising. Aged 32, this was my first pregnancy. The gynaecologist presumably decided that I was the right age to cope and I was spared the question.

An abortion costs between 70,000 and 100,000 yen

Open *Tôkyô, onna o tasuke hon*, an information book for women who live in Tokyo, and in the section dealing with 'Safe Sex' (p. 18) there is advice not only on different forms of contraception but also on how much an abortion will cost depending on how many months pregnant the woman is.

An abortion can be carried out up until week twenty-two (until recently week twenty-four),[5] but the cost fluctuates between 70,000 and 100,000 yen (excluding the cost of hospitalization) depending on whether it takes place before or after the third month,[6] and between 100,000 and 200,000 yen if it takes place after.[7] Each additional day spent in hospital can cost anything between 10,000 to 20,000 yen which makes abortion relatively accessible to the majority of budgets.

Officially there are 500,000 abortions a year

Fujita states

> It is surprising that only the Ministry of Health appears to believe the statistics it conscientiously publishes each year at the tax-payer's expense, when doctors themselves have calculated the actual number of abortions carried out to be double, if not triple this figure.[8]

In the course of his research, Fujita ascertained that some private clinics carry out an average of five to twenty abortions a day, which means that at the rate current at that time, they were making a profit calculated to be 75 million yen a year.[9] However scandalous this might be, these figures do highlight the very substantial income earned by doctors. Worse still, they explain why doctors are opposed to the contraceptive pill being made freely available in Japan. Salaried gynaecologists employed by state hospitals, or those managed by local cooperatives, do not spurn these second jobs which supplement their income and if official figures are inaccurate this is no doubt because gynaecologists do not publicize the facts.

Medical science to encourage birth or death?

While Japan is the country with the lowest number of perinatal deaths in the world, we should not forget that it still favours the first-born and second-born – the 'precious children'; the others are more often than not destined to become water-babies or *mizuko* (a term used to denote aborted features: see pp. 130–40). It is difficult to speak of a child-based society when we examine these sad facts. And yet this was the interpretation put forward by the anthropologist Hara Hiroko, to explain the relatively high mortality rate among women in childbirth.[10]

Women will abort in pain

It is difficult to believe, as Ogino Miho or Tanaka Kimiko maintain, that abortion is a routine operation over which the woman experiences not the slightest feeling of remorse – witness this touching statement by a 45-year-old woman who had two abortions during her eighteen-year marriage: 'As an act of penance for what I was doing to my foetus I asked not to be given an anaesthetic.[11] I felt it was the least I could do for him.[12]

THE TORMENT OF WATER-BABIES

The *mizuko* trade is the speciality of some Buddhist temples which have become experts at instigating or exploiting women's feelings of remorse. An advertisement which appeared in a daily paper promised (for a fee) to protect the family against 'the harmful effects of the little souls who come to torment the living'.

In reality the facts are extremely complicated and require further explanation. First, while abortion and infanticide have been practised for a very long time the water-babies business is much more recent, originating at the beginning of the 1960s and peaking around 1965 and 1970. The evolution of the meaning attached to the term *mizuko* is in itself revealing since it used to refer only to foetuses who died before or just after birth but now it also denotes aborted embryos.

Brochures produced by the new temples which specialize in the repose of these souls are careful to perpetuate the ambiguity for they explain that whatever the circumstances, parents are nevertheless responsible because they were unable to do what they should have done for them, had their lives not been terminated.

The semantic shift is all the more astounding since Shinto eschatology exempted children who had died in infancy from the cycle of purification which adults had to undergo before being reintegrated into the pantheon. In a way they were placed in moratorium or in transit while awaiting a better reincarnation.

The 'return to sender' (see p. 116) was supposed to put off reincarnation without denying the child the possibility of one at a later date. During a period of famine or extreme poverty the parents were in a way doing the child a favour by returning them since this meant they might have a more clement reincarnation. Seen in this light abortion or infanticide were the lesser of two evils.

This is none the less a fairly dubious attitude, because in Buddhism there is no worse Karmic act than to take a life, however this is done. Moreover it is clearly stated in Buddhist texts that life begins at the moment of conception. Besides, the way the Mahayana Buddhists describe the fate awaiting the water-babies is enough to make their parents tremble. Thrust into a corner of hell on the banks of the River

Sai, they are doomed to the interminable task of building pagoda- or stupa-like towers by stacking pebbles which symbolize prayers for their parents:[13] fragile constructions which wicked demons then take fiendish delight in demolishing. They are condemned to these eternal tortures because they were unable to carry out their filial duty towards their parents, to whom they are indebted despite everything for the gift of life, however brief this was.

While emphasizing the source of this legend to be very much Japanese, placing its origins well before the Edo period (even though it was propagated in the eighteenth century),[14] Yanagita Kunio explains that its assimilation into Buddhism was much later no doubt because he wanted to influence parents by describing the tortures they were inflicting on the children they were depriving of life.[15]

Here are extracts from a Buddhist song *Sai-no-kawara Jizô wasan* ('Hymn of praise to the Jizô of the River Sai') sung in Japanese, which describes these tortures:[16]

Not of this world is the story of sorrow.
The story of the Sai-no-Kawara,
At the roots of the Mountain of Shide; –
Not of this world is the tale; yet 'tis most pitiful
to hear
for together in the Sai-no-Kawara are assembled
Children of tender age in multitude, –
Infants but two or three years old,
Infants of four or five, infants of less than ten;
In the Sai-no-Kawara are they gathered together.
And the voice of their longing for their parents,
The voice of their crying for their mothers and
their fathers –
'*Chichi koishi! hana koishi!*' –
Is never as the voice of the crying of children in
this world,
But a crying so pitiful to hear
That the sound of it would pierce through flesh
and bone.
And sorrowful indeed the task which they
perform, –
Gathering the stones of the bed of the river,
Therewith to heap the tower of prayers.
Saying prayers for the happiness of father, they
heap the first tower;

Saying prayers for the happiness of mother, they
heap the second tower;
Saying the prayers for their brothers, their sisters, and
all whom they loved at home, they heap the third tower.
Such, by day, are their pitiful diversions.
But ever as the sun begins to sink below the
horizon,
Then do the Oni, the demons of the hells, appear,
And say to them, – 'What is this that you do
here?
'Lo! your parents still living in the Shaba-world [i.e. this world]
'Take no thought of pious offering or holy work:
'They do nought but mourn for you from the
morning unto the evening.
'Oh, how pitiful! alas! how unmerciful!
'Verily the cause of the pains that you suffer
'Is only the mourning, the lamentation of your
parents.'
And saying also 'Blame never us!'
The demons cast down the heaped-up towers,
They dash the stones down with their clubs of
iron.
But lo! the teacher Jizô appears.
All gently he comes, and says to the weeping
infants: –
'Be not afraid, dears! be never fearful!
'Poor little souls, your lives were brief indeed!
'Too soon you were forced to make the
weary journey to the Meido
'The long journey to the region of the dead!
'Trust to me! I am your father and mother in the Meido,
'Father of all children in the region of the dead.'
And he folds the skirt of his shining robe about them;
So graciously takes he pity on the infants.
To those who cannot walk he stretches forth his strong
shakujô;
And he pets the little ones, caresses them, takes them to his
loving bosom.
So graciously he takes pity on the infants.
Namu Amida Butsu! [I take my refuge in the Buddha Amida]
(*Source*: Hearn Lafcadio, *Glimpses of Unfamiliar Japan*,
Tut. Books, 1894, pp. 56–61)

The origins of the Jizô worship

Bodhisattva Jizô is one of the most popular bodhisattvas in Japan,[17] whereas in India he would seem to be the least so.[18] Described by Lafcadio Hearn as 'the most Japanese of all the Japanese divinities',[19] whose worship probably goes back to the Edo period (1600–1868) together with the custom of erecting statues to him, presenting him with toys, clothes, offerings or small stones as symbols of prayers with a view to putting dead children under his protection.[20] Introduced at the end of the Heian period (794–1185), the worship of Jizô is not associated with any sect in particular for he saves anyone who prays to him for he has made himself guardian of the place between the two worlds so that he can shield humans from the tortures of hell.[21] The earliest stone representations of him go back to the beginning of the eighteenth century and were destined to facilitate births, to protect children as well as the victims of infanticide, famine and abortion.[22]

Over a period of time Jizô also came to be the boddhisattva who helps the dying to be reborn in the Pure Land of Miroku. Jizô is usually depicted as a very young monk or child with the detached air of those fulfilled beings who have reincarnated through compassion with the sole aim of relieving a suffering humanity. It might be more correct to say that he is asexual. As we saw in the *Jizô wasan*, he is at the same time the father and mother of children. Indeed he is sometimes represented as having a woman's breast (notably in the Shiunzan Jozôdera Temple of Chichibu). Symbolizing the purest form of love which never passes judgement, if he remains impersonal this is because he shines on all those who have need of him.[23]

Yanagita Kunio states that the small pebbles piled up in front of representations of Jizô symbolize the torture of the perpetually demolished gravel towers 'that no human would have the heart to knock down', and that in the reconstructions of the Sai-no-kawara, at the foot of certain mountains, the little stack of stones are so fragile that they look as though the slightest breeze would blow them down.[24] He writes, 'It is said that when they do fall they are immediately picked up, for no self-respecting father – and not only the recently bereaved ones – could pass them by without being moved to pick up a few stones to add to the pile, even though no one is ever caught doing this.'[25]

Jizô, protector of living or dead children?

Originally the protector of children (*kosodate Jizô*), we have seen how he was by extension also that of the aborted foetuses condemned to the torments of the River Sai. That is why he saw himself in the 'specialist' role of saviour or mediator on behalf of aborted embryos, hence the juxtaposition of *mizuko* to his name, turning him into a symbol of hope and compassion – a rare quality in that kingdom.[26] Though he is now often represented holding a baby in his left hand, with crowds of them pleading at his feet, more modern representations give him a uterus containing an aborted foetus in place of the *hôju* or *cintamani* (the onion-shaped mystic jewel by virtue of which all wishes may be fulfilled), which he traditionally held in his left hand.[27]

Although religious services destined to appease the suffering of aborted foetuses is no doubt several hundred years old, the form which they take these days, institutionalized by new Buddhist sects, has been around for over twenty or thirty years. It exploits what Werblowsky (see n. 27) defines as 'the booming business of Terror' because it dwell on the curses or malicious acts possibly resulting from the hostile emotions of foetuses who have more or less been assimilated into the *muenbotoke*, or spirits abandoned after their death which no one has taken the trouble to lay to rest through the appropriate ritual.[28] Denied their earthly incarnation, these little beings are prone to become malicious, as they constantly strive to avenge themselves on their sires or phratry. That is why the *mizuko* are sometimes compared to the *gaki*,[29] or skeletal demons whose bellies are swollen with rickets, condemned to be tormented by hunger, so much so that they are often depicted in rolled paintings, hurling themselves onto human excrement on which they start feeding.[30]

On the other hand the water-babies' resentment is likely to degenerate, hence the temptation to draw a parallel between them and the legend of the *kappa*,[31] or mythical, malevolent, amphibious animals and vampires,[32] who constantly torment the living in an attempt to drown them so that they can feast on their blood, which unquestionably follows on from what was said in Chapter 5. Indeed it is somewhat disconcerting that the characters for 'river' and 'child' are used to write *kappa*.

The *mizuko*'s vindictive influence on brothers and sisters can be exercised in different ways. They can communicate a great fear of the dark to them, make them act impulsively, make them susceptible to violent mood swings (from hyperactivity to extreme apathy), they might have exhausted their parents' patience by becoming obsessed with sex or prone to repeated illnesses or accidents.[33]

Miura Dômyô, a monk of the Jôdo sect (School of Pure Land Buddhism) also mentions what he calls *jibyô*, psychosomatic illnesses or chronic pains which no medicine can treat, which can be accompanied by occult manifestations such as the distant vision of a perpetually weeping child, the impression of seeing a strange shape through the *shôji*,[34] or hearing a funeral slab repeatedly falling; or even mysterious traffic accidents, professional disasters and other signs suggestive of unnatural misfortune.[35]

The prospectuses I possessed also dwelt on the foetus' anger and vindictive nature which has the potential to put the rest of the household in danger. They warn against the possibility of heart diseases, cervical or lower back pains (particularly in the mother), or even a sustained phase of extreme violence against the phratry, a nervous breakdown or suicidal tendencies interpreted as being the *mizuko*'s revenge against those who prevented the foetus from living. We read that: 'The souls of aborted children are trying to tell you this: "What! After having taken my life, you have the audacity to ask me to rest in peace? Really, you are quite irresponsible. Don't count on me to forgive you!"'[36]

This is why the *mizuko kuyô* ritual is so important.[37] Defined by Werblowsky as being a pacification rite for the souls of unborn (i.e. naturally or artificially aborted) embryos it is also a kind of exorcism destined to appease the living as well as the dead but more particularly a form of therapy for the mother who is given no emotional support by the medical team (apart from the possibility of having a *kuyô* said at the hospital itself).[38]

Many are the researchers who stress how the decision to have an abortion has become a terrible burden for the family since it no longer shares the responsibility with the rest of the household or the village community.[39] These days, when another mouth to feed is no longer a threat to the survival of the family, this decision is all the more difficult since it can hardly be prompted by anything other than purely egoistical reasons, such as the preservation of the family's standard of living or providing the two oldest children with a better chance for success.

A professor at the University of Tôyô states that the majority of city dwellers find themselves caught in a vicious circle where they are perpetually striving for a better life.

Although they can feed and clothe themselves and sleep in comfort, they nevertheless still want to improve their standard of living, which explains why they are no longer willing to spend time bringing up children and why they certainly do not want more than two. The moment another pregnancy is confirmed their first thought is to have it aborted.

This is why 90 per cent of the time the reason given and readily accepted by the medical profession is that the family has financial difficulties.

Passed in 1948 (it is sometimes claimed) to help Japanese women get rid of the souvenirs left them by passing GIs, the law allowing abortion was completed the following year with the addition of the famous financial clause which means that a woman can never be refused an abortion. These days, when women turn up for the routine operation they never seem to have to give the doctor a reason. As we have already seen, it is married women with two children who have the most abortions.

The pictorial votive offerings (wooden plaques on the back of which pilgrims write their wishes or, as is the case here, their repentance) which are found in temples not only corroborate the true relevance of this act, but also on occasion, make it less alarming: 'Please, forgive us' or 'We promise never to do it again'.[40]

This votive tablet was also discovered by me at the Kinshôji (fourth station of the Chichibu pilgrimage dedicated to Kannon):[41] *May my child live happily ever after in Heaven. I know this might sound selfish but you can be sure that your mother will never forget you as long as she lives* (signed Setsuko 9 February 1992).

Some of the inscriptions are quite surprising; even verging on the cynical: 'We shall make good with the next baby where we failed towards you, please protect it'. Similarly this message signed by a 29-year-old mother: 'Sorry, my babies. Get along with each other in heaven and have a good time there'.[42] And again: 'Baby, we are really sorry. Please come back into my womb in five years time' (signed by a young couple of 23 and 24). This last plaque is strangely reminiscent of the *kogaeshi* 'return to sender' concept (see p. 116).

Since 1965, the Jikishian temple in Kyoto, known to be a *naki-komidera* (a temple where one comes in to weep or grieve) has put at the disposal of the pilgrims, books of grievances which they can either read or write in, in order to ease their consciences.[43] There are several hundred of these books already in stock.

Here are some of the comments found in one of the Shôjuin books, a temple in Tokyo which specializes in the *mizuko kuyô*:[44]

'My baby, I am sorry. You came just too early for us.'
'I feel very guilty.'
'I have come to beg your forgiveness.'
'Please forgive your foolish father.'[45]

And the following, also found in a book of grievances:

After having had one miscarriage and an abortion we were blessed with two children – a boy and a girl – and I am now very happy living with my husband and aunt. And yet, I cannot help but have a heavy heart each time I think of the child I aborted and I wonder what it would have been like if it had lived. Now, at the age of 36, I see that the experiences of life help you grow up and mature, even though some are very painful. I remember a sleepless night I had when I was younger, nursing a broken heart. And yet that experience made me stronger. I would like to tell the young that they should have the courage to face life and not allow themselves to be disheartened. As for me, I am going to do all I can to improve myself.[46]

WATER-BABIES AND THE RITUAL OF APPEASEMENT

The ritual of appeasement these days consists of having a *bonze recite sutras*, for a donation in the order of 20,000 yen. As the aborted embryos and foetuses do not usually have a first name, it is not the custom to give them one posthumously, although this is done in some temples.

They are on occasion also given a funeral slab. Although the majority of temples do not house foetal remains, the Shôjuin Temple in Tokyo, known as the 'baby temple' (*akachan dera*), will take in their ashes, since the so-called law on eugenical protection, permitting abortion, made the cremation of foetuses aborted after the fourth month of pregnancy, obligatory. In 1981, the ashes of 550,000 foetuses were deposited there. In Yokohama, the Sôjiji has a tower where the bones of the *mizuko* are conserved.[47]

Richard Fox Young divides the temples specializing in *mizuko kuyô* into three groups:

- those which inspire fear, by dwelling on the vindictive nature of the *mizuko* (as is the case of the Shiunzan Jizôdera at Chichibu);
- those which promise peace of mind, by emphasizing the benefits they and their families will enjoy as long as the necessary ritual is accomplished at regular intervals;
- and finally those which require the couple to be genuinely repentant and to promise they will never again find themselves in the same situation, the Shiunzan Jizôji, at Chichibu, suggest that as a penance they go on a pilgrimage: that of the Shikoku henrô or the hyaku Kannon.[48]

My own observations led me to believe that the three categories often overlapped. To these, could be added the temples which do not practise the *kuyô*, but which never refuse a request for one. Having found that around 33 per cent of Zen temples carry out the *mizuko kuyô* ritual, while 56 per cent do not – though he does not rule out their usefulness – Werblowsky quotes a Zen monk who told him that when a woman comes to him to request a *kuyô* or the reciting of sutras, he does not have the heart to refuse. He related the story of a woman who was suffering from different ailments (probably due to the menopause) that no doctor could alleviate, who blamed these on an abortion she had had a few decades previously. He carried out the ritual she had requested but also advised her to seek specialized medical help.

Though the *mizuko kuyô* ritual appears to be very much rooted in Buddhism it has what William La Fleur describes as hints of neo-Shintoism.[49] Although quite rare, some Shinto temples, for example the Ishikiri Jinja, do practise it, substituting the readings of sutras with *norito*.[50]

Finally, it is not only Shinto temples but also Buddhist temples that organize *kuyô* ceremonies for inanimate objects which have served their purpose and which cannot be discarded without an expression of gratitude for services rendered. And so there is a *kuyô* for needles, chopsticks, dolls and even, more recently, for worn-out razor blades and bras. The dividing line between animate and inanimate objects is somewhat hazy.[51]

Although it would be difficult to say whether this was some kind of recent anthropomorphism resulting from the fashion to keep pets, the need to have a substitute for love (or children?) or the Buddhist respect for life, but these days *petto kuyô* are also celebrated in Buddhist temples for domestic animals which have passed away.

Therapy for the mother or the child?

Werblowsky is of the opinion that mothers if not parents are in greater need of being placated than are the foetuses, for they have a great need to harness their grief or at least to relieve their consciences. Hence his definition of *mizuko kuyô* as being 'the projection of painful traumas', for the reciting of sutras is supposed to offset the absence of psychological help as it replies to 'an overriding need to pacify something in the subconscious'.[52]

Bardwell Smith also describes the *mizuko kuyô* as being an essential element in helping women get through the period of mourning whether or not the death of the foetus was deliberate.[53]

Water-babies – a lucrative business

When you discover how lucrative the water-babies business is, it becomes all to easy to criticize the monks. As an example, the cost of buying a statue in the Shiunzan Jizô temple in Chichibu is 150,000, 180,000 or 230,000 yen plus a charge for engraving (300 yen per character) and the right to have it placed within the temple complex (5,000 yen a year). As these prices are the fruit of a dubious compromise, it is difficult not to feel somewhat uncomfortable given that in theory no act is more despicable to a Buddhist than to take a life, however insignificant that life might be.

The only (ambiguous) position taken by the Buddhist clergy was spelt out during an international conference (World Buddhist Conference) in response to a declaration which described Japan as an 'abortion paradise'.[54] It would appear that while in theory the monks condemn abortion, they find themselves more or less compelled to accept it as an inescapable evil.

Without wanting to minimize the scandalous trade surrounding water-babies, it must nevertheless be acknowledged that temples are responding to a genuine need on the part of women who require psychological assistance when the burden of guilt they have to carry becomes too heavy for them alone. In Japan as elsewhere, there are many reasons why women resort to abortion – the fear of bringing into the world an abnormal child, marital infidelity, the mother's age – but the vaguest and most common reason seems to be that economic clause which allows abortion whatever the grounds (at present 90 per cent) if a mother does not feel up to coping with the responsibilities of motherhood. It would appear that the Japanese are happy to maintain this obscurity since they sometimes prefer not to see too clearly.

Finally, we focus on Japanese doctors who are frequently accused of shamelessly taking advantage of a situation with a view (through the carrying out of abortions) to inflating their earnings. It is often said that it is they who are opposed to the introduction of the pill, for fear of losing out on what has become a lucrative business. There is probably some truth in this but a number of discussions have made me moderate my judgement. Although the Ministry of Health has just rejected a proposal that the pill be available over the counter, it should be said that many doctors are actually in favour of the idea, and contrary to popular opinion, the pill is not illegal, any more than it is prescribed – as Werblowsky claims – only as a remedy. I know of many Japanese women who have been on the pill and who were given a three-month rather than a one-month prescription which was the norm until quite recently. However the Ministry of Health's position is still somewhat ambiguous: indirectly it seems to endorse the pill by allowing it to be used as a treatment but not recommending it as a contraceptive 'because this might encourage the young to become promiscuous and that could lead to the spread of AIDS'. It would seem therefore that while the ministry objects to it being freely available over the chemists' counter it chooses to ignore the 'abusive' use of the contraceptive pill which already goes on, especially as this use remains the privilege of a small, well-informed intellectual elite (in 1986 barely 4.5 per cent were on the pill).

Those who have used it are not always enthusiastic. Many resent having to take it every day but even more object to the fact that it interferes with their normal hormonal functions. One woman confided to me that to her it was a breakthrough 'like tampons compared to sanitary towels' although she admitted that at the age of 46, it had taken 'a lot of courage' to go and ask to be put on the pill. Proof again no doubt, that it is not appropriate to discuss such matters, particularly as the consultations are semi-public.

In the face of the reticence feminists have observed, it is difficult for me to accept absolutely Werblowsky's view when he says that the Ministry of Health is wittingly 'brainwashing' women to discourage them from taking an oral contraceptive because they want to maintain the status quo. My view is that there is a genuine cultural reticence among Japanese women not only with regard to taking the initiative where contraception is concerned (for fear of being regarded as loose women) but also because it means that each day they have to take a drug that will disrupt their metabolism.

'We are not just talking about a psychological rejection,' one feminist confided, who had never felt she wanted to take it. To her and to many women, oral contraception is against nature and that is why they decline to use it.

To those tempted to point out that in fact the Japanese are the world's biggest consumers of medicines, all that can be said is that this is because of the way the medical system works. If it suits doctors to write prescriptions so that they can make a profit, if does not mean that the Japanese will actually take all the medicines they have been prescribed.

7 The new order

It is young women who hold the future in their hands, so let us take a brief look at their values and lifestyles. Are they prepared to follow in their mothers' footsteps or have they decided to rebel?

THE HANAKO SYNDROME

Named after a magazine targeting the 'single aristocrats' who still live with their parents, and whose earnings are therefore more like pocket money, the Hanako type with her air of a 'little girl well brought up though it doesn't mean she is', is considered to be intelligent and cultured but also frivolous, egocentric, epicurean and a slave to fashion. In short she is the ideal consumer who goes out of her way to avoid *a priori* anything difficult or which requires effort. Single – between the age of 20 and 29 – she has adopted the magazine's motto which proclaims that she expects more from life than a career and a Prince Charming.

There is no question of having both either, for she knows exactly what she can expect from the Equal Employment Opportunity Law: only those who belong to the small intellectual elite who have done the rounds of the competitive circuit can fight next to men, they know how much effort is required of them and know the price of the reward. The others, ejected from positions in those elitist circles, serve as excuses to employers to say they can offer young girls only clerical positions. Despite the lack of objections, no one is really fooled and this flexibility on both sides allows the status quo to be maintained. Thus the 'turnover' of the workforce continues without anyone complaining about it, least of all Hanako who can also leave the battlefield when she decides she has had (more than) enough and that now is the time to look for a husband. The retiring warrior in some ways resembles Princess Masako who after having experienced the dizzy world of diplomacy chose to become the wife of the Crown Prince.

There is no question of Hanako emulating her mother either who, like 60 per cent of women aged 40 or over, and in present employment, threw herself into a part-time job, only to be mercilessly exploited through having to do extremely insipid and repetitive work with hours equivalent to full-time. Hanako takes a detached look at the results. What has her mother gained? She does two jobs a day for she and her husband are not emancipated since he continues to expect all the usual little comforts. To see her looking chronically exhausted and neglected, Hanako does not consider her to be either fulfilled or happy. The game is definitely not worth the candle and this is not an example Hanako would wish to emulate.

Looking for a husband

While she is searching for her (wealthy) Prince Charming, why should she not ask for a little more but she must keep a cool head for the future is at stake. To the three obligatory *kô* (rich, educated and tall),[1] she has added the three *ryô* (handsome, good-natured and from a good background).[2] However, income remains the determining factor and this must be sufficiently high to allow her to have a house which is both functional and congenial. This is in fact the motto of *Muffin*'s readership (*Hanako*'s counterpart for the married woman and mother): 'A touch of luxury in the family'.

Moreover she wishes to find a good man (malleable) who will grant her a certain amount of freedom and who will not have the same machismo temperament as her father. Not just any one will do either, far from it. She does have a considerable advantage however, for there are more young men than young women, thus giving her a choice. She will therefore do all she can to find the rare pearl.

As the feminist Ueno Chizuko writes, a child is of course a necessary part of the married woman's accoutrements, society is no nearer to accepting the status of a dinky couple (*d*ouble *i*ncome, *n*o *k*ids), any more than it is closer to accepting that of the 'married woman without children'. Hence the child is Hanako's excuse for staying quietly at home. But, for everything to be perfect, she wants not only the tailor-made husband but also the tailor-made child. The child should look like the ones she has seen in the magazines for mothers-to-be – cute and chubby – and never prevent her from looking around the shops whenever she feels like it. In other words she wants a decorative child she can take anywhere.

Sensational mothers

The archetypal mother 'who loses none of her charm' is provided by the singer Matsuda Seiko, the Japanese Madonna whose wedding and pregnancy caused widespread press coverage. If the public found her so fascinating it is probably because she succeeded in steering her ship so well, successfully meeting the criteria to which Hanako subscribes. In contrast is Yamaguchi Momoe, actress and dancer, renowned for her part in *The Izu Dancer* (based on Kawabata's novel), who after her marriage 'discreetly' slid into the role of a mother (three children in eight years). If Momoe-chan conforms to an ideal, this is because her decision was painful and irreversible (she wept as she put down the microphone during her final performance). Seiko meanwhile steered her way through marriage and motherhood without sustaining the slightest damage.[3] But she achieved much more, for by becoming the heroine of magazines for expectant mothers (*Balloon. P. and*, etc.) she was working for Japan by making motherhood fashionable,[4] it could even be said, that she 'commercialized' it. She created and propagated what Ueno Chizuko called the model of the Holy Family, based on the Oedipal triangle: father, mother, child or children, plus grandmother sometimes, as long as it is the Holy Family who needs her and not the other way round.

In addition to a tailor-made husband and baby, the grandmother should be tailor-made, ready to (lovingly) take on the baby in question the moment he or she becomes a nuisance. It suits Hanako to have the three generations under the same roof (as they need a nanny might as well take granny in) but unlike previous models it is her mother rather than the husband's who moves in, which places him in the position of a *mukoyôshi*.[5] The expression 'Masuo syndrome', an ironic term for this phenomenon, was inspired by the husband of the heroine of the famous cartoon *Sazae san* who lives with his in-laws and who, like the rest of the household, obeys the dictates of her father.[6] This underlines the husband's inferior position. He is, moreover, a man more often than not chosen because of his lack of personality and who is of course no threat to the mother–daughter relationship.

Equipped with a suitable husband and mother, Seiko-chan was very popular when she set off to Hawaii to get over the birth, without taking her baby with her. Her admirers were astonished, however, when a short while later she went off to New York. Some began to think she was a bit too eager to get away from her child.

Agnes-Chan is a Hong Kong Chinese woman who began her singing career very young. It was her appearance (sweet, verging on the insipid) rather than her voice which people found so endearing. Her popularity did not prevent her from spending four years at Sophia University in Tokyo or from completing her masters degree at Stanford. She is somewhere between Momoe and Seiko inasmuch as she wanted to continue teaching, studying and making television appearances as a *talento*,[7] while being the epitome of the loving mother, ever mindful of her children.[8]

And yet the day Agnes arrived at NHK's (state-run television channel) recording studios with a baby in her arms, feminists seized upon the situation and debated whether or not anyone had the right to work under such conditions. When NHK improvised a nursery, Agnes was accused of wanting to have her cake and eat it by refusing to make the choice which no woman can escape. And that is why with her big bag full of nappies, toys and feeding bottles, she was even denounced as an Asian-peasant-who-smells-of-milk.[9] In the face of these attacks, this 'bashing', as the feminist Ochiai Emiko put it,[10] Agnes decided at the end of an interview with the anthropologist Hara Hiroko,[11] to head back to Stanford to do her PhD as soon as she had brought her second child into the world. I should like to say in her favour that, unlike Seiko, she takes her responsibilities for the offspring seriously, although her Japanese husband (of whom there is never a mention) seems to have no say in the matter.

Has twenty years of feminism achieved no more than this?

Hanako's philosophy might well be to go her own sweet way and live life to the full but she has never been through a rebellious phase: indeed since the Meiji period (1868) the dream of becoming a housewife does not seem to have changed much. It was out of favour for a while but its popularity would seem to be soaring once more. 'With its insinuation that she lacked personality, it used to be said that she smelled of *nukamiso* [salted rice-bran paste for pickling vegetables],' Ueno writes, 'but these days housewives are smart, well-dressed and tanned from all that outdoor tennis.'

It must be acknowledged that the 'three meals a day and an afternoon nap' (see p. 28 and 197, n. 34) is not all bad, for there is nothing like a good sinecure.

'When you consider that all we have to show for twenty years of feminism is *kattena obatarian* (the egocentric middle-aged woman) and the flighty Hanako, it's enough to drive you to despair',[12] laments Ueno, who makes no distinction between the two categories except to say that the latter is not prepared to wait until her husband is dead to start enjoying herself. And if she reproaches her for being a merry widow while her husband is still alive, this is because in her heart of hearts her husband is already well and truly dead and buried.

Not all Hanakos have the perseverance necessary to carry this through and the main criticism aimed at Ueno stems from the fact that however irresponsible she might seem,[13] the average young Japanese woman in no way resembles Matsuda Seiko for she takes her maternal responsibilities so seriously (even if her child is the first she has ever come into contact with) that she is sometimes in danger of becoming neurotic (see Chapter 1). If Seiko is discussed as much as she is, is it not just because she is the incarnation of so many young women's wildest dreams – because she frees them of the myth of the pelican mother who sacrificed herself body and soul in the service of her nearest and dearest? She has doubtless created new yearnings which the average woman will never be able to satisfy (how many women could afford to go to Hawaii to recover from childbirth?). But who can blame them for dreaming when they have witnessed the previous generation slaving away?

'Ueno is also mistaken when she says that a child is just an excuse,' argues the mother of a 3-year-old girl who describes herself as having been an 'intellectual Hanako', 'for in the present social climate you need to have two. There will always be some kind soul, eager to whisper in your ear that you're not really an adult until you've had the second and that it is this one alone, who makes a complete and whole woman of you.'

While feminists complain, we might wonder whether, beneath that conformist appearance of hers, Hanako is not in the process of inciting a revolution, for by expecting so much, she is telling men that she is not prepared to accept just anyone nor for that matter just any old lifestyle. In an article in *Asahi*, Hanako relates how whenever she takes a taxi to go home at night, the driver berates her for going out and enjoying herself instead of getting married and that it is because of women like her that the men in his line of work can no longer find a wife. She was stunned the first time it happened but by the third, she was getting annoyed with being lectured to like that, considering it was years since her own father had dared do so.

THE DECLINE OF MARRIAGE

An article in *Asahi* (17 June 1992) entitled 'The proliferation of celibacy' pointed out that, coinciding with an ageing population, celibacy had gone up two or threefold. The Centre studying demographic problems outlined the trend revealed by a national survey carried out in 1990 and published two years later, thus: 'Women *could* marry but they don't; men *would like* to marry but they can't'.

The survey found that up until 1970, a little over 40 per cent of men and under 20 per cent of women were still single, but that five years later 20 per cent of young women between the age of 25 and 29 were still single, a figure which doubled over the next five years.

That the percentage of single women between the age of 30 and 34 has gone from 8 per cent to 14 per cent is just about acceptable but for celibacy to have doubled among those of childbearing age (25–35) is the cause of great concern to demographers.

However, taking into account that there are twice as many bachelors aged 30 to 34 and three times as many aged 35 to 39, the situation is such that of the men aged between 40 and 44 the number who will remain permanently single has jumped from 4 per cent to 12 per cent: the real problem of celibacy is among the male population.

Though the public is very much aware that there is a dearth of wives in rural areas it is not so well informed when it comes to the disturbing increase in the number of single men in the 30–49 age range, not only among white-collar and blue-collar workers (see pp. 162–3) but also those involved in the fishing industry.

There are many difficulties such as plummeting birthrate, fewer marriages, increase in the number of divorces, and the problems of an ageing population made all the more acute as life expectancy continues to increase.[14] Yuzawa Yasuhiko has come to the conclusion that the actual institution of marriage is under threat.[15] Yet, considering the acute 'marriageitis' which the Japanese have always suffered from – 98.8 per cent of Japanese born during the Meiji period (1868–1911) were married at least once in their life – Yuzawa speculates that if they are the victims of a shortage of women of marriageable age, perhaps men who are still single at the age of 35 or 40 have deliberately followed a 'strategy of delay'.

In a survey carried out by the Altman Marriage Bureau, though 25 per cent of women interviewed declared that marriage did not necessarily lead to happiness, 95 per cent of them did admit that they still wished to get married.[16] There was a small proviso, however: not just anyone would do, for 60 per cent of the 95 per cent who said they wanted to get married declared that they would do so only 'if they met someone decent and who fitted the bill'.

On the whole men seemed much more anxious to get married, even though these *toshikoshisoba* (see p. 221, n.21) were laying down identical conditions in their eternal search for the perfect woman. The reason why marriage is regarded as an 'option' is of course connected to the fact that it is no longer considered to be an absolute necessity, as was the case not so long ago when women had no other alternative and when families were trying to find a husband for their daughters as quickly as possible so that there would be one mouth fewer to feed. 'These days,' maintains Madoka Yoriko, a delegate from the research centre on family problems, 'women no longer need to marry in order to live and as parents have fewer children, they aren't under the same pressure to get rid of their daughters.'

THE 'IMPOSSIBLE TO MARRY OFF' GO SHOPPING

Why not go for a beautiful Asian girl?

For five years now farmers have been travelling to South East Asia in search of a wife but this practice is no longer restricted to those from rural areas, writes Kajiwara Hazuki, who decided to go along to a marriage bureau situated in the Ikebukuro area of Tokyo, whose operation extends 'beyond the borders of Japan' and who, according to their publicity, can find you a 'charming Asian'.[17] When he arrived on the seventh floor, he was struck by the fact that the agency (*Nippon bridal kyôkai*) was full of young men and their mothers, who were moreover the only ones to specify their requirements.[18] 'You see, he's already 30. "We" would like someone who's cheerful. Yes, we have our own business. And we own our house.' The sons involved gave their embarrassed assent.

The managing director of an agency which was set up in 1978 explained that Chinese women were now the most popular.[19] Originally this bureau did not go beyond the borders of the archipelago in its search for wives; however, in 1990 having realized that some of its clients were absolutely 'impossible to marry off', it moved into the specialized market of mixed marriages. With offices in China and Taiwan the bureau now offers young women from those two countries.

Toshikoshisoba or old bachelors

The managing director Mr Suzuki explains:

> As far as our Japanese male clients are concerned, it really is quite hopeless. No Japanese girl wants them! To begin with Japanese

men have no idea how to behave. When we arrange for applicants to meet in a café they can find nothing better to do than enumerate their requirements one by one without showing the least interest in those of their companion. And that's the last thing they should be doing! Then add to this the problem of the *ie* (family: see p. 215, n. 24). It's incredible to think that a society as modern as this one has a family structure which hasn't changed since before the war. There is nothing guaranteed to scare off a Japanese woman more than these kinds of conditions.

Another establishment which arranges mixed marriages supports this claim. Its director specializes in Koreans and justifies this by explaining that they are the only ones capable these days of living up to the 'despotic' expectations of Japanese men who have become discouraged by the excessive demands of their compatriots. 'I am sometimes tempted to ask them if they can cook and do the laundry,' was the comment from one of them, 'you just don't get those problems with Korean women!'

If the director stresses the fact that Japanese women no longer correspond to the type sought by the more traditional Japanese male, it is to justify why marriage bureaux specializing in mixed marriages have expanded their activities beyond their national borders.

It goes without saying that all our clients would much rather marry a Japanese girl but the facts speak for themselves since barely 10 per cent get as far as a *miai*, though this in itself is *no* guarantee of marriage.[20]

Taxi and lorry drivers, blue-collar workers (see pp. 162–3), farmers' eldest sons and traders are in the worst position. For them to insist that they will take only a Japanese woman for a wife is purely and simply to live in cloud cuckooland; in any case they always end up realizing this themselves after many months or even years of fruitless searching. It was all very well to be ironic over 'Christmas cakes', saying that once a woman was over 25, she was 'on the shelf', these days it is the men who are described as *toshikoshisoba*.[21] After the age of 31 there are no more takers!

Mr N, a 39 year old who runs a *râmen* restaurant, is not without charm.[22] Yet he has two handicaps: first he is short, and second, his job 'classification'. He has had six *miai*, five with Japanese girls and one with a Chinese girl, so far without success. He explains:

To pay 2 or 3 million yen for a foreign wife is not exorbitant when you consider that going out with a Japanese girl means you soon get through 1 or 2 million! You know, when you go out with them, they never offer to pay! When you think of how much we do for them, all that just to be jilted, you get to a stage where you've had enough! At least if you go through an agency you know what you're in for!

Another bachelor, aged 36, working in the field of naval construction, pours out his heart unable to look his interlocutor in the eye: 'There are quite a few problems these days. If you want to get married you have to be prepared to compromise, for the women of today won't. In a way, living alone isn't such a problem'.

He came to Tokyo after spending nine years trying to get a job as an accountant. It was those nine 'moratorium' years which were so damaging. He goes on to say how he approached different marriage bureaux after having completed a course in a cultural centre in order to become 'attractive' (see pp. 165–8) but when he heard what his compatriots expected, he realized they were out of touch with the men of today. 'How many young men are there, of marriageable age who earn an annual salary of 10 million yen? It's absolutely absurd!'

Another reject aged 37 explains: 'I am an only child with a mother to look after who is also an only child. A Japanese wife? Out of the question!' He has his own house and works for a large food manufacturer, but his mother is about to move in with him, so he has few illusions left. This has not prevented him from having ten *miai*, but as soon as he broaches the delicate subject, the candidate immediately disappears. 'They're interested in the house but without the old girl!'[23]

Mr Y is smart, tall (1.75m), and blames his prolonged celibacy on his sobriety. 'Chinese women are fine,' he says, 'they don't need to drink or smoke to be happy.' That is why he decided to ask the agency to find him a wife from Peking, where women have the reputation of putting their husbands first. In his opinion, the women of Shanghai are too spirited. He has not given up hope of finding that rare pearl who would be willing, without complaining, to look after his mother in her old age.[24]

A 'risky' investment

Mixed marriages are not always successful. A Japanese man spent 3 million yen on his marriage to a Filipina only to have his wife disappear after three days. 'All she wanted was a visa (see p. 157),' he lamented, 'She obviously thought the easiest way to get one was to get married'. The bureau refuses to intervene in such cases as it no longer considers itself to be involved once the marriage has been consummated.

To judge by the proliferation of marriage bureaux since the early 1990s, it would appear that almost anybody can open one (Iwao Sumiko reckons there are around 5,000 of them),[25] with taxi drivers in Manilla or Seoul acting as their agents.

The prosperous and highly regarded Altman Marriage Bureau in Tokyo's Nishi Shinjuku area restricts itself to Japanese women 'on principle', for they regard mixed marriages as presenting too many linguistic or cultural problems. This opinion is shared by the director of the Nippon Seinenkan Marriage Bureau (near Shinjuku) who, after having travelled throughout Japan to interview wives 'imported' from the Philippines and Communist China, considers the global consequences of these marriages to be too negative to envisage extending her activities beyond Japan's borders. The Altman Bureau maintains that very few of its male clients have the level of education or earnings to fit the requirements laid down by their female clients and that even those who have not been eliminated have very little chance of getting as far as a *miai*. 'Sub-contracting' is the only alternative left to the others.

The director of Vivas International has no illusions:

> Those who come to us have the choice of marrying for love (which, let's be realistic, is highly unlikely!), of remaining bachelors or of opting for a mixed marriage. The men who choose the last alternative are clearly those who have usually worked their way through countless bureaux or intermediaries and had *miai* after *miai* without ever getting anywhere. Many have already spent millions of yen and have no idea where to turn to next. All they can do is go to the smaller bureaux who specialize in 'charming Asian women'. At least with us they are confident of getting some- where. It is a kind of *kakekomidera* (see p. 219, n. 42) for men! We began with Taiwanese women and then Korean but now tend to concentrate more on the Filipinas.

Half of all foreign wives actually come from the Philippines. However, this is where most of the problems arise when the goal of getting a visa substantially transforms the deal. Although marriage by correspondence initiated by the 'suppliers' in June 1990 has now been made illegal, it would seem that a underground network continues to function in secret. It is estimated that a man needs to invest around

2,380,000 yen to conclude a marriage, an all-inclusive price which covers airfare, wedding ceremony and honeymoon. This is not an extortionate sum when the end result is marriage.

The wife trade (*jinshin-baibai*)?[26]

Although advertising the service has been banned, it continues to be perpetuated on the basis of word-of-mouth and through those Japanese-speaking institutions which also often act as intermediaries between purchaser and provider. Potential 'fiancées' are tested not only on their punctuality and diligence but also, on occasion, their ability to adapt (one wonders how?). They are also sometimes instructed to take classes in cookery and/or the Japanese language and have to vouch that they have never had a child. Filipino families merely ask the candidates to provide a medical certificate to confirm that he is not HIV positive.

These precautions having been taken, 'group *miais*' are arranged during which time charter-loads of suitors – of a certain age – are given a few minutes to make their choice. If there were any expectations then it would appear that the results are often disappointing. The Vivas Marriage Bureau has already recorded between ten and thirty divorces, 90 per cent of which were caused by sexual problems. 'And that can be blamed on porn videos,' declares the director Mr Kikuike, who acts as a 'wholesaler' in mixed marriages.[27]

> The 40-year-old men who make up the bulk of our clientele might not have chased after women very much but on the other hand they are unbeatable when it comes to porn videos. When they get married they are deluded into thinking that it will be the same scenario! They also expect Filipinas to be emancipated but these young country girls sometimes turn up in floods of tears in search of a refuge;[28] the disillusioned ones who end up returning to their villages invariably give our men the reputation of being 'perverts'. I learned of one divorce case where the young woman had been forced to drink her own urine because it was supposed to be a 'natural remedy'.[29]

Another major problem arises from the fact that Japanese men marry foreigners as a last resort and so they are reluctant to make the slightest effort to try to understand the other culture.

The proprietor of the *Barrio Festa* (a restaurant in Ikebukuro (Tokyo) which specializes in Filipino cuisine), who speaks fluent Tagalog, describes Filipino–Japanese couples as being bogged down in a veritable quagmire. From having put himself at the disposal of many of his clients, he knows what it is all about.

Without a shadow of a doubt they are attracted by the visa and the living allowance. As for the rest – they put up with it. It should be said that they're not exactly spoilt, their husbands are 'short, pot-bellied and bald'. If they happen to love one another then so much the better, but the poor things can hardly stammer three words of Japanese and their husbands have no intention of learning Tagalog.

And yet he admits to being astonished by the effusiveness of the latter who would never chat as much to a Japanese wife. 'Probably because they know from the outset that communication will be distorted', he adds, his expression thoughtful.

One client explained

We are criticized for going to Asia 'to buy' a wife, but when you consider that Japanese women want a husband who earns over 10 million yen a year, that also means that they evaluate themselves in monetary terms. If I have married a Filipina, it is because I couldn't afford to aim any higher. What do you expect, I had to come to terms with it.

IMPORTING FOREIGN WIVES FOR FARMERS

This is how Marian (aged 24) ended up married – supposedly successfully – to Mr Yamada (aged 36).

Originally from a village near Manilla, Marian looked after her family (seven brothers and sisters) as best she could by working in a small factory which manufactured pharmaceutical products. One day she found herself in a *miai* group, 'just like that', without having planned to. That is how she met her husband whom she married three days later.

'Once you've made your choice you have to get on with it', Mr Yamada explained. After a dozen fruitless *miai*, he had felt very disheartened and had reached the stage where he could not bear seeing his friends getting married one after another. By chance he learned from a television programme that some of the villages in his prefecture arranged group marriages so he decided at once that he would enrol. A month later he was married. He went on to explain: 'I wanted her to know that she'd be living with my parents. I was so nervous I could feel my heart thumping loudly but to my great surprise she didn't say anything. She looked taken aback but said nothing.'

His village town hall has already organized several dozen marriages in this way. In one village the ratio is 48 women to 209 men of marriageable age (25–40) that is, 1 woman to 4.4 men. The village's survival is therefore reliant on group mixed marriages, which are easy to identify because of the enormous age gap between husband and wife: the men can be anything between 30 and 40 (very occasionally 60) whereas the women are between 18 and 25.

Mr Yamada does not consider his life to be particularly 'out of the ordinary' and regrets the fuss made by the media about this kind of union. Marian, who is expecting their second child, describes her life speaking in the Tôhoku dialect she has mastered in the space of two years:

> When I lived in the Philippines I always dreamed of going abroad. I wanted to travel of course, not get married! However I met five Japanese men in Manilla and that's how I ended up coming here to live. Initially I had no idea that the purpose of the venture was marriage. The man who recruited me had made no mention of that! All he said was that five Japanese men wanted to invite me to dinner in the Five Stars Hotel. They were supposed to be celebrating their birthdays and just wanted us to show them the sights afterwards.
>
> He was a good liar for I had no idea that these men were looking for Filipina wives. We were eight women to nine men. It is always the men who choose – I had no say in the matter. Be that as it may, I was flattered that I was my husband's first choice! Apparently he was attracted by my personality and healthy appearance. Actually, I thought he was a bit old.
>
> Next day he was eager to meet my parents. He showed us a photo of his parents and presented us with a cassette player from them. He also gave us 10,000 pesos (1 peso = 7 yen). As far as surprises go, that really was one! All we had to do was come to a decision. On the third day we were married at the town hall! I wore a Filipino dress. We spent our honeymoon in Baguio (north-east of Manila).
>
> I was actually really nervous, there are so many stories going around about *yakuza* (gangsters). I was so worried he might be one of them. I wondered who this man could be, but as the mayor of my town was acting as sponsor I decided he must be an honest man. The man recruiting had to be OK too, even though he had

me well and truly fooled! When we got married (in 1986) my husband promised I could go home at the end of the year, but that was a lie too.

He's not a bad person and he treats me well but money's a bit tight. Having paid out 1,380,000 yen to cover the cost of the trip and wedding, he took 300,000 yen with him to the Philippines, but as it was the first time he'd been there he had no idea about prices. To begin with the plane is not cheap and then people were forever asking him for 50,000 yen here and 50,000 yen there. He was really taken for a ride! He paid up without complaining but when we arrived in Japan, I thought: 'We're flat broke!' He had spent so much money that he had none left! He wasn't in debt (thank goodness!) but he was penniless! He apologized and asked me to be patient, to make an effort.

Eight days after we were married all the husbands returned to Japan and we followed on two weeks later. They had hired a minibus to bring us here. On the motorway we stopped every now and then to take a rest and we did some shopping. God, how good it was! I was so excited to be going abroad at last! But when we arrived in the village I was struck by how many mountains there were. I had never seen so many!

In the September, I went to work in the paddy-fields for the first time. I'd lived in the country before but there hadn't been any paddy-fields there, just factories, not farms like here. My in-laws wondered how I would cope but I found the rice harvest great fun! But I was always asking them if I could have a rest! I feel so ashamed when I think about it! . . .

As my husband works for a company outside the farm, grandfather looks after the paddy-fields and grandmother is in charge of growing the vegetables. She brings us some every day which means we don't have to go and buy any. He is a good man, my husband. My in-laws too, for that matter. I'm happy but life isn't without its problems. For example my husband hadn't told me we'd all be living under the same roof. There's no way we can have our own space. I find that rather hard.

When I was first pregnant I was extremely irritable and I really resented my husband. I found it so exasperating that my in-laws couldn't understand my mood swings. I suffered from terrible nausea. Sometimes it was so bad I had to stay in bed all day. Mother-in-law would then bring me hard boiled eggs and milk and force me to eat them. Yes, at the I beginning it really was hard.

Grandfather was also in the habit of coming along to ask me

why I was idling in bed like that, but honestly, there was no way I could have got up! I was so upset I wept! My husband explained that I was doing everything I could for him and the baby and that we should all be patient. Even when I was giving birth I was all agitated.

Marian went to work in a confectionery factory less than a month after her arrival. The husbands had not originally intended that their young wives should go to work but the town hall supplied an interpreter while they learned the routine. Now they do the job as well as the others. It is even said that they liven up the atmosphere.

I get paid 400 yen an hour and by working from 8 to 5 I end up earning 80,000 yen a month. I can also do overtime if I want to.[30] It's not terribly well paid but it's better than back home! When I was younger I worked in a factory and earned 35 pesos a day.[31] I would give it all to my mother to help her out but the factories went bankrupt one after another. It was terrible.

I applied to be allowed to send my family money and have also arranged to have a credit transfer of 30,000 yen made two or three times a year. They are really happy. That's why I put up with it. I deprive myself of everything but my parents-in-law are very helpful. Anything left over I put aside for the children's education.

I have a good husband but he does get angry sometimes especially when I ask him to take me somewhere. He always says he's too busy. One day I'd love it if we could all go to the Philippines together. Sometimes I go along and listen to *father* (the priest) when he's in the neighbourhood but my son's a Buddhist like his father which saddens me sometimes.

When my husband comes home from work he's very talkative. He's told me about his life and the time when he was single. He told me that it was so depressing before I came to live here that he would always come home as late as possible. Sometimes he'd go out drinking. Life was so monotonous that's what decided him in the end to go to the Philippines and look for a wife.

When I still lived there, I had a boyfriend who went off to work in Saudi Arabia. He'd sometimes send me money. His mother had told him to go as she thought we were still too young to get married. He wrote to me recently. My parents sent the letter on to me here in Japan. I was really embarrassed but my husband was very understanding. Just as well really! My mother told me to forget all about him now that I was happy: she must have been joking! It took a long time to forget he was my boyfriend after all.

You can't forget, just like that! As it happens, I have no regrets. I'm fine here and I'm not interested in him any more.

And yet even though I'm happy it doesn't stop me from sometimes feeling homesick. After all, life in Japan hasn't been easy for me but the hardest thing of all has been my in-laws' attitude. They are forever telling me off. Most of the time I don't know why but I say nothing, I just let them get on with it.

Japanese fathers are strict, but then so was my father so nothing much has changed there. Fortunately my mother-in-law is very kind. When she goes off on a trip she asks me to take over from her instead of going to the factory. The first day I do the cooking and the housework but if she's not back the next day I return to work leaving the baby with my father-in-law. I try to get home as early as possible so that I can get every thing done. It's grandfather who baths the baby. He's a good man after all!

My plans for the future? Because I love my husband we plan to have four children. He says that the number four represents happiness.[32] Two's a bit cheerless. He's always saying that four is synonymous with happiness.[33]

Marian's case might appear to be very encouraging. After all she says she is happy and has no regrets, not even with regard to her Filipino boyfriend. Her husband is willing to act as arbitrator between her and his parents and even goes so far as to stay with her while she is in labour which is still a fairly rare occurrence, especially in rural communities. Moreover he is talkative, a quality which is as rare in Japan as it is appreciated.

However, the fact remains that Marian was 'bought' for 70,000 yen while the total cost of the operation amounted to 2 or 3 million yen once all the deductions had been made to pay the intermediaries and cover the cost of the ceremony. As far as the Japanese are concerned, this is not expensive since a wedding in the archipelago can cost a minimum of 6 to 8 million yen, a price which includes the hiring of the bride's clothes, the ceremony, a night in a hotel and the honeymoon. Although in Japan a sum of money is usually handed over to the fiancée's family during the engagement party,[34] in this context, this 'gift' (fairly small when we consider Japanese prices) smacks rather uncomfortably of the 'wife trade' (*jinshin-baibai*). In this particular case Mr Yamada can see that he is forcing Marian's hand by plying her family with gifts. Indeed, Ochiai Emiko cites the case of a Filipina woman who admitted that she had found it difficult to adjust to the idea that she had been 'bought' from her family for the same amount.[35]

Japanese women have objected to the system, on the grounds that the transaction is carried out so swiftly that it challenges the whole question of free will. This comes to the fore in Marian's account when she says that it is the men who choose and that the women have only the right to accept.

Ochiai Emiko has no hesitation in including this 'trade' in the *Japayuki-san*,[36] term used to refer to South-East Asian prostitutes who come to Japan on artists' visas,[37] to work as hostesses, entertainers, dancers or call-girls.

The fear expressed by Marian ('I wondered who this man could be . . .'), the intermediary's somewhat dubious character, the lies she was told serve only to underline the similarity, together with the rapidity with which the deal was concluded. Barely three days after the 'fortuitous' meeting, Marian's fate was decided. She obtained her visa and left the Philippines within a fortnight. This hasty departure, with neither psychological nor linguistic preparation, meant that she would have a difficult time adapting.

Her first disappointment was that the money had been used up. The most painful repercussion for Marian is that the prospect of returning home is very remote. The linguistic problems are far from being inconsequential. Itamoto Yôko, who has interviewed some sixty foreign wives in the prefectures concerned explains,

> The popularity of Filipina wives is understandable if we remember that they come from an Asian country where English is spoken. Japanese men tend to think that if they can say 'yes', 'no' and 'I love you', that communication is possible.

Nevertheless cultural and sexual problems do occur, which is why the market is now turning towards Communist China. Japanese men are capitalizing on the fact that Chinese women are looking for a way of getting out of their country.

> They think that moving to Japan is a foot up the ladder, but in the first three cases I recently studied only one could be judged a success. The second disappeared into the wild (to return to China would be to lose face) and the third lady is contemplating a divorce.

'Their problems are insurmountable', she told me on her return from Niigata in September 1995, where she had just been to meet another woman, already pregnant but still unable to communicate.

> In the case of the Chinese, it is still much too early to speak of success or failure. The young woman I met yesterday for example is

in a state of total dependence. Unable to communicate with anyone she is completely dependent on her husband (assuming she can communicate with him, which is highly unlikely). She can't converse with her gynaecologist or understand the health record she's been given. She was in a total panic. And as she can't read any of the books on childcare, all she can do is telephone her mother every now and then to ask her advice. A rather unsatisfactory course of action – if you consider how differently things are done in the two countries – which can only confuse the issue.

If the experiment with the Chinese is no more conclusive than with the Filipinas this is no doubt because Japanese men are not predisposed to making the slightest effort. Marian's husband's indifference regarding a visit to the Philippines is a prime example of this. Having reached his goal, he has, it would seem from the evidence, no reason (desire?) to return there. Mrs Itamoto adds

Any effort made is very much one-sided, but it is the sexual problems which remain by far the most worrying. These young women very soon find themselves with two or three children and end up in the depths of despair.

Somewhere between a beast of burden and a baby-machine

A further upsetting aspect of Marian's account is just how much was expected of her. Although her in-laws were supportive, their attitude to her when she was first pregnant and therefore less useful was quite deplorable. Was it because they saw her only as a 'beast of burden without horns' (a term which actually originated in Tôhoku)? Would their behaviour have been the same had she been Japanese? An embarrassing question in the light of its racist overtones.

Will the Japanese only ever consider Filipinas to be 'dancers', maids of all work in embassies or foreigners' houses (Japanese people are not allowed by the immigration office to be sponsors for Filipina maids), or what Hirai Nobuyoshi calls (not without a note of nostalgia) 'baby-machines'? Whatever the case, there is no doubt that in the Japanese psyche they will always be regarded as second-class citizens. Itamoto maintains that:

The major problem facing these women continues to be the insufferable dependence accorded them by their status as illiterates they are completely helpless when things go wrong. When they arrived in Japan everything had been sorted out for them: passport, visa, ticket. All they had to do was jump on the plane. Sometimes this turns out to be more of a curse than a blessing for when all is lost they haven't the slightest idea how to get home. They would need to demonstrate far greater strength and independence than they actually have especially since they are incapable of even taking the train to Tokyo. I know of one woman who ran away leaving her three children behind. She begged me to help her get home. When I explained that what she had done put her in the wrong, the sobbing woman told me she would rather die. In an attempt to reassure her I told her she could try going to court, but how can you go to court when you're illiterate? You've lost before you've even started!

Apart from that there is the cultural gap, which, according to Itamoto, is reinforced by the Japanese temperament. She criticizes Japanese husbands for being reserved (they never express their feelings, never tell their wives they love them), for lacking a sense of humour (they never laugh or smile) and because they are *workaholics* (they work too much and refuse on principle to make a space in their lives for living).

But without doubt the most difficult aspect of their lives is the lack of privacy which results from living with their in-laws. They all tell me that there should be a way of creating and maintaining two family units under the same roof so that they are not always under their in-laws' thumb.

It is significant that what most worries the Filipinas is what Japanese women were wanting to escape.

'If it's difficult for men who live in towns to find themselves a wife, then for those who live in the country it is virtually impossible,' declares Mitsuoka Kôji, author of a book on the problems that farmers encounter. He knows the situation from personal experience since he lives in the Aichi prefecture.[38] If in his view it is the problems of succession which lie behind farmers' constant setbacks, Mitsuoka nevertheless admits that the problems of women who have parents to look after (oldest daughters and/or families which have only daughters) are even greater.

For them, marrying an oldest son is quite out of the question as he has to take over as head of the family. Second or third sons have two alternatives; either they have left the village years ago to go and work in the city or they are honour bound not to become a *yôshi* (see n. 5). It has reached the stage where the parents of young women are ready to welcome their future son-in-law – not to mention their issue – while their daughters are still at school!

However, though the youngest choose to run away, the oldest cannot escape the constraints of tradition.

Why can farm workers no longer find wives?

In the inland sea the problem is now so acute that the council of a village near Niigata – where in twenty years the population has halved – decided to carry out a survey and asked the women who used to live in the village whether it was their intention to return one day. Although they seemed to appreciate the village lads – and referred to them as being 'decent sorts', far superior to those from the city – none of the women questioned said she would have wanted to marry one nor was it their intention ever to return there.

> However much we try to paint a glowing picture of the advantages of living in the country they continue to choose to live in *rabbit hutches* in town and however much they claim they wanted to escape the snow or the mountains, it is clear that what they dreaded was in reality agricultural work but more especially having to live with mother-in-law.[39] In the country this is of course taken for granted – it would be unthinkable to live side by side but separately.

'It is a fact,' adds Madoka Yoriko, for thirteen years coordinator of classes on 'how to get divorced without losing your smile' and founder of a society for divorced women,

> that most of the country women who come and see me want to divorce their in-laws rather than their husbands.[40] While father's hold and the mother complex remains unchanged,[41] it is more than likely that farmers will find it increasingly difficult to find themselves a wife.

The problem stems from the fact that those who put their family's interests before their own are committing themselves to a life of celibacy, for maternal duty is even greater than filial duty. As Suzuki Katsuko puts it,[42] these men have been brought up by their mothers to be 'good little boys' and any appeal they might have had to young women is lost.

Silent and clumsy suitors!

With their reputation for being reserved, uncommunicative and surly,[43] there is the added disadvantage that they have only two days off a month.

'Even though they might come to an arrangement about days off, the mother-in-law would encourage her daughter-in-law to work at home,' states Mitsuoka Kôji who claims that this is yet another handicap farmers have to deal with.

> When they take a girl for a drive they never say a word. I heard of a case where, after driving for an hour, the girl said 'Let's go back!', to which the gentleman replied 'Right! Let's go back then, shall we?' It was the first time he'd opened his mouth since they'd set out! Another man chain-smoked and never said a word. Is this really going to achieve anything? And when they say they've had lunch together, do you have any idea what that means? It means they've sat in the car and eaten a chunk of bread and drunk a glass of milk, and when they take a girl to a *drive-in*, they expect them to go halves![44]

Mitsuoka had a string of examples to substantiate his claim and told us the story of a function which had been organized for the young people who lived in the same prefecture, where as arranged the young women arrived early to get everything ready. After lunch, instead of taking the opportunity to chat to the young women, the men went off and left the girls on their own. Since there was no point in staying the girls went home. 'To crown it all,' he goes on, 'the young men's parents went and lodged a complaint at the town hall! It's a bit much coming from those who are to blame for having brought their sons up to be like that!'

There is a Confucian tenet which contends that once boys and girls reach the age of 7 they should no longer sit together. This goes a long way to explaining why, apart from a handful of easygoing and resourceful Hanako (see pp. 141–2) and *city-boys*, the majority of young people do not have many opportunities to mix. A survey carried out among single people found that 50 per cent of men and 40 per cent of women questioned had never had relations with the opposite sex because their work left them with neither the time nor the energy to 'lark around'.

'It's a feeble excuse,' Suzuki Katsuko concludes coldly, whose belief it is that relationships are actually distorted from the outset because of the importance accorded the family,[45] the reputation of the university they go to and how prestigious the employer of course.[46]

THERE IS MORE TO LIFE THAN SEX

Author of *Sekando vâjin* ('Second virgin') and of *Sekando vâjin shôkôgun* ('The second virginity syndrome'),[47] Mizuno Mari has detected – in young men as well as in young women – a general lack of interest in sex. While the women of her generation (she is 33) deliberated over whether or not to remain a virgin until they were married, she claims that young women these days go out of their way to lose their virginity (because it is what everyone else is doing or because they are curious) and then return to their original state by becoming what people call 'second virgins'. She has observed a similar trend among young men who claim they no longer have the energy nor the time to court girls and who profess that it is far less tiring to make do with porn videos. 'It's not so much that they are not interested in the act itself but rather all the energy required to get them there (dinners, dates, not to mention the risk of being jilted and all the stress and humiliation associated with that).' 'If that's the price to pay,' one young man explained, 'I'd rather go without.'[48]

The more resourceful blue-collar workers

However, not all young men are affected in the same way by the shortage of wives. A survey carried out on the female workforce in one factory by the students of Yuzawa Yasuhiko revealed that they had never heard of the three *kô* (see pp. 142 and 220, n. 1) and that besides they had had no problem finding a husband. They also said that what they valued more than anything else were feelings and that although higher education might lead to an easier life financially, it frequently meant that their husbands would be constrained to do such things as overtime. All things considered, they would still rather marry a worker who usually came home at 5 p.m. and who was willing to take the time to live.

The workforce of this factory, which manufactures electrical equipment, has a ratio of six women to four men; 60 per cent of its male workers were marrying colleagues while the remainder had found their spouses in neighbouring factories. Neither male nor female workers seemed to be in any hurry and calmly replied that they were waiting to reach the respective ages of 27–28 and 23–24 before marrying.[49] They at least did not feel there was any kind of crisis.

The balance between the sexes is not usually so well established in other factories. In the car industry there are very few women, which presents an enormous problem since the factory is like a small city. The situation is so bad in Toyota-town for example that when some employees join Toyota they feel as though they are condemning themselves to a life sentence of celibacy. In oil refineries and the petro-chemical industry, which is concentrated in the prefecture of Chiba, 90 per cent of the workforce is male. The opposite problem exists in textile mills where the workforce is almost exclusively female.

Of those who sign up with the Altman Marriage Bureau 45 per cent are scientists who have graduated from single-sex schools or colleges where boys never had the opportunity to fraternize with girls.[50] 'In this exclusively male preserve they obviously never have the chance to fall in love,' Suzuki explains, 'Consequently they don't understand the female psyche and are extremely gauche when it comes to relations with the opposite sex.'

The economic journal *Nihon Keizai Shimbun* (23 June 1992) revealed, in an article devoted to the problems encountered by young men of marriageable age, that since February 1992 there had been a new service available to employers (for the moderate sum of 200,000 yen for the whole of the male workforce) aimed at helping their un-married employees find a companion. For example, 27-year-old Mr X, at present residing in Osaka, works for one of the large construction companies. He received a note from his company's information department informing him that a marriage bureau affiliated to the company was 'kindly' offering to introduce him to a companion and that all he had to do was fill in an application form. Once he had over-come his initial indignation he contacted the bureau because they were undertaking, over a period of two and a half years, to introduce him to three applicants a month. Surely out of ninety he would find one that suited him.

Sixteen months after the service was first set up, the bureau already had some twenty companies join the scheme. Eighteen per cent were quoted on the Stock Exchange and nine were connected to the building trade. 'If this helps our employees find a wife so that they become even more committed to their jobs, the outlay will have been more than worthwhile', was the comment from one company execu-tive. However much the journalist found that this was 'pushing' the 'services' supplied by the company 'a bit far' we should not forget that employers have always been very much involved in their employees' unions, on occasion going so far as to recommend female relatives, proposals which are moreover very difficult to turn down.

When I read this article however, I was tempted to suggest that employers should reduce the hours of overtime they expected their employees to do even though this was a more expensive alternative than the one proposed by the bureau in question. Another suggestion was that unmarried employees be allocated mixed living quarters. An article in *Nikkei* (27 June 1992) revealed that a move in this direction had been well received by employees of both sexes.

After a certain age, celibacy wears badly

It is undeniable that beyond a certain age (thirties), the single man, never particularly well regarded, becomes a burden. A bachelor's life expectancy is lower than that of a married man (which in 1992 was 76 years of age).

Madoka Yoriko has the same observations to make about divorce: admittedly her women clients express no regrets at having divorced but they do admit that they wished they had not had to resort to it.

There is a distinct difference in attitude between divorced men and women: while the former would like to remarry as quickly as possible the latter would rather wait. In Japan (and everywhere else for that matter) petitioning for divorce is nearly always initiated by the woman. However once they have breathed a sigh of relief which signifies 'I won't ever get caught out like that again', they realize to their cost how little society tolerates single people, and once their children begin to leave home (these women are around 45–46) their confidence begins to waver. When they reach 50 they end up wanting to find a companion for their later years.

One option available to these women is known as *kayoïkon* (which could be translated as 'living apart together') where the couple choose not to have their union legalized so as to avoid friction with the children of the first marriage.[51] Other couples opt for this because they want to safeguard their children's inheritance. But what might be appropriate in the city is unacceptable in rural communities, even though trial marriages or pre-nuptial cohabitation used to be the norm, so that the compatibility of a daughter-in-law with her in-laws could be tested before her name was added to the family register together with the first-born's name.

Nowadays marriage is no longer as appealing as it used to be. From having observed her elders' monotonous existences, a young woman will hesitate for some time before committing herself to marriage and motherhood, to having to reconcile work and children – a quasi-utopic gamble given the physical exertion and extraordinarily strong constitution this demands – or resign herself to the gloomy, empty tedium of a housewife's life. Whatever path she chooses, marriage is no longer synonymous with happiness and young women are openly admitting that these days they are not interested in the traditional male who expects his wife to take on all the domestic chores or who only will 'tolerate' her job as long as this does not impinge on his comfort. These days there is no reason to have a mediocre marriage.

SCHOOLS FOR HUSBANDS

Old bachelors before their time

Men's attitudes have evolved much less rapidly than women's. They still expect their wives to put their bedding out to air in the sunshine or to prepare their meals or baths with the same devotion that their mothers used to display. However, with the proliferation of automatic launderettes, restaurants and convenient stores open 24 hours a day, there is no longer that same urgency for men to get married; this no doubt explains why they want a marriage which will prove to be really worthwhile.[52] According to Madoka Yoriko:

> The great problem is that the young men who enrol at marriage bureaux are exhausted by their week of working until ten o'clock every night. All they want to do once the week is over is spend Sunday in bed so that they can 'recharge their batteries'. . . . When I interview them, I soon realize they meet all the criteria needed to find a wife: a three-roomed flat with dining room and lounge, a job in a respectable company, a good salary, they're smart and not below the minimum height requested by the young ladies but they are always taken aback when I ask them if they think that women these days are happy to have a husband who comes home at ten each night and who is only interested in sleeping at the weekend.
>
> I try and get them to give some thought to the kind of home they would like to have by asking them how they envisage married life but their responses reveal that they do not want their way of life to change once they are married. I have also realized that they are quite incapable of putting themselves in the woman's position and that they do not have the slightest idea about the female psyche.

And so, while the young women of today yearn for a relationship that is above all else based on absolute equality – where there is no dominant/dominated partner and where they can at last make themselves heard due to the shortage of women, men who want to get married have no choice but to acquiesce whether they like it or not. This conspicuous time-lag in the male–female evolution inspired the feminist Higuchi Keiko to open a 'school for men' (*hanamuko gakkô*) with a view to reforming these gentleman.[53] Two and a half hours a week for three month will cost them 40,000 yen, but will give them the 'know-how' which will allow them to 'deserve' a Japanese wife.[54]

The idea came to her, as it did to Itamoto Yôko and the freelance journalist Saitô Shigeo, to run a school for husbands – in collaboration with the Nihon Seinenkan Marriage Bureau – after she had heard some of the questions their clients were asking over the telephone, a sample of which follows:

- Where should I take a young woman for a romantic date?
- What kinds of outings are likely to appeal to a young woman?
- What should I wear to go on a *miai*?
- What should I talk to a young woman about?
- How should I go about seducing her?
- When is the right moment to hold her hand?
- How long should I wait before I kiss her?

The first time I heard these questions I was quite shaken, for apart from their blatant awkwardness they revealed a crass ignorance of the *other*. This deficiency was also noticeable in the young men inspired to enrol at the bureau. To the question: 'Why do you want to get married?', while the young women would simply reply that they wanted to live with a man they loved and/or create a home, the young men nonchalantly replied that it was normal to get married at their age,[55] that they would lose their social credibility if they were not married by a certain age,[56] or else that they wanted to please their parents!

If by constantly changing jobs young men sometimes give the impression that they are insecure,[57] the 'blue-bird syndrome' does not continue beyond the age of 26–30 for they are very quickly sucked into the system and from then on cannot help but do what everyone else does and the first thing they have to do is find a home. They claim there are no opportunities to do this but the future will prove them wrong for the young women who enrol in our bureau all say that 'there are no more blokes' and that they have been unable to find a decent husband among the men they come into daily contact with. However outraged men might be by what they regard to be one-sided demands, they explain that they are not looking for anyone out of the ordinary, just someone 'normal' or 'average' in a word 'acceptable'! And they should be able to communicate, an area in which they seem to be particularly inept (they read at the table, fall asleep on the train when they're travelling with girlfriends, etc.). But what really hurts is that the sympathy which used to be felt for these workaholics has vanished – paradoxically young women no longer find these *economic animals* as they call themselves the least bit attractive. Men unwittingly drop their arms stating that they no longer have the desire nor the energy to communicate. . . .

Men who have not grown up but remained trapped in their traditional roles have not emulated women's evolution and a reversal has taken place in as much as it is they who want to get married whatever the cost, whereas women are backing off.

Using their mothers as their point of reference they complain that Japanese women are no longer 'kind'. It is perhaps time they cut the apron strings and learned to stop seeing their wives as mother substitutes.[58] In their defence it should be said that they have become 'economic animals' not to say robots as a result of being sacrificed to Japan's economic growth. However young women are not interested in going to bed with a robot! And that is why, in response to all these problems, we decided to open this school. We offer classes in reflecting on and becoming sensitive to issues such as marriage, the family of tomorrow and also female psyche, sexuality and sexual harassment.

Unlike the classes offered by their rival Kansai school (*Hanamukô kôza*),[59] which emphasizes the 'how' and concentrates on the art of showing yourself off to advantage (how to smile, how far away to sit, where to look, how not to be found wanting by always having something to say), this is more of a 'theoretical' or conditioning class, a group *miai* which takes place twice a month where thirty young men and the same number of young women are brought together. They 'go round' just like in a game of musical chairs and each has three minutes to 'catch' a partner but if the *miai* yields nothing, it does not matter, they can start again in two months' time. Anyway, even though that is what both parties crave so badly, it is not the aim of the exercise. As the director explained, the intensive summer weekend courses which take place at the foot of Mount Fuji in Yamagatakô are also much appreciated:

The aim of the participants is above all to learn to understand the female psyche and to appreciate their values. They want to know what women mean by a good man and what they should do to find a good woman. Moreover they want to learn how to become good husbands and to feel ready and able to match their ideas to those of their future wives. Others say they want to improve their relationships, to become more diplomatic, more eloquent, etc.

Others want to be 'reformed', so that they end up more open, better balanced, more attractive or more comfortable with themselves. What emerges from all this data is that you need more than the famous *kô* to find yourself a wife.[60] Those whose wives have left them would like to understand why. One of our first participants told us that our classes had helped him *in extremis* prevent his heart's desire from running away. Another told us he had managed to 'repair' his marriage and that we had supplied him with an inexhaustible number of topics to discuss with his wife.

Around a hundred men can take advantage of the three month course, together with sixty women, who are charged only half price, although not all the sessions are open to them.[61] The majority are aged between 25 and 39. Almost all are private sector employees though some do come from the public sector.

It was impossible at the graduation ceremony in September 1992 not be reminded of a support group meeting. They could have called themselves 'Unloved Anonymous'. To demonstrate how seriously they took it all, the 'graduates' requested that an association of former students be formed. One 'young man' of 54 spoke of how his wife had said that he did not deserve his diploma but he had not given up hope of one day deserving it for the classes had given him a 'body blow'.

Another man, nearly 40, explained that he had come to learn, gather information and take advantage of the opportunity to meet people, in a word, he wanted to understand why things had gone so badly wrong between the sexes. By the end of the course, and after having devoured some twenty books on the subject, he felt enlightened: 'The answer is simple,' he explained, 'the male–female relationship is founded on misunderstandings. If we circumvent what should not be said but say what is in our hearts, we should avoid them in future'. Another said that Japanese men are as clumsy as they are because they are inhibited by the fear of making a mistake.

At the end of the ceremony a (very pretty) Japanese girl took the microphone and announced that the sight of men so sufficiently reformed and open that they took the course, was extremely heartening. Could this school really hold the solution to the problem?

8 The achievement of working mothers

VARIOUS ACCOUNTS

Here is a selection of accounts from women who have managed to survive the difficult challenge of holding down a job while not having to give up the idea of having children. Here is the story of their lives, their struggles, their frustrations but also their victories.

'Nothing irritates me more than to hear my colleagues telling me that there's really no point in working if it means leaving my children in a crèche'

Mrs S (aged 32) works in a department store from 9.40 a.m. until 5.10 p.m. She lives 70 minutes away from work. Her husband (aged 31) works in the pharmaceutical industry and their 3-year-old daughter goes to the crèche. Her monthly income is 180,000 yen.

I have been working ever since I heard that in China it is only the old, the infirm and children who are exempt from working. I don't work because I have to,[1] but I certainly don't want to be thought of as a woman who wants to have a career. Apart from the financial considerations I find my job personally enriching and most gratifying.

My salary goes towards repaying the loans on our apartment and towards improving our daily life; also I manage to save a little. My job has helped me understand the mechanics of selling and as I work in the tea department I read the specialized magazines to ensure that I am well informed. When I had to leave after the birth of my daughter I got back into the habit of doing the tea ceremony.

You ask me to describe how I manage to get the housework and cooking done. First of all I programme the rice cooker for dinner while I'm preparing breakfast so that all I have to do in the evening is heat it up. On my days off I give the house a thorough clean, the rest of the time I just clear up after my daughter.

What does my husband do? The bulk of it, for he's much better at doing the housework than I am! He's also very good at looking after his daughter who has become a real 'daddy's girl'! When we were first married he started by doing the washing up but as he works in the pharmaceutical industry it wasn't a problem because he was used to washing pipettes and other laboratory apparatus. Then I showed him how to organize the washing and after our daughter was born I showed him how to give her a bath. Since then, it's become his speciality. At night he was the one who got up to make her bottle and comfort her and as he was better than me, he took on that responsibility too! There were times where he would cradle her in his arms until the early hours of the morning. It wasn't long before he was changing her nappy as well. We don't work on the principle that absolutely everything must be shared equally, it's more a question of who has their hands free at the time. My husband clears up, does the housework, cleans the bath and it is always him who takes the rubbish down early in the morning before he goes to work.

As a general rule I'm the one who does the cooking but if I ask him to give me a hand he is always willing to help out. He maintains that cooking is easy as long as you follow the recipe and that it's a lot easier than a chemistry experiment.

As his mother was a housewife it wasn't until we were married that my husband had to do anything around the house but because I carried on working he just automatically began to help out as he considered we were equal. This has been a great example to our daughter who also does her bit. Sometimes she's more of a hindrance than a help but I'm not one to discourage good intentions.

Nothing irritates me more than to hear my colleagues (especially men of a certain age) telling me that there's really no point in working if it means leaving my children in a crèche. If I choose to have a child it is for me and certainly not for my country that I do so. I'm not asking for mothers to be given preferential treatment but up to now Japanese companies have had too little regard for people's private lives. They still can't tolerate anyone leaving work early because they have to collect a child from the crèche. So I don't want to hear them complaining about the drop in the birthrate or the shortage of labour. The larger companies are sensitive to change and have reacted promptly by bringing in new measures, but what's the point if we don't have the right to avail ourselves of them?

Crèches should be better subsidized, the carers better paid and they should be granted better working conditions (more staff, a shorter working day, more holidays).[2] They have a difficult and tiresome job to do and parents should be able to entrust their children to people who are less stressed. Moreover, it is also imperative that private crèches should be subsidized so that they can be on an equal footing with those administered by local cooperatives.

My husband wonders why no surveys have ever been carried out on working fathers! In his opinion he does just as much as I do but women invariably end up automatically being put first! I think men should be encouraged, for you can get so much more done when there are two of you sharing the load rather than always expecting the mother to do everything.

'I get very upset when a housewife asks me why I work and tells me she feels sorry for my children'

Mrs K (aged 36) is a civil servant and works every day from 8.30 a.m. to 5 p.m. and has a 45-minute journey to her place of work. Her husband (aged 35) is also a civil servant. They have two sons aged 5 and 9; the younger is in a crèche, the older is at primary school. Her monthly salary is 200,000 yen.

It is difficult to explain why I work, all I can tell you is that I worked before I was married and that in the civil service a female employee is not necessarily expected to hand in her notice either the moment she gets married or when she has her first child. The whole of my salary goes into the family purse. It goes towards repaying the loans or paying the insurance premiums. It also means we have some savings.

How has working enriched me? As I had learned to type Japanese characters,[3] I asked to be transferred to a more appropriate department but since the introduction of word-processors I have taken up law.

My time-saving secrets? I do the bulk of the housework on a Sunday but as one of my principles is not to stint on the cooking, I never resort to frozen meals.[4] I always make lots of dishes to go with the rice because my role as a working mother is largely dependent on my remaining healthy and on the rest of the family being so too. I have a semi-automatic washing machine (automatic wash, manual spin)[5] as well as a dishwasher. My older son does what he can and on a Sunday my husband gives me a hand with the housework. He drops the younger son off at the crèche and gives the children their bath but I would like them to look after themselves and for the older one to help me more during the summer holidays.

I get very stressed out. Nothing irritates me more than the PTA meetings where I find the deliberate lack of understanding towards working mothers particularly irksome. I've got into the habit of letting off steam by confiding in colleagues. Do I detect any understanding whatsoever towards working mothers? In a way yes, since in the civil service they don't oblige us to give up work. However, I would like to see a system introduced whereby we could take time off to get our children vaccinated,[6] or to look after them (a child or an old person); even though legislation covering maternity leave exists, I find the attitude of housewives very dubious. There is nothing more trying than to hear a housewife who is convinced that she is right, ask me why I work and then tell me that I am inflicting unnecessary suffering on my children. It takes me months to get over it! It's the same when I'm told (nicely) that just because I work doesn't mean I shouldn't attend PTA meetings at the school or crèche even though they invariably take place during the working day – it makes me want to cry. I'd like there to be more crèches or after-school clubs for I have personally suffered a lot from the dearth of crèches adapted to my full-time working day.

I have no long-term plans and take each day as it comes but I do stand by the principle that we'll always manage as long as everyone is in good health.

'I sometimes ask myself what on earth possessed me to have children'

Mrs A (aged 34) works from 9.30 a.m. to 5.30 p.m. for a market research agency which is an hour away from where she lives. Her husband (aged 36) works in the service industry. Her son and daughter (3 and 5) are still in a crèche. Her monthly salary is 220,000 yen.

I've been working for eleven years although I had to stop when my first child was born (I could have taken maternity leave but as there was no precedent and no crèches in the area, sadly I had to stop). During the first six months I continued to work from home but since all I wanted was to return to the office I applied to the director of the agency for a dispensation and he agreed to take me back part-time. But with the birth in May of my second child I had to go back to working from home until he started at the crèche in April of the following year.[7]

All the time I was working part-time my hours were equivalent to a full-time job, but last year I was at last able to return to full-time work. I immediately received training in marketing and research strategies since my work is study-related.

I'd like my husband and children to become more self-reliant, without my having to force them to help me with the household chores. I'd like to get to the stage where our roles are completely interchangeable, for I never want to be treated only as a house-wife.

My children are in a council-run crèche but when I have to work past its closing time, I have to ask another mother to collect them and give them their evening meal.

I suppose it's because I've always put my job first and the children second but I find my older son to be deceitful. The child-minder never stops commenting, indeed complaining about it – which makes me even more depressed (let's face it, nobody at the crèche ever congratulates us mothers for doing a good job!).

I don't want to unburden my domestic problems at work for none of my colleagues has children; I also make sure I work just as hard as the others, as though I didn't have children, and that's why I get so exhausted. On the other hand I have to keep going for the sake of the women of tomorrow. I have a very determined streak in me and tend to think I would never be forgiven for making a mistake. And I could be right.

Whatever people say, children are irreplaceable and when I see on television some of the atrocities that go on I feel guilty too. However, when I look at my life I feel resentful and sometimes wonder what on earth possessed me ever to have children. These days more and more women are choosing not to have any and I have to admit that I sometimes envy them. Rather than regretting it afterwards it might have been wiser not to have them at all. People no doubt think I'm one of those terrible feminists but I often wonder why it's always the woman who has to decide whether or not she should continue with her career. I think this is most unjust. When a woman gets married she becomes Mr X's wife and even gets to be called 'mother' by people from outside the family as though she has no identity of her own. The expression *sengyô shufu* (literally: professional housewife) is strange in itself, but the expression *yûshoku shufu* (working housewife) is even more so! I really do feel it is a great pity that a housewife who has been through higher education should interrupt her career because of family pressure or any other reason. If public opinion needs to be changed then so does the attitude of crèches and there should be contingency plans for the care of children who fall ill. We should also stop automatically inculcating children with such notions as 'masculine' and 'feminine' behaviour.

I can't wait for the day when we can all play *mah-jong* together and the loser gets to cook the dinner!

'Now that my husband is home earlier, I've started to live again!'

Mrs U (aged 38) works part-time (from 9.30 a.m. until 4.30 p.m.) for a publishing house which is 45 minutes away from her home. Her husband (aged 38) is also in publishing and their three sons (aged 7, 9 and 11) are all at primary school.

This is my fifth job since I completed my studies but I don't want to have to change again. My present job is more like *arubaito* and I have become quite skilled since what I do is write and correct proofs.[8] At the moment I work just to get out of the house but I can envisage working from home in the future.

Once children start school they become more self-sufficient but we are very concerned about their studies and their future. This is why I do not wish to work more. Of course it goes without saying that I work for the money and to pay for their studies.

My husband used to do a lot of overtime and so everything else was left to me. Now that he comes home earlier (7 p.m.) we all eat together and have time to discuss the children which takes quite a load off me. He does the washing up once or twice a week but it does annoy me to see them all playing computer games while I do all the work!

In my opinion there's nothing quite like confiding in a friend or going to an aerobics or gymnastics class to combat stress. I still feel guilty though for although my children were in a crèche, they eat anything they lay their hands on and refuse to eat vegetables.[9]

As far as future improvements are concerned I see no point in setting up company crèches; I think it's better for children to stay in their neighbourhood. When you have very young children it's impossible to commute during the rush hour; a better idea would be to give parents an extra 30 minutes morning and afternoon so that they can take and fetch their children to or from the crèche.

All three of my sons are now in primary school and since the spring of last year I was nominated parent representative on the PTA. Unfortunately it meant I had to take time off work to attend meetings as they were always held in the day. It was terrible! The mothers can be divided into three groups: the housewives who stay at home, those who work part-time and those who work full-time. The association works on the principle that each mother must have a term in office (once for each child) and there is no question of a working mother being exempted on the grounds of extenuating circumstances! That's their bad luck!

I do understand the importance of PTAs but why are meetings always held during the working day? It creates an enormous amount of antagonism between mothers who work and those who don't (some of whom would like to work but who for one reason or another cannot).

At the crèche, meetings were always held in the evening or on a Saturday so there wasn't ever a problem, but now they're at school it's quite different. I think it's high time PTAs were regarded as a social problem, otherwise this alienation between mothers will continue to exist.

My dreams for the future? I would like my three sons to become more independent (not only from an economic point of view) and self-sufficient, for there is every chance that they will still be living with us when they go to university and I really would like some time to myself.

'For me there is nothing like work as an antidote to stress'

Mrs U (aged 34) works for a commercial company. Her husband (aged 33) is in company management. They have two daughters (aged 3 and 5) who still go to the crèche.

As I couldn't take maternity leave I had to give up my job when my daughters were born. I stayed at home for a year to look after the older one but for only six months when I had the second. But I always made myself read so that I could keep up to date.

Even before we were married my husband had always been an advocate of working wives so it was never a problem as far as I was concerned but he wasn't expecting me to ask him to help out with the children; consequently if I rely on him too heavily I end up losing my temper.

My daughters have been going to the crèche since they were tiny. Adjusting to life in a group presented no problems and everything went extremely smoothly. In any case we had no choice since both our families live a long way from here.

You want to know if I get stressed? Yes, when I'm up to my eyes in work or I have to take time off because one of the children is ill because my job is the best antidote I have to stress.

Of course there's always room for improvement, particularly when it comes to men's attitudes which still have a long way to go, for it is pointless to bring in a whole lot of new measures while their implementation relies on these male moods. It's quite disgraceful that mothers still find it difficult to continue in their jobs unless they bust a gut or have a will of iron. On the other hand if a couple never has time to relax or live a little, then life becomes very dull.

I look forward to the time when I can not only take pride in my job but also feel that I am enjoying life to the full. I would also like the next ten or twenty years to be a lot calmer.[10]

'NEW FATHERS' AND 'NEW HUSBANDS'

These appear to be very optimistic accounts and tangible proof that, as long as they are iron-willed, some women will lead a life – if not fulfilling, at least satisfying – without having to sacrifice their family life or motherhood.

A closer examination of these different stories, particularly their hours of work, makes it feasible to calculate the cost of their victory, for not all of them have the constitution or courage to get up at 5 in morning in order to prepare the evening meal while getting the breakfast ready. And yet if these accounts are striking it is because we can detect issues which herald change.

The willingness of many fathers – in their early or middle thirties – to help, bears out an observation (which at the time seems very optimistic) made by the anthropologist Hara Hiroko, when she said that it was becoming 'more and more natural' for young fathers to help their wives with the domestic chores and childcare. Their spouse's job is usually a *sine qua non* condition; although, in the first account, Mrs S's husband had never helped with chores before he was married, it did not prevent him from 'automatically' helping his wife because he felt they were in a similar situation.

In the course of an interview, Hara Hiroko stressed just how different this attitude was from that of the proponents of the ideals of May 1968 who, as victims of the egalitarian ideas for which they had fought, helped their wives unenthusiastically.[11]

As one of them, a university academic of aged 43, explained:

> Compassion and selflessness – that's why I help. How else could she cope with three children and a full-time job? Personally I have nothing against sexual equality but there again it was never my ambition to marry a feminist! As it happens she never browbeat me, she just presented me with a *fait accompli*. I never thought kids could be so time-consuming! Mind you, I never asked her to have three. It was her decision. I just had to get on with it! What else could I have done? But she shouldn't expect me to be always sweetness and light. I too have my limits.

That this breach, opened by those who participated in the events of May 1968, has not been closed up again allows a ray of hope to shine through.

This new breed of willing fathers is sometimes referred to as the *sanji no anata*, 'the three *ji* man', that is the one who looks after the children (*ikuji*), the cooking (*suiji*) and the housework (*sôji*), distinctions which do not, however, exempt him from also doing the washing and shopping. The last part of the article in *Asahi* which introduced him (31 May 1992) was tempered by the findings of a survey carried out in 1986 by the Sômuchô (Management and Coordination Agency), which pointed out that, among working couples with children, the women on average devoted four and a half hours a day to household chores as opposed to the eight minutes that their husbands contributed.

The employers' role

The passing of the law on parental leave was a step in the right direction towards sexual equality. On the same day that the law came into effect on 1 April 1992, *Asahi* cited several companies which had foreseen the legislation. Different packages had been implemented (one to three years' unpaid leave, six months to a year on half salary, and so on) but in theory all of them included men, giving them the same rights as their wives.

The case of 33-year-old Mr Ota, employed by NEC and a pioneer of paternity leave, is particularly informative inasmuch as his reactions are strangely reminiscent of the women's accounts related in Chapter 1. For example:

> Days spent with our baby *almost drove me to a nervous breakdown* [added emphasis]. It was not until I found myself forever giving him his bottle or changing his nappy that I realized how tiresome

it can be to look after a child. However, now that I know what to do I am ready to start again for the second one.

The advantage of this brief six-month apprenticeship (he and his wife shared their parental leave) was that he experienced the reality of this 'leave' which is leave in name alone.

Sighing as he admitted to being extremely bored and that he could not wait to return to work, albeit for a few hours a day, probably he did not realize that he was using the same words as women use. Although from the evidence available this case remains extremely marginal, it nevertheless represents a (small) step towards equality.

This move is asking to be encouraged, not only by wives but also by employers who should allow their employees to get home early so that they have the chance to enjoy family life. The well-known psychiatrist Saitô Satoru explained that the reason Japanese men arrived home late from the office was not because of their interest in or passion for their job but because their colleagues and superiors did not go home early. No one dared to be the first to leave.[12] 'One can feel the change that still is to be done in the mentalities of workers', added the founder of a support group for 'workaholics' which he described as being an introspective group set up to help salaried workers consider the role that their families have in their daily lives. He went on to say, with a wry smile, that since creating the group which meets every Sunday morning he had actually become a workaholic too.

It is indeed significant to hear the fourth woman quoted, say how her life had been transformed just because her husband came home before 7 p.m. Many Japanese women made the same observation, for example Yûki Misae who said that just having her husband there at the weekend had finally helped her find her children 'lovable'. When women say that their husbands always come home at night by taxi because they have missed the last underground train, or that they never come home before 1 a.m., without having been able to find the time to have dinner and that five hours later they are off again, it is apparent just how much companies have contributed to women's childrearing educational neurosis.

Another important consideration (in the second interview) is the possibility of coming to an arrangement with employers as long as they are willing to prove their good will. In the current climate there might be many Japanese women interested in coming to a similar arrangement. Perhaps parental leave will encourage a move in this direction, since the future seems to be linked to it.

WHAT PRICE SUCCESS?

'It's quite disgraceful that mothers still find it difficult to continue in their jobs unless they have a will of iron.' This statement accurately describes the situation and emphasizes the high price which must be paid in order to reconcile family and work (never is it considered to be a 'career').

The impossibility of employing domestic help makes the situation so different from the one in France for example. Domestic staff agencies (half-heartedly) make a note of one's requirements and never bother to follow them up since they have so few applicants. Furthermore, with the exception of embassies and foreign companies, one wonders who could possibly afford the prices charged by cleaning agencies.

If a mother finds she is having to deal with the ordeal on her own, with no cleaner or baby-sitter, it is because society still considers that any self-respecting woman should be responsible for doing these herself. The many schools without a canteen feel that this 'gives' mothers the opportunity of expressing their love for their children (see pp. 90–2). Another example is that of a woman who, unable to secure a place for her child in the council-run crèche, was told by an official from the department of social welfare that her children were indeed very fortunate since she would be able to devote all her energy to them.[13] What more can be said? Is there really no alternative to being either bored to death or exhausted by your job?

'Nothing irritates me more than to hear my colleagues telling me that there's really no point in working if it means leaving my children in a crèche', said one of the women quoted above (pp. 169–70). Her colleagues are expressing the view of the majority of men. Most men would not admit to what they really think, either through cowardice or more probably because it is worthy to appear to be a 'feminist' (again it is important to clarify the meaning of this word, for most of the men who use it do not have any idea of what feminism entails).

It is not only employers and colleagues who psychologically abuse working mothers, but also the carers from whom one might have expected a little more understanding given that they share their destinies and that their livelihoods are dependent on working mothers.

In so far as housewives are concerned – boosted by their clear consciences – they dispense crushing remarks and advice, their beliefs dominate the heart of the PTA and there is never any question of someone being exempt from holding office; the day or the time of a meeting are never changed to accommodate a working mother. PTA debates frequently end with the two enemy camps settling old scores.

Many crèches hold their meetings in the middle of the afternoon on a working day, and then the insinuations come pouring out ('Make a little effort, after all it is *your daughter* we're discussing', for example). Judging by the level of subjects discussed, it would seem that it was a conspiracy. I have vivid recollections of an afternoon in 1992 where the carers could find nothing better to do than to get each of us in turn to describe the consistency of our respective (5-year-old) children's faeces. Bearing in mind that the twenty-three mothers present were taking time off work to discuss this particular topic, the farce was successful.

As the third women to be interviewed said 'Let's face it, nobody at the crèche ever congratulates us mothers for doing a good job!' This is confirmed by another mother when she says that every time the childcarer comes running after her she automatically wonders what the criticism is going to be this time.

Another carer told me (and with such tact!) that after having seen the way mothers dropped their children off at the crèche in the morning ('as though they were an awkward bundle') she could never leave her own in one. We find in this statement the influence of the ideas of Hiraï Nobuyoshi, Kobayashi Noboru, and others.

A KIND OF HAPPINESS

I should like to conclude – if that is at all possible – by anticipating already current criticisms. 'You're exaggerating!' some say, 'There are many women who say their lives as wives and mothers are fulfilling!' Of course there are many mothers who are always in a good mood, a baby on their back, forever willing to cart buckets of water to and fro so that they can fill the moats of the sandcastle the oldest has just built. And there are small friendly groups of women, each with a baby on her arm, chatting merrily away in the park. Here are two examples of the kinds of lives these 'fulfilled mothers' lead. The first is of a mother aged around 45–50. In theory she has finished bringing up her children but still enjoys their company: although they are grown up they still live at home. She is an even-tempered housewife who does not find housework a burden and who enjoys life without ever envying those who rush around and call themselves 'working women'.

Whenever she hears the front door bell ring she calmly goes to answer it, calling: 'Coming!' I walk in and deliberately say without bothering to butter her up: 'I'm starving! Is there anything to eat?'

'There's no time to get bored while you're around!' she says instantly bringing me some hot dish or other.

While we're eating I give her a blow by blow account of my day. She's very attentive and occasionally makes a comment. Not long after that Father comes in and then it's his turn to tell us about his day. Mother is always there to listen to us.

And then my brother comes along and puts his oar in. While father sips his whisky we secretly pinch his snacks. When he realizes what we're up to he accuses us of being a couple of opportunists – we just let him get on with it for it's the same every day. Around nine o'clock we get together again in the sitting room to chat over the coffee Mother's made us. Although she puts plenty of sugar in it, Father always complains it's not sweet enough.

It's always the same but as soon as I'm home I get a new lease of life. Perhaps it's because I can at last be myself. I'm sure it's the same for my father and brother. The day I have my own home I'd like it to be no different from this one. I think I'm really lucky to be living with my father, mother and brother. I am also fortunate to have a well-paid job.

We drink instant coffee, but it's what I like best. I can hear my mother calling me from the bathroom to tell me that the bath temperature is just right. I must go and see to my ablutions.[14]

This is very revealing in several ways, especially because it was written by a 21-year-old woman (rather than by her brother) who allows herself to be pampered by her mother in much the same way as a boy would. Chapter 1 described the other side of the story, as being brought up like this puts women at a great disadvantage for they are incapable of coping with the harsh reality of life when it is their turn to be a mother. In her eyes her parents' home embodies the kind of happiness to which she aspires.

While the mother successfully creates the illusion of happiness, upon closer examination, not content with preparing her 21-year-old daughter's dinner she actually checks the temperature of her bath water. She also puts sugar in her husband's coffee; rather than add more sugar, he complains that it is still not sweet enough. Tanaka Kimiko comments

The terrible thing about this situation is that everyone finds it quite normal and the mother, without a word of complaint but with a smile, puts up with it because she enjoys this dependence so much.

In fact she considers these 'services' to be her job without realizing that some thirty years ago they would have been absolutely unthinkable.

A survey carried out by NHK into how Japanese women organize their time has found that though the nature of housework has changed there was little variation over a period of fifteen years in the number of hours spent doing the chores each day (seven hours ten minutes as opposed to seven hours twenty nine minutes between 1960 and 1975). It is in fact the nature of the work which has changed: the heavy duty jobs (such as preserving vegetables in brine or jam making) have been replaced by 'services' such as putting sugar in one's husband's coffee or running a bath for one's 'little' 21 year old.

Tanaka quotes another informative survey which shows just how far a mother's service can go, whether or not she has a job. One-third of mothers who have 20-year-old children wake them up each morning to get them off to university or work, clean their rooms, take them shopping or wait up for them at night. Taking into consideration that these percentages were even higher among working mothers and that two-thirds of the young people interviewed were girls, the only possible conclusion is that their mothers have inadvertently created a race of macho women who use and abuse them and who will be incapable of coping with motherhood later in life.

Although these services can take a thousand different forms (squeezing the toothpaste onto your husband's toothbrush, picking up the clothes he drops on the floor when he come home from work and hanging them up, unfolding and unbuttoning his shirt for him and even helping him to put it on, putting his shoes the right way round so that he can just slip his feet into them, handing him the shoe-horn, and so on), they are not necessarily carried out with enthusiasm. Couples might seem to be living happily together, but they do not spend much time together. On retirement, the situation becomes critical when the wife announces she cannot bear to be permanently at the beck and call of a despot. Although they do not all sue for divorce, many become depressed while they wait to be liberated (death of the spouse, of the 'awkward furniture'), and some even dream of it out loud under the influence of alcohol.

My child, my reason for living

Here is the second account of a 'fulfilled woman', taken from the diary of a 32-year-old woman living in Tokyo with her husband and 2-year-old daughter.

Monday 14 January 1991

Saori had barely opened her eyes at half past eight this morning than she was rushing into her father's room demanding: 'Daddy, change my wee wee (nappy)!' Whenever her father hears her voice, however late (or early) it is, he always gets up saying: 'Good morning Saori!' and then changes her nappy and gets her dressed.

'Daddy, I want to see Mickey!'

He puts her Mickey Mouse video on for her to watch.

'Read me the fish story!'

And he does. As I watch them from my bed, Saori comes over to demand something to eat. As I don't react, she says: 'Mummy, get up!' In the end I do. When I ask her what she wants, without hesitation she replies: '*Râmens*!' [Chinese noodles in hot soup]

When I suggest that she choose something more nutritious, my husband tells me it's too late, after all I did ask her what she wanted. He's right of course, so I apologize and go and prepare it. I am careful to add seaweed, cabbage and an egg so that the dish will be more nourishing.

She settles down to eat and watch *With Mother*. By half past nine she's finished and it's time for her father to leave for work. He's setting off relatively early today! She goes to the door with him and says: '*Itte rasshaï*,[15] and then presses her mouth, nose, eyes, forehead, cheeks and chin up against those parts of her father's face. He's barely shut the door behind him than she's on the balcony waving and shouting for everyone to hear: 'Daddy, *Itte rasshaï*!' He makes his way to the station, turning around to wave back until he's out of sight.

10 o'clock   I do the housework and washing while Saori watches Channel 3 or declares: 'I'm writing!', 'Bricks' or 'I'm reading!'. Every ten minutes or so she wants to do something different and keeps interrupting me because she wants me to keep her company. We have the complete collection of Disney educational games (picture books, cassettes, toys) as well as the *Gakken Mami setto* and *kumon* ones,[16] but any doubts I might have had as to whether or not this was a good investment were soon dispelled – she doesn't miss a thing. And then after this, it's that. Ah! I never stop! She has homework to do every evening for the *kumon* but rather than force her I wait until she wants to do it.

11.30   Although she had a mandarin and a boiled potato after breakfast she says she's still hungry. As it's the day we go to the *kumon* I decide it would be a good idea to eat early and so I ask her what she'd like to eat. Without hesitating she says: 'Rice, fish and leaves.' I set to and make her some spinach soup and fish to go with the rice.

12.30 It's time to get ready for the *kumon*. She takes longer than usual to decide what to wear as she's developing an interest in her appearance. 'That's nice!' Or 'No, I want to wear that!' And how she loves her pushchair, she says: 'We're going in the push-push!'

We go to Ochiai station with the pushchair (it's 15 minutes on foot) before taking the train to Nakano. The *kumon* is a 15 minute walk from the station. She loves going there and full of enthusiasm, she says: 'We're going to the *kumon*!'

13.30 The class begins. Saori gives the teacher her homework before taking her thirty-minute break. From the mountain of toys she picks out her favourites. Half an hour later the children are invited to sit down and listen to the teacher sing them a song, teach them hand games or read them a story. The time flies past.

14.30 After saying goodbye to the teacher, little Kuni (aged 3) invites Saori to escort him on the way home, an invitation she's happy to accept as her usual boyfriend is absent. We stop at the Lotteria (local *fast food*) to have a mother-to-mother and child-to-child chat over a fruit juice. Then we have a look round the sales but come away empty handed.

17.30 Already! We've missed *Ampâman*![17] Never mind!

18.30 For want of anything better I put on a video which we watch together as we eat our dinner. Just like a big girl and with-out having to be prompted Saori says '*Itadakimasu!*.[18] Then when she's finished eating she says: '*Gochisôsama*'[19] before clearing away her plate. I can honestly say that she's been a great joy to me over the last two years!

19.30 It's bath-time and how she loves it! She always has *Ampâman* in the bath with her and washes him with the same zest as I wash her. As it's always so difficult to get her out I try to switch the light off or to sweet-talk her, but it has been easier since I noticed she wanted to get out when she started feeling dizzy.[20]

20.00 We watch *Chikyû Family*, a fascinating documentary on the flora and fauna of the Australian continent. She loves natural history programmes, documentaries on people, in fact anything to do with the universe. This 45 minute programme has her absolutely riveted.

21.00 This is a difficult time for me as I'm beginning to get tired whereas Saori is still full of beans. It begins with 'Let's read!',

'Let's write!', 'Let's do this or let's do that!', 'What shall we listen to?'. Whatever it is, I do it while I clear up. It's like being assistant to a demanding boss.

23.00 Having played to her heart's content, Saori at last admits that she's feeling sleepy. Aah! God be praised! She drops off almost as soon as I lie down next to her.

It's one in the morning as I finish writing this diary and I'll soon be going to bed. Her father's not home yet but there's nothing unusual in that. When I hear him come in, I get up and we spend two or three hours chatting together non-stop. This time is very precious to us as we watch our daughter while she sleeps.

My husband works in the media and so he's always back late (or early!). Unfortunately he never has the opportunity of having dinner or of taking a bath with his daughter, but as it happens I'm quite glad we have this opportunity of spending some time alone together once Saori has gone to bed; for whatever time he comes home he always makes sure we have a long chat, just as he makes time to see to his daughter in the morning. When I watch her as she sleeps I realize just how lucky I am.

One of our principles is never to tell our daughter off and it must be said that it is unconditional for we have never had occasion to do so. Of course, I get angry if she walks around with a kitchen knife, but . . .

The people around here are always telling her that she's so adorable she couldn't possibly ever get told off. Even though I've only ever had dealings with one I am aware of course that there's a certain amount of luck involved as to the kind of child you get. I am perhaps very privileged to have had one who is so easy to raise. Be that as it may it's thanks to her that I'm as gentle as *Moomin*'s[21] mother. Ah yes, little Saori, it's all thanks to you!

All I want out of life is for her to be well educated, for my husband and me to have a good relationship and for me to get on well with other people. I know neither the whys nor the where-fores but fulfilment comes to me from my husband and little daughter. Because I radiate happiness Saori is always in a good mood and my husband's career progresses in leaps and bounds. There are times when I see the two of them together that I want to go and shout my joy to the sea.

Clearly, I am once more extolling my good fortune.[22]

Here is a portrait of a woman who says she is happy and who is fully conscious of it: she has fulfilled her closest dreams and has had her full share in life. A closer examination will reveal the fragility of this happiness, which is completely tied up with the two beings who occupy her life. Few Japanese women can boast that they have such an attentive husband, willing to take the time to listen to her every evening, whatever hour of the night or morning he might arrive home. But what would happen to this happiness if her husband were ever unfaithful to her or he lost his job? Would she be able to deal with the situation, she who regarded the only job she ever had as a stopgap until she got married?

Little Saori represents the other source of her happiness: her dearest wish has come true, her daughter is adorable, intelligent and well behaved. Indeed, what more could she want but what will happen to this happiness when Saori goes through that inevitable argumentative phase for it is highly unlikely that she will continue to allow herself to be manipulated. 'In ten years' time,' states Tanaka Kimiko, 'this woman will go through a kind of existential "empty nest syndrome" crisis from which she will only be able to emerge if she finds a reason for living which has nothing to do with Saori.'

However, we can see how this child 'who is so easy to raise' takes up all her mother's time and energy for the latter lives through her alone, so much so that the television – and for that matter the video – have become Saori's exclusive property. The mother would never dream of letting her miss *Ampâman*, but not once does she ever think of watching the news.

Another incredible factor is that the mother's manipulation of the daughter has its counterpart in the child's manipulation of the mother. By the age of 2 Saori has succeeded in reducing her parents to a state of slavery, which she would be wrong to sacrifice as they seem to derive masochistic pleasure from it. Followers of Hiraï Nobuyoshi's educational principles,[23] they never contradict her which in simple terms, relates to carrying out her four wishes.[24] However, her mother is a skilled facilitator since Saori delights in all the educational activities her mother casually gets her to do as though they were 'a game'.

A significant amount of money has been allotted to stimulate the intellect of a 2-year-old child, already enrolled in a *juku* (private crammer), whose mother buys her – without thinking twice about it – the Disney collection (which costs 400,000 yen). Moreover, having enrolled her in the *kumon* (10,000 yen plus 6,000 yen a month) means she has to go to the trouble (which in a city like Tokyo is not inconsiderable) of taking the train to get her child there twice a week: two whole afternoons for half an hour of games and a half-hour 'class'.

A personal frustration translated into a desire to make her daughter do the studies she never did might be one of *Kyôiku mama*'s motivating factors. Although this is the case here, it is not an absolute rule and educated women often display the same determination, indeed the same symptoms. It is probable that Saori's mother, in a few years' time, will enrol in classes at the same time as her daughter, not so much for her own edification but rather to keep up with and help her daughter. (One woman who did this succeeded in getting her daughter into the prestigious university of Keiô while she herself had studied only to A level standard.)

There is nothing exceptional about this case. There are many mothers who willingly traipse across Tokyo through the morning rush-hour to take their children to a super-nursery-school which will take them to the bottom of the 'escalator'.[25] Some have time to go home before returning to collect them to take them on to other classes (music, calligraphy, sport, and so on). Others prefer to wait in a café or a McDonalds.

In return, these small children, who effortlessly realize their mothers' dreams, succeed in chasing their fathers from the marital bed. These 'little couples' are so common that they have almost become the norm.

Finally, however fulfilled Saori's mother is, she does not talk of having another child, a factor which, linked to the fact that it is working women who have the most children,[26] should be considered by demographers, paediatricians and other experts.

'Apart from the fact that 20 per cent of women claim to be "extremely happy", the great majority of them say they are "relatively satisfied" with their lives,' states Tanaka Kimiko who reminds us that behind Japan's success story lurks a yearning to lead an 'ordinary life' which has been described earlier. A life which would elsewhere pass for a mediocre existence is perhaps the expression of the purest of wisdom since it is modest, realistic and therefore human.

Although Japanese mothers would seem to be moved by their offsprings' academic performance they actually yearn to have children who are neither better nor worse than the others. This no doubt explains why 70 to 75 per cent of Japanese women are willing to put up with a marriage which is (if not mediocre) then at least average.

My little mummy is completely off her head

Finally, here are the remarks of a little girl in primary school, whose essay was selected by Hiraï Nobuyoshi to illustrate why the ordinary is so appealing. Although Hiraï read it out as though he were confiding a little masterpiece, it actually gives the impression that any significant revolution in people's attitudes had still not happened.

The other day mother left the vegetables to simmer while she went off to put the washing out in the garden. As the saucepan began to boil over my father shouted: 'Hey! It's boiling over!' Dismayed, doesn't she just drop the pole and rush into the kitchen . . . and wham![27] The washing lands straight in the mud!

'Oh, really!' says Father, 'you're always making a mess of things!'

'Sorry,' mother replies in a jokey way.

And yet this same father who scolds mother is just as crazy! One morning, when he's barely got out of bed, doesn't he go and shout: 'No need for breakfast this morning!' Then he jumps into his clothes, rushes to the door and with his briefcase under his arm, runs out.

'Oh, really!' says mother, 'Have you forgotten it is Sunday? Honestly, you're really not thinking straight!' With a couple of parents like these, how do you expect me to cope?

Needless to say, my younger brother is just as nutty! We're all a bit cracked! And yet when I'm older, I'd like to be like my mother. I'll marry a blockhead like my father and we'll have children as cracked as my brother! Ah! We'll have such fun together! Dear idiotic little mummy![28]

By way of a conclusion

The object of this book was certainly not to paint a depressing picture, or for that matter to criticize Japanese mothers. I believe that they display a most praiseworthy devotion which for their children definitely represents a priceless asset which will help them to confront life. The effect that childcare books have had in making mothers feel guilty proves beyond a doubt that they wish to carry out their duties as best as they possibly can. These books do of course contain some good advice and no one would dare challenge the benefits of 'bonding' or of breast-feeding.

The problem is that these books cannot replace the personal knowledge that was once passed down from mother to daughter; there has been every opportunity since then to reproach mothers for being 'incapable of functioning without an instruction manual' or of having lost what Kyûtoku calls their 'educational instinct'. It is important to emphasize that the women who call the baby help line are not 'cases' (Jimba Yukiko, who has spent so much time listening to them, has repeated this frequently) even though different problems have been emerging more recently which reflect greater material comfort – small recompense for the solitude they endure – which remains reliant on the ups and downs of the economic climate.

It would appear that France and Japan have much more in common than people might think. For example judging by the recent importance being given to relaxation therapy and haptonomy, Japan is far from having exclusive rights over *taikyô*. The popularity of the Arthur method or Glenn Doman's books (now available in French) where readers learn how to raise 'outstanding' geniuses proves that the desire of parents to force nature 'gently' is not restricted by national boundaries.

Nevertheless, even Hiraï Nobuyoshi has distanced himself from what he used to preach since his own daughter-in-law proved to him that it was possible to have a career and bring up three children without their ending up deprived, autistic or neglected. It was particularly interesting to hear him admit this in June 1991. The problem is that at the age of 70 experts do not renege in print on the theories which have made them famous. That is why his books continue to be bestsellers and continue to do the damage we have observed.

My meeting with the author of *Illness Caused by Mother* was less reassuring. Kyûtoku continues to believe that his theories are well founded; indeed, since he wrote his first book he has produced four more which have particularly provocative subtitles: for example: *Profile of the Bad Mother*.

If Michel Lemay's book,[1] *J'ai mal à ma mère* (Illness Caused by Mother), also reminds us that with the best will in the world mothers can sometimes cause untold damage, it is important to explain that he deals with inadequate relationships, which makes all the difference. Kyûtoku's books are so overwhelming because he wants his theories to apply to all Japanese mothers. Although his theories are at last being criticized it is disconcerting to learn that those who make a point of reading him are the parents of children with school refusal syndrome on whom he would probably have a disastrous impact.

It is surprising to learn of the undeniable influence in Japan of the thoughts and theories of Harlow, Bowlby, Klaus, Kennel and René Spitz given that they are more relevant to conditions in the United States. In Japan there are no single or teenage mothers (they have abortions), any more than there are 'blended' families where the children – the product of more than one marriage – live together. 'Crack babies' (whose mothers were crack addicts during pregnancy) are still unknown; only one HIV positive baby has so far been recorded.[2] No Japanese child goes hungry (which is not the case in the United States where 5.5 million children under the age of 12 (12.7 per cent) are hungry, to which we should add 6 million children considered to be 'at risk of being under-nourished').[3] Japan has the lowest infant mortality rate in the world; the rate in the United States is still at 9.7% placing the country in seventeenth position in the world, with the district of Columbia alone coming twenty-third after Jamaica and Costa Rica. While many American children never receive medical check-ups and are once more at risk from tuberculosis, Japanese children are spoilt, mollycoddled and over- rather than under-fed. Finally, child abuse may well be a much debated subject but children are no more mistreated than were their parents, except that before it was never discussed.

Although paediatricians like Môri Taneki, Yamada Makoto and, to a certain extent, Ikegame Ume have essentially taken the opposite view to the theories of the 'great masters', they have in no way established their reputation. All they have done is give the ant-hill a hard kick,[4] without actually coming up with an alternative to the *laissez-faire* attitude which not only produces egocentric and extremely spoilt children but also can lead to neglect. As Tanaka Kimiko says,

to go from one extreme to the other has never solved anything and since the collapse of the country's previous social support structures, there has never been a time when mothers have devoted so much time to bringing up their children and when, psychologically speaking, this task has been so hard.

However, without being at all aggressive, Japanese women are making their silent little revolution, instigating change by what I would call a gentle resistance. Hanako marries but she has had the opportunity to live life to the full. Although, until the mid-1960s, a young woman had to be a virgin when she married, this is no longer the case. Not only is this concept outdated but also anyone insisting on marrying a virgin might have to wait a long time. While marriage has not been completely rejected, there is no reason to rush into it. Young women intend to take their time: these days it is they who choose – yet another significant development in the way the couple has evolved in Japan. By asking for so much more they are expressing their desire to see men evolve and become more compliant husbands. It is sometimes the case that a mother-in-law lives with them when it suits the daughter-in-law (and not the other way round). To be tolerated – indeed sought – a mother-in-law must be ready (to bend over backwards for her grandchildren), willing and able – a new and free version of the much-sought-after post-war live-in maid of all work. If mother-in-law is a widow with a nice house she will be more than welcome, for she will obviously go and work for her daughter-in-law, who expects her to die suddenly without being a nuisance (*pokkuri*).[5] The mother-in-law who belongs to the old school is loudly and emphatically rejected and rural marriages are boycotted.

Despite this evolution, deciding to become a mother remains a difficult step to take. Yet, once they are over the initial shock, the majority of young women come to terms with it, thinking that perhaps it is easier to cope with an unplanned child rather than have to deal with the dilemma of when the 'ideal moment' is. Thus 'the unexpected baby' is actually a good thing since most women want a child and because it is better to have one when the mother is young. Later (their duty done) they make a conscious choice to limit their expenses, for however real the joys of motherhood are, once is enough. Everyone knows that life with two children can be incredibly busy. That is why it is not until afterwards that young women take control of their fertility. If contraception does not work they can always have an abortion, but to judge by the number of articles on 'sexless couples' it would seem that there is no longer a great need for contraception.

Though some might interpret this to be a deliberate stance (a kind of sexual and womb strike) never before have women been in such a good position to put pressure on the politicians. 'We have to submit our demands – it's now or never!' said Jimba Yukiko who, at 57, does not mince her words.

They must provide us with crèches which are better-equipped, adapted to the hours we work and more open to our suggestions, jobs should introduce flexi-time, longer maternity leave of two or three years with a guarantee that our jobs will still be there for us, not forgetting the need for more congenial working hours so that our partners have the chance to help us. Women must stand firm until these conditions are met. At least give them the choice and if they choose to continue to work, no one should throw sexual equality in their faces under the pretext that they have the same opportunities as men. Is it progress if like men, women die of over-work? Let's be reasonable! We must make it absolutely clear to the government that by having two children we are working for the future of the country and must therefore receive some compensation. It is imperative that employers adapt working conditions to accommodate pregnant women and young mothers instead of treating them as commodities to be discarded after use.

The time is fast approaching when the country will be forced to choose between opening its doors to foreign workers or making intelligent use of its female workforce.

Tanaka Kimiko has also observed that since the mid-1980s a new and stronger husband–wife relationship has been developing.[6] If women reproach their husbands for being condescending and making them feel that they are no good at anything, they are unanimous in their acknowledgement that their chief quality is that they leave them free to do as they wish. This could of course be interpreted as indifference but also as being a formidable permutation of power in the couple. The *breadwinner*/housewife blueprint certainly does not make for an easy life but Japanese women may feel that there is some advantage in it.

Moreover, even though barely 26 per cent of women questioned said that they enjoyed looking after their children,[7] almost all made the sacrifice required of them while never losing sight of the fact that it was an obligation and not for their personal betterment. They are finding it increasingly difficult to sustain the self-denial which is expected of them but however frustrated they might feel when they see their western counterparts, they nevertheless persevere; and to the Japanese child, this self-denial is a capital investment of inestimable value.

I am not saying that western values should be taken as a point of reference, for the Japanese seem far better equipped when it comes to dealing with situations or conditions of life which might be judged intolerable in the eyes of another culture. I am convinced that Oshin (see Chapter 5) is still alive in the hearts of all Japanese women. In a similar situation they would certainly do everything just as well, for their strength resides in their extraordinary ability to adapt and their courage is never far away. What could be mistaken as passivity should never be taken to be resignation. Patiently they put up with the situation, but the old ten-year 'moratorium' has been considerably shortened for they do not necessarily wait for their child to start primary school before going back to work; if they have only one child, it is likely that the break will be shorter still.

A return to part-time work implies that their skills are being devalued and exploited in the interests of the country and company but at the moment this is still a better alternative to the overwhelming effects of always being alone with a child.

We could ask just how much of themselves women actually want to invest in a career which might not, apart from the odd exception, be terribly enthralling. To see their husbands slaving away they might decide that after all their lot is not so bad.

Taking everything into account, maybe part-time work fulfils a need, maybe it distracts women 'just enough' without encroaching on their private lives?

Some would (misguidedly) contest the expression 'distract', for, whatever the job, it means that every single one of them has access to the outside world and to other people. It also means that they can place their child in a crèche which often gives them the help and support they need which is sadly lacking in the nuclear family.[8] Their jobs also allow them to be part of a whole network of female solidarity, whose therapeutic value is inestimable. The women can give one another support, advice, the opportunity to express their resentment, help, cosseting, congratulations and praise. It is somewhat ironic that at night, their husbands can be found in bars in the centre of town, paying a fortune to get these same things from a hostess.

This is no doubt why the part-time job is so successful for it gives everyone what they need: wives have a clear conscience, and husbands because – while they cannot help but see how this benefits their wives who come home refreshed and rejuvenated – their wives' work can also improve their daily lives. Finally, both country and company benefit, for the vigorous economic system has an extraordinary safety valve in this intelligent, hard-working and over-qualified workforce, which not only is happy to work for a pittance but also is dismissible if the fluctuating needs of the economy require it to be. Everyone breaks even. That's how life is.

Notes

1 YOUNG MOTHERS IN A DILEMMA

1 In this context the most appropriate explanation of *amai* would be gentle, indulgent, spoilt, easy; the psychiatrist Doi Takeo sees this word as being the key to understanding the Japanese mentality: see *Amae no kôzô*, Kôbundo, 1971 (English translation *The Anatomy of Dependence*, Kôdansha International, 1973). (See also Chapter 4, n. 95.)

2 Taken from *Ikuji noiroze* ('Childrearing neurosis'), collection, ed. Yûhikaku Shinsho, 1982, p. 186.

3 *Ibid.*, p. 225.

4 *Wife*, 188, July 1984, quoted by Tanaka Kimiko, in *Hataraku josei no kosodateron* ('The educational theories of working women'), Shinchô Sensho, 1988, pp. 77–8.

5 This ancient custom is known as *satogaeri*. It is an opportunity (still much appreciated) for the woman to be pampered, indeed cosseted by her own mother. This invaluable reprieve generally lasts for one or two months but can sometimes go on for as long as six months.

6 Tanaka, *op. cit.*, pp. 79–80.

7 Yûki Misae, *Minna nayande mama ni naru* ('We all learn to become mothers on the job!'), Chôbunsha, Tokyo, 1990.

8 From *Wife*, 188, quoted by Tanaka, *op. cit.*, p. 80.

9 An identical account can be found in an article in the economic journal *Nihon Keizai Shimbun* of 14 May 1991: 'Without hesitation they stated quite clearly: "Ah! If only I hadn't had him!"'

10 *Ikuji noiroze, op. cit.*, pp. 209–10.

11 *Ibid.*, p. 211.

12 Maternity leave benefit has been available (in some professions which have a high proportion of women) since 1975, because of a fear of a short-fall in the labour market (as in the case of nurses) or because women are in the majority or members of a union (for example teachers and child-carers). (For more information on the legislation covering maternity leave passed on 1 April 1992, see pp. 46–7.)

13 From the article on the battered child help line, in the magazine *Como*, 11, entitled, 'Help! I don't find my child lovable!', November 1991, p. 89.

14 See Ariyoshi Sawako's historical novel, *Hanaoka Seishû no tsuma*,

Shinchôsha, 1970 (English translation, *The Doctor's Wife*, Kôdansha, 1978).

15 Tanaka, *op. cit.*, pp. 80–1.

16 From *Ikuji noiroze, op. cit.*, pp. 194–5.

17 It is customary in Japan to leave the front door unlocked. The postman or delivery boy usually enters without ringing, shouting: '*Gomen kudasai*' ('Excuse me'). The bell is used only if the door is locked.

18 The *tandai* diploma corresponds to two years' post-school studies.

19 *Ikuji noiroze, op. cit.*, pp. 222–4.

20 In an article entitled 'Appel à la conscience du corps médical' ('Appeal to the medical profession's conscience'), the writer Endô Shûsaku denounces the lack of dignity of this production line style medical care (see '*Nihon no "ryôi" ni uttaeru*', in *Chûô Kôron*, July 1982, pp. 128–37), which appeared in *Les Cahiers du Japon* (15, spring 1983, pp. 73–8).

21 This is why psychiatrists' consulting rooms are designed to look like those of general practitioners.

22 Morita, in his famous and very Japanese style psychotherapy, advises people to learn to live with their neuroses and/or obsessions. His whole philosophy is encapsulated in the expression *aru ga mama*, in other words we should learn to accept ourselves for what we are. (For further details, see David K. Reynolds' excellent book, *Morita Psychotherapy*, University of California Press, Berkeley, 1976.)

23 It is extremely rare for a man to invite his colleagues home; it is customary to take them to a restaurant rather than to his home.

24 *Ikuji noiroze, op. cit.*, pp. 221–2.

25 *Minna nayande mama mi maru op. cit.*, pp. 81–2.

26 Rich, pp. 24–5.

27 This relates to a Japanese educational principle on which teachers and parents always agree: that the child must eat everything.

28 From *Ikuji noiroze, op. cit.*, p. 215.

29 Christiane Olivier, *Les Enfants de Jocaste* ('Jocasta's children'), Denoël-Gonthier, Paris, 1980.

30 Jimba Yukiko (co-author of *Ikuji noiroze* ('Childrearing neurosis') recalls a family therapy session where the therapist set the husband a 'homework' task to express his love or gratitude to his wife at least once a week. After a week of embarrassment, the approach of the deadline made the husband suddenly turn to his wife just as he was about to go out and tell her he loved her. She was so taken aback by this that she became concerned over the state of his health.

31 *Tanshinfuninsha* refers to employees who are transferred by their companies and who, for a variety of reasons (usually the children's education or the care of elderly parents or in-laws), leave their wives behind. (For more detailed information on this national problem, see Chapter 3.)

32 Halfway between an arranged marriage and a love match, these *shanai kekkon* appear to be very popular in the mid-1990s, both in the eyes of the employers – who can as a result politely dismiss their staff – and the OL (*office ladies*) who often wish to work only until they have found a husband (see Chapters 2 and 7).

33 This kind of suicide is called *boshi shinjû*.

34 This was a slogan popular in the 1970s to describe a housewife's life.
35 13.5 per cent had 15 minutes' daily contact, 20.3 per cent had 30 minutes' and 15 per cent over an hour (from *Nihon no chichioya to kodomo* ('Japanese fathers and their children'), Tokyo, p. 32, graph 2.1).
36 A synopsis of this was published in Germany in a collective work, *Zur sozialgeschichte des Kindheit*, Verlag Alber, 1986.
37 This theme became the subject of a programme on the national television channel (NHK), summer 1989.
38 From *Como*, 11, November 1991, p. 86.
39 *Kyôku mama* is a mother obsessed with her children's education.
40 The *hiragana* is a phonetic and cursive alphabet comprising 51 signs which all Japanese children can already read – and often write – well before they go to primary school.
41 The development of these theories can be found in, among others: *Bogenbyô* ('Illness caused by Mother'), Sun Mark Shuppan, 1979, where Kyûtoku Shigemori deplores the loss of the 'childrearing instinct' inherent in today's Japanese mother. See also Hiraï Nobuyoshi, *Ushinawareta boseiaï* ('The disappearance of maternal love'), Reimei Shobô, 1981; and see also Chapter 4.
42 She is referring here to what the Americans call *quality time* (this subject is dealt with by, among others, Brazelton, in *Working and Caring*, Addison Wesley, 1983, and by Anita Shreve, *Remaking Motherhood*, Fawcett Columbine, New York, 1988.)
43 From *Wife*, 188, quoted in *Hataraku josei . . . , op. cit.*, p. 83.
44 From the article on the battered child help line ('*Watakushi, "ochikobore mama" kashira?*', 'Am I an unworthy mother?') in *Como*, 11, November 1991, p. 14.
45 From *Ikuji noiroze, op. cit.*, p. 224.
46 See the articles devoted to Dr Saitô Satoru in *Asahi*, 22 October 1991 and 5 December 1990, and in *Nikkei*, 3 January 1992 (see also Chapter 8, n. 12).
47 *O-migiri* is a triangle of cooked rice, equivalent to a bowl of rice.
48 Literally, the temple in which one seeks refuge. Traditionally forbidden to men, these temples, which are reserved for Buddhist nuns, also serve as safe havens to women who want to escape their husbands or difficult situations.

2 WHY HAVE CHILDREN?

1 The English expression in *katakana* was used in the interview.
2 Statement taken from Amano Masako, lecturer at the University of Chiba (see interview in *Croissant*, 306, 10 August 1990, pp. 50–1).
3 Of the young women the Recruit Centre interviewed in 1991, 83.3 per cent replied that they did wish to marry; of these, 37.4 per cent said 'whatever the cost', while 16.6 per cent stated that they were not particularly interested in getting married (of these replies 41.5 per cent were from those who had taken the equivalent to A levels, 17.5 per cent were from those who had followed vocational courses, 23.9 per cent were from those who had the equivalent to HND and 14.5 per cent were from those

who had graduated after four years at university). Taken from *Working Women ni kansuru chôsa* ('Survey on working women'), Recruit Centre, 1991, p. 59.

4 In reply to a questionnaire distributed to several employers, the cinematographic company Tôwa replied that it expected its male employees to get married when they were around 26, because allegiance to a family engendered allegiance to the company. For a more in-depth study see Muriel Jolivet, 'L'intégration sociale par la voie du mariage' ('Social integration through marriage') (unpublished), DREA, Paris-III/ INALCO, 1977, pp. 49–53; Jolivet, *L'université au service de l'économie japonaise*, Economica, Paris, 1985, pp. 122–3; Jolivet, 'Le consensus dans l'entreprise' ('Company consensus'), in *Japon, le consensus: mythe et réalités* (coll.) ('Japan, the consensus: myths and realities'), Economica, Paris, 1984, pp. 139–70. (See also Chapter 7.)

5 Quoted by Charles Whipple, *The Hanako Syndrome*, Media Watch, 1991.

6 Tsushima Yûko, *Hikari no Ryobun* (French translation, *Territoire de Lumière* ('Land of light'), Des Femmes, Paris, 1986).

7 Tanaka Kimiko is editor-in-chief of *Wife*, and author of several books, including *Hataraku josei no kosodateron* ('The educational theories of working women'), 1987.

8 *Hataraku josei... op. cit.*, pp. 78–9. During a conference in Tokyo in December 1992, the Marxist Feminist Ueno Chizuko said that the secret desire of today's *career woman* was to have her mother-in-law at home so that she could look after her offspring.

9 Questioned on what they thought of couples who chose not to have children, 58.2 per cent of women replied that it was a personal choice and that it was normal for some couples to be different (from *Kateikan ni kansuru ankêto chôsa* ('Study on the concept of home') Economic Development Agency, 1990).

10 76.5 per cent of single women interviewed by the Recruit Centre in 1991 replied that they would like to bear their children between the ages of 26 and 32, with the majority of these (30.9 per cent) favouring 28 to 29 (according to *Working women ni kansuru chôsa, op. cit.*, p. 60).

11 Statistics provided by Ministry of Health, 1990.

12 The presumption that all women dream of becoming mothers means that this question was not so much based on whether or not the woman wanted a child but rather on the number of children she wanted to have. Interviewed by the Recruit Centre in 1991, 45 per cent of young women replied that they wanted to have two children while 33 per cent stated they wanted to have three. However, 22.5 per cent thought they would have only one and nearly 60 per cent, two. The difference between the number of children desired and the number of children they actually had was 0.3 per cent. While 12 per cent of young women admit to not wanting children, only 5.5 per cent think they might not have any (from *Working Women ni kansuru chôsa, op. cit.*, p. 61).

13 Extract from *Minna nayande, mama ni naru, op. cit.*, p. 98.

14 According to a survey published by the *Asahi* newspaper, 3 March 1995 this includes the cost from birth till end of university at 22 years.

15 *Nihon no kodomo to hahaoya* ('Japanese children and their mothers'),

Prime Minister's Office, Youth Headquarters, 1981 (not updated since), p. 165.

16 Statistics provided by the Ministry of Health, 1989. This is the archetypal scenario, but since caring for elderly people very much depends on the state of their health, it is not possible to make too sweeping a generalization. However, in show houses for prospective buyers, there is an area traditionally reserved for the grandparents. This is a ground-floor room of around eight *tatamis*, cut off from the rest of the family whose bedrooms are upstairs. *Tatami* mats are straw flooring materials in traditional style. A *tatami* (1.76 × 0.88 metres or 5.8 × 2.9 feet) continues to be used as a unit of measure for the area of a room.

17 *Atarashii josei no ikikata-o motomete* ('The demands of the new women'), published by the Economic Development Agency, 1987, see Figure 8, p. 123.

18 A survey carried out by the Prime Minister's Office reveals that in 1992, 75.7 per cent of parents preferred a girl to a boy (24.3 per cent). In *Josei no gendai to shisaku*, 1995, printed in Itoh Kimio, *Dansei gaku nyûmon* (*Introduction to men's studies*), Sakuhinsha, 1996, p. 29. An article (14 February 1993) in the newspapers *Asahi* and *Mainichi* on choosing the sex of a child, revealed that those parents who chose gender selection nearly always did so because they wanted a girl.

19 *San K* was a term originally used to refer to heavy manual labour which the Japanese (particularly the young) are no longer interested in.

20 *Il oppai, warui oppai* (English subtitle: *The Good Breast and the Bad Breast*), Tôjunsha, 1985, and *Papa-wa go kigen naname* (*Papa, You are Cross!*), Sakuhinsha, Tokyo, 1989 (in Japanese).

21 39.4 per cent of women questioned replied that they felt that the children's education fell mainly or only to the mother, against 54.3 per cent who did not agree (from *Atarashii josei no ikikata-o motomete, op. cit.,* Figure 39, p. 71).

22 For *yoïko* see the survey carried out by Merry White and Robert Le Vine, 'What is an li ko (Good Child)?', in *Child Development and Education in Japan*, Harold Stevenson, Hiroshi Azuma and Kenji Hakuta, 1986, pp. 55–62. See also the work by Hiraï Nobuyoshi, *Yoi ko, warui ko* ('The good child and the naughty child'), PHP Kenkyûsho, 1990; and also 'The good child', in Joy Hendry, *Becoming Japanese, The World of the Pre-School Child,* University of Hawaii Press, Honolulu, 1986, pp. 86–98. In an article entitled 'Education', Saitô Jirô also deals with this question (see 'Inside the "Good Child" factories', *Omni Magazine*).

For further information regarding children being dropped into the adult world, see Ezra Vogel, *Japan's New Middle Class*, University of California Press, Berkeley, 1963 (particularly Chapter 3, 'The gateway to salary: infernal entrance examinations', pp. 40–67). See also Vogel 'Entrance examinations and emotional disturbances in Japan's new middle class', *Japanese Culture*, 34, pp. 140–52.

23 It is customary in Japan for the whole family to expect to benefit from the spin-offs of their children's success (particularly that of the oldest son), as revealed in the saying: 'make a triumphant entry into your birthplace where success equals filial duty.

24 This trend can also be found in France: see for example, 'Tu seras un raté mon fils' ('You will be a failure my son'), *Le Nouvel Observateur*, 1461, 5–11 November 1992, pp. 9–11.

25 Thomas Rohlen stresses that a person will be judged according to his ability, thus turning a child who has problems at school into a failure (see *Japan's High Schools*, University of California Press, 1983). The sociologist Takeuchi Yô emphasizes that in his opinion the comparison made in Japan between professional and moral values, and the opinion the company has of its employee, become synonymous with the opinion he has of himself (in *Nipponjin no shussekan* ('The concept of success in Japan') Gakubunsha, 1978). In the article from *Le Nouvel Observateur* quoted in n. 24, it was also written: 'To children, not to be performing well at school, is to lose the love of their parents.'

26 The number of children suffering from school phobia or school refusal syndrome is in the order of 75,000 (statistics supplied by the Ministry of Education, 1993). 'School refusal' is defined as being absent more than 30 days, apart from illness or injury. See also on this subject, Muriel Jolivet, 'Le revers de la médaille' ('The other side of the coin'), *Le Monde de l'Education*, 110, November 1984.

27 This is well portrayed in Ozu Yasujirô's films, for example, *Bakushû*.

28 From the article on the declining birthrate in *Croissant*, 306, 10 August 1990.

29 At the time of writing, the total number of female students attending this university is around 10 per cent. However, parents who are intellectually motivated, or who do not have sons, encourage their daughters these days in the same way as they would a son.

30 Statistics for 1990, supplied by the Ministry of Education.

31 From *Nihon no kodomo to hahaoya, op. cit.*, cf. 'Kodomo no shokugyô kibô ('A mother's expectations for future occupations'), pp. 214–24 and figure on p. 26.

32 From *Kyôiku mondai (gakureki) ni kansuru yoron chôsa* ('Public opinion survey on study related problems'), Prime Minister's Office, Shoukadoh Booksellers Pr. Co., Kyoto, 1985.

33 From an interview in *Croissant*, 306, 10 August 1990, p. 57. Essayist, critic and lecturer, Higuchi Keiko is the mother of a female doctor and also the author of *Onna no ko no sodatekata*, Bunka Shuppankyoku, Tokyo, 1978 (*Bringing up Girls, Status of Women in Japan*, 1985).

34 Statistics released by the Ministry of Health, 1987, *Kekkon to shussan ni kansuru zenkoku chôsa*, published in *Nihon keizai shimbun*, 5 May 1988.

35 From *Shigoto to ikuji dochiramo taisetsu ni shitai* ('The art of reconciling work and children'), Ministry of Labour, Women's Headquarters, p. 3.

36 Only large companies were liable to grant this leave; small to medium-sized companies were exempt until 1995.

37 For the few examples who have applied the law before it was passed, see Chapter 8, pp. 177–8.

38 From *Ikuji shûgyô seido no susume* ('Proposal to encourage women to take maternity leave'), Women's Headquarters, 1987.

39 Although not as well paid as childcare assistants of crèches managed by local government, who belong to a union and strike for more money, the

former have the advantage of being able to keep their children with them, which the latter are not permitted to do.

40 On the subject of this law, see Muriel Jolivet, 'Femmes en retrait' ('A few steps behind'), *Le Monde*, 14 November 1986; and Jolivet, 'L'Avenir à armes égales' ('The future on equal terms'), in the report, 'L'emploi au féminin', ('Employing women'), *France-Japon Éco*, 35, 1988, pp. 27–30.

41 See interview, in *ibid.*, pp. 30–1. Regulations limit overtime to 150 hours a year; hours worked over and above this number are undeclared and unpaid. Some companies simplify the problem by paying only for the hours worked after 7.30 p.m. while others make it quite clear to their employees how many hours they are allowed to claim each month.

42 This is why there has been talk recently of creating what Alice Lam refers to as 'middle-of-the-road' career tract without transfer (in Equal employment opportunities for Japanese Women changing company practice, in Janet Hunter (ed.) *Japanese Women Working*, London, Routledge, 1993). However, transfers are considered to be the *sine qua non* prerequisite to being in line for promotion. Could this be a clever ruse to eliminate women from posts of responsibility? Be that as it may, 21.6 per cent of female students surveyed in 1992 by the Recruit Centre replied that they longed for one of these non-specialized posts, while 39.5 per cent said they would possibly like to have one, which represents a drop of 7.5 per cent and 0.8 per cent in relation to 1990 (from *Yonensei daigaku joshi gakusei no shûshoku jittai chôsa* ('Research into the actual working conditions available to female university graduates'), Recruit Research, 1992.

43 For the rare instances where Japanese women have dared to defy this custom, refer to the excellent work done by Alice Cook and Hayashi Hiroko, *Working Women in Japan, Discrimination, Resistance and Reform*, Cornell International Industrial and Labor Relations Report, 10, Cornell University, 1980.

44 As Mary Ann Mason (assistant professor of Law and Social Welfare at the School of Social Welfare, University of California, Berkeley) states in *The Equality Trap* (Simon & Schuster, New York, 1988, p. 16),

Equality is a two-edged sword that can cut women down as well as help them up. Equality works as a strategy only in the limited situations where women are actually in the same situation as men. It can therefore be a useful strategy for young women students, or for women who will not have children and wish to compete with men. Women with children will always get the sharp edge of the sword.

45 An evolution which is in no way revolutionary, the child arriving on average twenty-two months after the wedding.

46 Here is that nonchalance which was talked about so much concerning the 'crystal' youth of the 1980s, described by Tanaka Yasuo in his best-seller *Nantonaku Kurisutaru* ('Like crystal'), awarded the Kawada Shobô prize, Shinchôsha, 1981. For more details, refer to Olivier Chegaray's excellent article, 'Une Jeunesse cristal' ('A crystal youth'), *Des villes nommées Tokyo* ('Cities called Tokyo'), *Autrement*, special issue, 8, September 1984, pp. 123–9. See also Wakabayashi Shin, 'Reflexions sur

la nouvelle génération' ('Reflections on the new generation'), *Cahiers du Japon*, 10, winter 1981, pp. 106–8.

47 From the White Paper on jobs done by women (*91 nen Fujin Rôdô Hakusho*), published in 1991 by the Ministry of Labour.

48 In reality 712 yen (statistics supplied by the Ministry of Labour 1990), the rate fluctuates between 688 and 748 yen according to the size of the company; for further information on part-time employees' estimated hourly rates, depending on the type of work and scale of the company, see *Chingin kôzo kihon tôkei chôsa* ('Investigation into the structure of salaries'), Ministry of Labour.

49 The extremely well-documented investigation carried out by Hara Hiroko also found that women who worked part-time were those who put their families first 'whatever the circumstances' (see Hara Hiroko-hen, *Hahaoya no shûgyô to katei seikatsu no hendô* ('Mother's occupation and home education'), Kôbundô, 1987 based on the 1985 investigation).

50 If these 'High Miss' have no other choice but to leave their company, there is always the possibility of their going to work for small or medium-sized businesses or a foreign firm, more interested in their employees' output or efficiency than in their civil status. See Muriel Jolivet, 'Que les femmes sachent se rendre indispensables ouvrira la porte vers l'égalité' ('The door to equality will open the day women become indispensable'), dossier on 'L'emploi au féminin' ('Employing women'), *France-Japon Éco*, 35, 1988, pp. 44–8.

51 From Alice Cook and Hayashi Hiroko, *Working Women in Japan: Discrimination, Resistance and Reform, op. cit.*, p. 28.

52 *Ibid.*, p. 46. In the mid-1960s women were still expected to retire five years earlier than men.

53 *Ibid.*, pp. 46–9.

54 *Ibid.*, p. 50.

55 The problem also arises when it comes to a part-time job whose hours can be equivalent to a full-time post excluding overtime.

56 From *Atarashii josei no ikikata-o motomete, op. cit.*, p. 99.

57 *Fujin no shûgyô ni kansuru yoron chôsa* ('Public opinion survey on working women'), Prime Minister's Office, 1983.

58 From *Kodomo chôsa (Tokyo, Yamanote)* ('Research on Tokyo's children who live *intra muros*'), Kokusai Josei gakkai, 1981. The results of this inquiry confirm in every way those of the inquiry carried out under the direction of Iwao Sumiko and Sugiyama Meiko, *Hataraku hahaoya no jidai* ('The era of the working mother'), NHK Books, 456, 1984, and the one carried out by Hara Hiroko and Sugiyama Meiko, *Hataraku onnatachi no jidai*, NHK Books, 479, 1985, as well as the extensive survey published under the direction of Hara Hiroko (see n. 49). (For a synopsis in French of these sources, see Muriel Jolivet 'Conjuguer travail et maternité au Japon' ('Combining work and motherhood in Japan'), *Projet*, 206, 1987, pp. 97–101.)

59 From the survey carried out by the Prime Minister's Office, Youth Development Headquarters, *Seishônen to katei ni kansuru kokusai hikaku chôsa* ('International study on young people and the family'), Sômuchô (Management and Coordination Agency), 1981 (not updated since).

60 See for example, *'Otto wa kaji, ikuji no dono teido sanka suru ka'* ('Constructive help from husbands with housework and childcare'), in *Kinrôsha oyobi kinrôsha setai no tsuma ni kazoku ishiki ni kansuru chôsa*, Ministry of Labour, 1981. See also *Hataraku hahaoya no idai, op. cit.*, as well as the study quoted in n. 58.

61 See, for example, *Nippon no kodomo to hahaoya, op. cit.*, which reveals that on average children spend 24 minutes a day helping with the chores as opposed to 72 minutes in the United States (see graph 2.2.12, p. 48).

62 Figures from students on two and four year degree courses respectively (from *Joshigakusei wa nani-o kangaete iru ka* ('What do the female students think?'), Recruit Centre, 1984, p. 32, not updated since).

63 These 'second jobbers' can be a risk for they soon tire of babysitting and a week after starting will stop work without a second thought.

64 In my experience Japanese babysitters cannot do more than one thing at a time, because nowadays young Japanese women are mollycoddled. An employee of 'Japan Baby-Sitter' went so far as to dictate to me over the phone what she expected to find on arrival (rice set to be cooked at a given time, menu written out in detail, etc.). They categorically refuse to administer medicines or to allow children to ride their bikes so as to avoid accidents. So far not one has shown herself capable of giving the children a bath. The only time I decided to risk it, the young woman (aged 29) forgot to heat the water and the children ended up having a cold bath.

65 Only in exceptional cases do crèches take in babies at the end of maternity leave (now eight weeks). Mothers normally have to wait until their babies are over 5, 6 or 8 months old depending on the town or district. Childcare thus remains a problem during the first few months of a baby's life. The lucky ones can call upon their mother's services (which often involves moving nearer to her, which can result in a much longer journey to work); others have no choice but to turn to the *hôiku mama-san*. These are more or less registered minders, who look after several children in sometimes extremely cramped accommodation.

66 Statistics supplied by the Prime Minister's Office, *Fujin no shûgyô ni kansuru yoron chôsa* ('Opinion survey on women starting work'), 1983.

67 Title of a guide for women who wish to return to paid work on a part-time basis, giving them advice on how to organize the family and prepare them psychologically for the transition.

68 Expression used in *Hataraku hahaoya no jidai, op. cit.* p. 16.

69 For more information on the principle of *risshin shusse*, see Muriel Jolivet, *'Shusse ishiki'* ('The race to success'), in *Nippon no shinchûkansô* ('The new middle class in Japan'), coll. Waseda University Press, 1982, pp. 57–104.

70 From the words *'madogiwa'* (near the windows) and *'zoku'* (tribe, clan). For further details, see Muriel Jolivet, *Le Consensus social dans l'entreprise* ('Social consensus in the company'), Economica, Paris, 1984, pp. 139–70.

71 In NHK's programme *Okâsan to isshô* ('With mother') for the under-threes broadcast twice a day, one sequence in three is devoted to the pleasure of being naked in the bath with daddy and of rubbing his back.

72 Statistics supplied by the Ministry of Health, 1988.

73 Kashima Takashi, *Otoko to onna kawaru rikigaku* ('The dynamics of change between men and women'), Iwanami Shinsho, 1989. Kashima Takashi, *Otoko no zahyôjiku – kigyô kara katei-he, shakai-he* ('Men's axes of coordination – company, family and society'), Iwanami Shinsho, 1993.

3 FATHERS

1 *Nippon no kodomo to chichioya* ('Japanese children and their fathers'), Sômucho Seishônen taisaku hombu (Management and Coordination Agency, Youth Bureau, 1987).

2 In *Papa-wa gokigen naname, op. cit.*

3 From *Nihon no chichioya to kodomo, op. cit.*, graph 2.2.2, p. 35.

4 See Table 2.4 on the topics of conversation between fathers and their children, *ibid.*, p. 39.

5 See graphs 2.5 and 2.7 *ibid.*, pp. 41 and 44.

6 See graph 2.1, *ibid.*, p. 32.

7 See *Nihon no chichioya to kodomo, op. cit.*, graph 2.8.10, p. 50.

8 See interview in *France Japon Éco, op. cit.*, pp. 44–5.

9 This was a method frequently used by women to get their children off to sleep. It was facilitated by the fact that the kimono was simply crossed over the breast. Today's habit of using the breast as a pacifier is a development of this tradition.

10 On this subject see '*Ryôsaikembô to atarashii onna*' ('The doctrine of "the good wife and wise mother" and the new woman'), *Asahi hyakka, Nippon no rekishi*, 129, 1988. See also 'The good wife and wise mother', in *Des Japonaises, Des Femmes*, Paris, 1987, ch. 3, pp. 71–86; as well as Tate Kaoru's contribution: '*Ryôsaï kembô*, in *Onna no mede miru* ('Seen by a woman'), coll. 1987, Keisô Shobô, pp. 184–209.

11 From Hara Hiroko and Wagatsuma Hiroshi, *Shitsuke*, Kôbundô, Tokyo, 1974.

12 One can cite the psychiatrist Saitô Shigeta for example, *Chichioya fuzaï shindorômu* ('The syndrome of the absent father'), 1987; or Tawara Moeko, *Fugenbyô no kodomotachi* ('Children who suffer from father-sickness'), 1981.

13 In *Kakyô no oshie*, Miraisha, 1967.

14 As far as we know there is no equivalent for fathers to the poems of Satô Hachirô who sings, in three volumes, the praises of his mother (see *Shishû Okâsan*, Kôdansha Bunkô, 1977).

15 From Hara and Wagatsuma, *op. cit.*, pp. 174 and 195. Yvonne Knibiehler also explains: 'The father goes off to work, his job becomes increasingly more absorbing thus distracting him from problems of a domestic nature. He becomes literally and metaphorically invisible: his work is no longer seen and the results remain unknown. His authority is unjustified, and merely felt as being repressive' (in *Les Pères aussi ont une histoire* ('Fathers also have a story to tell'), Hachette, 1987, p. 174).

16 Paul Federn, *On the Psychology of Revolution: The Fatherless Society*, 1919 (quoted by Doi Takeo, *Amae no kôzô*, Kôbundo, 1971) (English edition, *The Anatomy of Dependence*, Kôdansha International, 1973, p. 152).

17 An expression borrowed from Neumann, *The Great Mother*, Routledge & Kegan Paul; see *Bosei shakai Nihon no byôri* ('Japanese society's obsession with motherhood'), Chûô Kôronsha, 1976.

18 *Bringing up Girls, op. cit.*, p. 233.

19 This also appears on another graph where fathers state that they love their children while the latter are a long way from expressing the same sentiment. They are in ninth position with 20.6 per cent, *Nihon no chichioya to kodomo, op. cit.*, pp. 115–16.

20 See *ibid.*, graph 3.2.1, p. 58.

21 See *ibid.*, graph 3.2.3, p. 60.

22 See *ibid.*, graph 3.2.2, p. 59.

23 From *ibid.*, graph 3.2.4, pp. 61–2.

24 In *'Gendai no oyako kankei'* ('Modern day relations between parents and their children'), *Gendai no Esupuri* ('Esprit d'aujourd'hui'), *Sociology Journal*, 113, 1976, pp. 110–21. (Yamamura Yoshiaki is the author of a classic on Japanese mothers, *Nihon no hahaoya*, Tôyôkan Shuppansha, 1971.)

25 27.2 per cent think their children respect them and 38.4 per cent think they do 'a little' (see *ibid.*, graph 4.1 (c), p. 76). Asked by the Recruit Centre who they admired the most, students still placed their father at the top of the list (see *Daigakusei-wa nani-o kangaete iru ka*) ('What do male students think?'), Chôsa geppô, 1979.

26 *Nihon no chichioya to kodomo, op. cit.*, graph 4.2.5, p. 80.

27 See *ibid.*, graph 4.2.1, p. 78.

28 In *Shitsuke, op. cit.*, Ezra Vogel also says that the mother skilfully uses the image of the father in order to manipulate the child (in *Japan's New Middle Class*, University of California Press, 1963).

29 From *Status and Role Behavior in Changing Japan*, 1970, pp. 334–70. See also De Vos and Wagatsuma, 'Perspectives on family life and delinquency', in *Heritage of Endurance Family Patterns and Delinquency Formation in Urban Japan*, University of California Press, 1984; as well as Hara and Wagatsuma, *op. cit.*, pp. 216–17.

30 20 per cent of fathers surveyed replied that they had quite often been to these meetings; of these 7.3 per cent participated actively (see *Nihon no chichioya to kodomo, op. cit.*, graph 1.12, p. 29).

31 Josei Kokusaï kôryû symposium (International Exchange on Women), Tokyo-to Itabashi-ku, 29 September 1988.

32 Sugiyama Akira nevertheless recorded his experiences as a 'childcarer' in a charming book *Kodomo ni moratta yukaina jikan* ('The wonderful moments children have given me'), 1989.

33 This no doubt explains why men look for another job the moment they retire. Their wish, even though their status drops as the years go by, is to have a place in society. On this subject see Muriel Jolivet, 'Jeunes loups et patriarches: les limites de la promotion à l'ancienneté' ('Young wolves and patriarchs: the limits of the seniority system'), *Le Monde diplomatique*, 24 February 1985.

34 op. cit. pp. 74 and 244.

35 Kittredge Cherry offers the metaphor of big, coarse, hard-to-dipose-of junk like a broken refrigerator, in *Womansword*, Kôdansha, p. 135.

36 On this subject see Okifuji Noriko, 'Ie kaerenaku natta otto tachi',

Voice, June 1989, pp. 182–91, an extract of which appeared in *Japan Eco*, XVII, special issue, 1990 under the title 'Men who can't go home', pp. 48–52.

37 For further details, refer to the following works: *Tôkô kyohi to wa* ('What is school refusal syndrome?'), coll. 1989; *Tôkô kyohi – gokai to henken kara no dasshutsu* ('How to be free of the misunderstandings and prejudices surrounding school phobia'), 1987; see also Muriel Jolivet, 'Le revers de la médaille', ('The other side of the coin'), *Le Monde de l'Education*, 110, November 1984, pp. 18–19.

38 Here she is alluding to aggression against the mother which is often associated with school refusal.

39 According to the proverb 'Children grow up seeing no more than their father's back'.

40 40.3 per cent of 40–44 year olds, 52.9 per cent of 45–49 year olds and 53.7 per cent of over fifties are transferred away from home (from *Tenkin-o meguru kakushû toriatsukai no jittai* ('A study on the transfers of the *tanshin funinsha*'), Research Centre on the Administration of the Workforce, 1986).

41 A survey found that the majority of men had agreed to a transfer without first consulting their families (from *Tanshin funin*, coll. under the direction of Iwao Sumiko, Saitô Hiroko and Fukutomi Mamoru, ed. Yûhikaku, 1991, especially the section entitled: '*Tanshin funin ni yotte, kazoku wa dô kawaru*') ('The changes inflicted on the family as a result of the father's transfers').

42 See Philippe Pons, 'Avec des fleurs, les employés japonais sont déplacés comme des pions' ('With a bunch of flowers Japanese employees are moved around like pawns'), *Le Monde de l'économie*, 11–12 May 1980.

43 Although it is rare for it to be the wife's career which prevents her from following her husband, this argument would probably be disguised for the benefit of her husband's employer – the children's education being more acceptable grounds since it is less controversial and the most common.

44 They also pose the most problems in the educational establishments they attend, particularly as far as school refusal, violence at school or in the home are concerned. For further information on school violence refer to: '*Kônai bôryoku*' ('Violence in schools'), coll. under the direction of Matsubara Haruo and Kumagaï Fumie, in *Gendai no Esupuri*, 180, Shibundô, 1982.

45 From *Des Japonaises, op. cit.*, p. 78.

46 2.7 per cent of Japanese fathers say they help their children every day with their studies, the majority (40.7 per cent) never help them at all or (38.6 per cent) only from time to time (from *Nippon no chichioya to kodomo, op. cit.*, Figure 2.2.3, p. 35).

47 Largely exploited by television dramas, the problems are invariably the result of the father leading a double life with an OL (*office lady* becomes *office love*) while the wife is left to cope with the family (and sometimes bedridden in-laws) on her own. This is illustrated in Hayashi Iku's best-seller *Kateinai rikon* ('Divorced inside the family'), Chikuma Bundô, Tokyo, 1986.

48 Surveys have revealed that financial assistance provided by the company

increases according to their importance (see for example *Gendai no katei kyôiku, op. cit.,* p. 219).

49 As well as the feeling of being 'divorced inside the family', the following problems can arise: the husband may feel superfluous when he is at home, he may suffer from alcohol dependency or even alcoholism to which he turns in an attempt to forget his loneliness or marital infidelities. See *Tanshin funin, op. cit.,* especially ch. 2: 'Tanshin funin to fufû seikatsu' ('The married life of the *tanshin funin'*).

50 An *ochazuke* is a snack often taken by men when they come in late at night: it is a cup of green tea poured over a bowl of hot rice.

51 This is in some ways reminiscent of what Japanese women who had gone into an arranged marriage used to say about their husbands: 'I neither love him nor hate him, and that's fine by me!'

52 Tachibana Yuri's account, *Wife,* 224, 1 July 1990, pp. 36–9.

53 *Chôju shakai ni okeru danjô betsu no ishiki no keikô ni kansuru chôsa* ('Study into men and women's understanding of social longevity'), Ministry of General Affairs.

54 Pensions vary depending on the establishment. White-collar workers usually receive a lump sum – in recognition of twenty-five years' service – together with a pension awarded five or six years later. In the larger companies, the lump sum is equivalent to around twenty months' salary and the pension 60 per cent or 70 per cent of the salary upon retirement, of which 30 per cent is met by the firm and 40 per cent by the state.

4 THE TEN COMMANDMENTS OF THE GOOD MOTHER

1 Thomas Verny is author of *The Secret Life of the Unborn Child,* Summit Books, New York, 1981.

2 Natsuyama Eichi, *Ni hyaku hachi jû nichi no taikyô* ('280 days of foetal education'), Furêberukan, 1989; he is also a member of Dr Kobayashi's study group at the Ministry of Health.

3 It is quite usual for a woman to be unaware that she is several months pregnant.

4 *Taiji kyôiku* ('Foetal education'), Goma Shobô, 1988, pp. 161–6. See also Oshima Kiyoshi, *Nobi nobi taikyô book,* ed. Nagaoka Shoten, 1989.

5 Oshima, *Taiji kyôiku,* pp. 116–19.

6 See 'San aku shokuhin' ('The three harmful foods'), in *Taiji Kyôiku, op. cit.,* pp. 81–6 (table p. 85).

7 *Ibid.,* p. 99.

8 *Ibid.,* p. 107.

9 *Ibid.,* p. 166.

10 *Ibid.,* p. 178.

11 *Ibid.,* p. 175.

12 *Ibid.,* pp. 182–3.

13 I should like to quote, for example, Tokizane Toshihiko, *Nô-o sodateru* ('How to develop the brain'), Mikasa Shobô, 1987; Shimokôchi Minoru, *Nôryoku-o sodateru* ('To develop a baby's mental faculties'), Osaka Shoseki, 1986, where the author points out that only families 'centred' on the child can develop the child's gifts; Ohara Keiko, *Kodomo no*

nôryoku no nobashikata ('How to develop a child's faculties'), PHP, 1989, among others.

14 For example, *Ibuka apiiru to zero sai izen kara no kyôiku* ('Ibuka's message on prenatal education'), Seiya Shoten, 1988; and *Yôchien dewa ososugiru*, Goma Shobô, 1971 (English translation: *Kindergarten is too Late*, Souvenir Press, London, 1979).

15 Like Suzuki Shin'ichi, the founder of the famous method for teaching young children to play the violin and director of the Talent Education Institute, Ibuka Masaru claims that *haïkus* have the double advantage of awakening children's artistic and aesthetic senses and of stimulating their synapses.

16 From Kobayashi Noboru, *Fureai no ikuji; taijiki kara no kosodate* ('How to achieve oneness during the foetal period'), TBS Britanika, 1988, pp. 55–7.

17 The method is named after its founder Ishii Isao and mentor Glenn Doman, the director of the Institute for the Achievement of Human Potential and author of best-sellers on the subject of *How to Teach Your Baby to Read*.

18 All these theories explain why Jitsuko and Joseph Susedix's book *Unborn Children can Learn to be Geniuses* (published in the United States in 1986, but impossible to find four years later) was immediately translated into Japanese. The book explains how to produce gifted children.

19 A parody of this advice can be found in the film based on Itoh Hiromi's book, *Ii oppai, warui oppai* ('The good breast and the bad breast'), *op. cit.*, which came out in June 1990.

20 *Taiji ni ongaku wa kikoeru ka* ('Can the foetus hear music?'), PHP Kenkyûsho.

21 *Op. cit.*, pp. 45–6.

22 These are the *Haha to ko no meikyoku kasetto* ('Well-known pieces for mother and baby on cassette'), Shufunotomo Cultural Centre.

23 One of the most popular and widely available is *Taiji-wa kiite iru* ('The foetus listens'), the Classic Music for the Unborn Child, Nippon Columbia.

24 *Akachan to mama ni okeru sekai no komoriuta* ('Lullabies from around the World for mother and child'), Nippon Columbia.

25 *Kotori no symphony* (Natural Sound Series).

26 *Mama no ongaku no komori uta* ('Lullabies based on Mummy's music'), *Nippon jidô katei bunka jigyôkai*.

27 *Norway no Mori* ('Norwegian Woods') A musical box of Beatles melodies will ensure that foetuses have beautiful dreams.

28 *Asa mezame no classic*, Polidor, BGM Classics.

29 *Chrystal Dew II* (this symphony, the sound of crystal glasses, is supposed to soothe both mother and foetus). This is one of many: the list is endless!

30 *Pachama*, by Toyoda Takeshi, which belongs to the series classed as 'musical tranquillizers'.

31 Kobayashi Noboru, *op. cit.*, p. 134.

32 For more information on the value of pain, see also Muriel Jolivet, 'Naître à Tokyo' ('Giving birth in Tokyo'), *Enfants Magazine*, August 1987; and Nancy Sharts engel, 'An American experience', *Birth*, 16, 2 June 1989.

33 Kobayashi Noboru, *op. cit.*, p. 77.
34 See the chart in R. Sosa, in Kobayashi Noboru, *op. cit.*, p. 87.
35 He also speaks (p. 141) of deepening maternal love or of triggering a communication (p. 221) or love (p. 170) programme.
36 From Taiji Kyôiku, *op. cit.*, p. 191.
37 Hiraï picked it up from an American professor who 'invented' it during a World Health Organisation seminar in 1953.
38 In other words lifting babies up and saying 'upsadaisy, upsadaisy!' to make them chuckle with laughter.
39 Kobayashi Noboru, *op. cit.*, p. 146.
40 These were commonplace in Japan until around 1955. For more information refer to two excellent works: *O san kakumei* ('Revolution in childbirth') by Fujita Shin'ichi, Asahi Shimbunsha, 1979; and *Nihonjin no ko umi, kosodate* ('The art of bringing children into the world and bringing them up, yesterday and today'), coll., Keisô Shobô, 1990.
41 This seems to be a little hasty: for while 30 per cent of deliveries in the Netherlands take place at home barely 0.4 per cent of them do in France (according to Laurence Pernoud, *J'attends un enfant* ('I'm expecting a baby'), Horay, 1990, p. 307).
42 For further information on this subject see Klaus and Kennel's article, 'Caring for the Parents of a Premature or Sick Infant', in *Maternal–Infant Bonding* (coll.), Mosby, 1976, pp. 99–166.
43 A tradition which survives to this day and which explains why so many children (until they are quite old) cannot go to sleep without stroking their mother's breasts. Hence the anxiety of some mothers after the birth of their second child: how can she satisfy both of them? In Hara and Wagatsuma's opinion this explains why alcohol is accepted in Japan for it is seen as a substitute for the breast to help men get to sleep (see *Shitsuke, op. cit.*, pp. 140–50).
44 This idea is fairly widespread in Japan (probably thanks to Hiraï), and many people asked us if we were in the habit of leaving our children alone when we went out at night. Kyûtoku Shigemori (see pp. 101–3) cites the case of a 3-year-old child whose trauma he cured by allowing him to call his mother an idiot: his mother had left him while she went out shopping.
45 Kobayashi Noboru, *op. cit.*, p. 144. Asked at what age they moved their child's bed out of their bedroom, 39.5 per cent of Japanese mothers replied 'once they were 3', while 34.3 per cent replied that they (4–9 age group) still slept in their room. By way of comparison, French mothers' responses can be divided thus: 'from birth' (44.9 per cent) and 'by the age of 3 months' (20.8 per cent), according to research carried out to compare how children in France and Japan are brought up, *Nihon no kosodate, sekai no kosodate – Nichi futsu kosodate ankêto chôsa kara*, published in 1990 by the Franco-Japanese Centre for Documentation on Women: replies to question 8. See also William Caudill and David Plath 'Who sleeps by whom? Parent–child involvement in urban Japanese families', *Psychiatry*, 29, 1966, pp. 344–66.
46 In Hiraï Nobuyoshi, *Ushinawareta Boseiaï* ('The disappearance of maternal love'), Reimei Shobô, 1981, p. 143.
47 In *Bogenbyô, op. cit.*, p. 35.

48 In Hiraï Nobuyoshi, *op. cit.* In the mid-1970s it was still a common sight to see women selling vegetables with their babies strapped to their back all day long. At the time of writing, our local butcher still ends her day serving customers with her baby on her back, after having been to fetch him from the crèche at 4 p.m. She keeps him there until the shop shuts (around 7 p.m.). It is not so much the child's age but his weight which finally forces the mother to give up.

49 Hiraï Nobuyoshi, *op. cit.*, p. 45.

50 By comparison, 37.7 per cent of Japanese women questioned by the Franco-Japanese Centre for Documentation on Women replied that they had bottle-fed their babies as opposed to 36.5 per cent who had breast-fed or 25.8 per cent who had partially breast-fed them (responses from French women were respectively, in the same order, 40.5 per cent, 31.3 per cent and 28.3 per cent) (*op. cit.*, question 1). Although the percentages of those who breast-fed appear to be fairly close, breast-feeding in Japan lasts for a minimum of six to twelve months.

51 *Bonyû hoiku hô* ('How to breast-feed'), Shufu no tomo, 1987.

52 *The Tender Gift: Breast-feeding*, Prentice-Hall, 1973.

53 Kobayashi Noboru, *op. cit.*, p. 182.

54 *Ibid.*, p. 197.

55 *Ibid.*, p. 194.

56 *Ibid.*, p. 200.

57 Kobayashi Noboru, *op. cit.*, p. 204.

58 See Itoh Hiromi's view in note 61.

59 *Bogenbyô*, *op. cit.*, pp. 40–5.

60 *Ushinawareta boseiaï*, *op. cit.*, p. 136.

61 What he is describing here as being a secondary factor, was in fact Itoh Hiromi's principal motivation. She quite openly gives a detailed description of the bliss she experienced when breast-feeding her two daughters and strongly urged her sisters to take advantage of this source of pleasure which nature had so generously put their way: see *Ii oppai, warui oppai* ('The good breast and the bad breast'), *op. cit.*

62 Namely 'they do not want to ruin their breasts and wish to delay the ageing process'. Funabashi Keiko, who gave birth to her third child in France, recalls how this question had come up during pre-natal classes, in her opinion a question unthinkable given the Japanese context: see 'Journal d'une Japonaise ayant accouché en France. Comparaison entre cultures et observation participante' ('Diary of a Japanese woman who gave birth in France. Cultural comparison and observant participation'), *Les Dossiers de l'obstétrique*, 161, April 1989.

63 *Ushinawareta boseiaï*, *op. cit.*, p. 137.

64 With its headquarters in Osaka, this school also has a branch in Tokyo which I visited in June 1990.

65 In *Bonyû hoiku* ('Breast-feeding'), Shufu no tomo, 1987, p. 192. Like Hiraï Nobuyoshi and Kyûtoku Shigemori, Oketani proposes that one should be suspicious of children who bring themselves up: a baby who requires a minimum of care and who sleeps a lot is a candidate for hospitalism, indeed autism.

66 *Ibid.*, p. 33.

67 *Ibid.*, p. 192. Empty bags to enable women to freeze their own milk are available from chemists, which is a great boon to the working woman.

68 In the film based on Itoh Hiromi's book (referred to p. 211, n. 68) it is amusing to observe the 'new father' juggling with frozen human milk and artificial milk, 'to ensure that the child will not develop a preference but learn to eat everything'. (See also Chapter 1, n. 27.)

69 At the Oketani School in Tokyo, 40 per cent of clients are well-educated working women, all products of the nuclear family.

70 The school offers a 'counselling service' but the listening is actually done by the masseuse during the thirty minute session while babies, on their mothers' abdomens, cry lustily.

71 *Bonyû hoiku, op. cit.*, pp. 145–8. See also p. 194.

72 In France the replies were as follows: myself: 36.5 per cent; commercial baby food 8.3 per cent; both: 55.2 per cent (23.1 per cent in Japan fell into this category). (From research undertaken by the Franco-Japanese Centre of Documentation on Women, 1990, *op. cit.*, see table 6.)

73 *Ushinawareta boseiaï, op. cit.*, pp. 152–3.

74 The Japanese mothers questioned replied that they prepared their children's food themselves 'because food prepared at home was better for the children' (54.4 per cent), 'because it was normal' (they did it automatically) (31.5 per cent) or 'because they felt guilty if they resorted to using baby food' (23.7 per cent). By comparison, in reply to the same questions, French mothers were grouped thus: 'better for the baby' (69 per cent), 'baby food is too expensive' (27.7 per cent) (from the study made by the Franco-Japanese Centre for Documentation on Women, *op. cit.*, question 7).

75 From *o-bentô*: arranged in a box this is a cold rice-based meal, served with vegetables, meat or fish; and from *kyôsô*: competition.

76 As it is impossible to hope to achieve this before 15 to 18 months, the Japanese mother is constantly putting her hand down her child's pants to check how wet the nappy is.

77 Taniguchi is also the author of a treatise entitled *Taikyô to sono shûsei* ('The reshaping of foetal education'), Ikuji bunka Kenkyûsho, 1990.

78 The jacket of Taniguchi's second book is adorned with a naked Cupid. His mother stands in front of him, ecstatic after having thrown the packet of disposable nappies in the bin.

79 He fails to mention the *ejiko*, baskets in which peasants would prop their babies on ashes, straw or a ball of rice, which allowed them to go to the toilet without getting wet or ending up with a rash, thus relieving the mother from the chore of having to do the laundry.

80 Notably expressed by Tanaka Kimiko in *Hataraku josei no kosodateron, op. cit.*, pp. 26–32.

81 *Yamete yokatta kami omutsu, op. cit.*, pp. 75–6.

82 *Ibid.*, pp. 79–80.

83 *Yamete yokatta . . . , op. cit.*, p. 155.

84 *Ibid.*, p. 55.

85 When this used to happen, because the mother was held responsible for the fruit of her womb, she was driven to infanticide; on this subject read the remarkable article 'Memento Mori' *Taiyô*, 30, September 1992.

86 In *Yamete yokatta kami omutsu, op. cit.*, pp. 163–5.

87 Taniguchi maintains in particular that disposable nappies keep a baby awake, while he also claims that mothers put their babies in disposable nappies because the mothers want to sleep. He therefore indirectly acknowledges that they are more absorbent, thus allowing the child to sleep longer.

88 A Japanese friend told me how her neighbours had hesitated before coming round to visit her after the birth of her daughter because, as they had not seen nappies drying in the window, they had assumed that the baby must be in an incubator.

89 *Ushinawareta boseiaï, op. cit.*, p. 109.

90 *Ibid.*, p. 125.

91 *Ibid.*, p. 123; the expression *petto-ka* is also used in this context (see p. 63).

92 *Ushinawareta boseiaï, op. cit.*, p. 123.

93 *Ibid.*, p. 126.

94 We can understand why some are apprehensive if we remember the conditions in which the husband forced his wife to have an abortion in Oshima's film *Shônen*.

95 There is no direct equivalent to *amae* in any western language though the English term dependence (used in the English version of Doi Takeo's book) comes close to embodying a concept which refers to the emotional interdependence which binds individuals together. Doi Takeo defines *amae* as being the feeling that infants normally have for their mother while they are still at the breast: it is a dependence, a desire to be loved passively as well as a feeling of repugnance at being snatched from the comfortable safety of the dyad to be projected into the world of harsh objective reality. This infant need explains why the child tries so hard to revoke mentally the separation from the mother. This also explains why men turn to their wives or to bar hostesses in search of their mothers. It is significant that both are addressed as 'mama'.

96 *Ushinawareta boseiaï, op. cit.*, p. 128.

97 This was observed by Spitz in children brought up in institutions or who had had a prolonged stay in a hospital.

98 See especially *Hospitalism: An Inquiry into the Genesis of Psychiatric Conditions in Early Childhood*, 1945, and *Anxiety in Infancy: A Study of its Manifestations in the First Year of Life*, 1950.

99 Although the Japanese educational system is based on this principle and claims to eliminate differences because it is basically egalitarian, it could never succeed without the help of private tuition and *juku* (kinds of 'crammers') which allow the democratic illusion to be maintained.

100 This book was followed by two others, *Bogenbyô zoku*, Kyôiku kenkyûsha, 1980, and *Bogenbyô zokuzoku*, Sun Mark Books, 1981, in which among other things is a description of the typical dangerous mother. The indefatigible Kyûtoku has also written *Bogenbyô-o fusegu tame no jû soku* ('Ten ways to avoid contaminating your child with the mother-sickness'), Sun Mark Shuppan, 1982, as well as *Shin bogenbyô* ('New illnesses caused by the mother'), Sun Mark Shuppan, 1990, which is addressed to all who are worried about the parent–child relationship.

101 *Bogenbyô, op. cit.*, pp. 116–17.

102 *Ibid.*, p. 75.

103 *Ibid.*, p. 39.
104 Kyûtoku Clinic, Nagoya-shi, Meito-ku, Kaniyashiro 5–201.
105 *Bogenbyô, op. cit.*, pp. 66–7.
106 This is fundamental to Japanese education, a tolerance of the cold is supposed to protect children from always catching colds, sore throats and 'flu. With this in mind, some playschools hold daily gymnastic classes where children go bare chested winter and summer. Most primary schools forbid the wearing of trousers and request that pupils come in shorts whatever the weather.
107 From *Bosei shakai Nihon no byôri* ('Japanese society's obsession with motherhood'), Chûô Kôronsha, 1976.
108 Although electrical appliances have greatly alleviated housework, the habit of putting the laundry out in the sun every day to dry, of airing the bedding on the balcony, or of doing the shopping on foot or by bike every evening (because vegetables must be eaten fresh) demands time and energy. Moreover washing machines run on a cold wash (which means that nappies in particular must first be washed by hand); the machines are often manual (not automatic) and take only between two and five kilos of washing at a time. Any self-respecting women owes it to herself to do all this with the minimum of fuss. As a 40-year-old bank employee said: 'I would never buy my wife a dishwasher. After all, it's her job. She has nothing else to do!' For further details, see Muriel Jolivet, 'Conjuguer travail et maternité au Japon' ('Combining work and motherhood in Japan'), *op. cit.*, pp. 97–101. Studies have shown that labour-saving devices mean that women must reinvest the time saved in the form of 'services' to the family (see Chapter 8).
109 Different from 'economic animal' or *workaholic*, greed or cupidity are inherent in this term.
110 For further details on Japanese crèches, see my account in Jolivet, 'Les surprises des crèches japonaises' ('The surprises Japanese crèches hold'), *Le Monde de l'Education*, 131, November 1986; as well as the article by Fujita Mariko, 'It's all Mother's fault', *Journal of Japanese Studies*, 15(1), winter 1989, pp. 67–91. For statistics on and opening hours of Japanese crèches – private and state, legal and illegal, see *Okâsan ga genki ni hataraku hon*, ed. Gendaishokan, 1987; *Hôiku hakusho* (White Paper on crèches), Ministry of Health, 1989. For unregistered establishments, see *Baby Hotel ni kan suru sôgô chôsa* ('Enquiry into "baby hotels"'), Banseisha, 1981.
111 *Ushinawareta boseiaï, op. cit.*, p. 194.
112 On this subject see Kathleen S. Uno, 'Day-care and family life in late Meiji-Taishô Japan', *Transactions of the Asiatic Society*, XIX, 1984, pp. 17–31.
113 Tokyo owes their proliferation to Minobe, the socialist mayor after 1971. There are at present 22,834 crèches in the whole country of which 13,518 are state run and 9,316 are private. They are open to children between the age of 6 months (in special circumstances 2 months) and 6 years. Tokyo has 1,600 crèches, of which 1,008 are state run and 592 are private (statistics supplied by the Ministry of Health, in *Hôiku Hakusho*, 1989, *op. cit.*).
114 *Ushinawareta boseiaï, op. cit.*, p. 115. By saying this he is lending his

support to the custom, practised *de facto* by the majority of Japanese companies, that the woman should give up work with the birth of the first child (see Chapter 2).

115 *Ibid.*, p. 195.
116 *Ibid.*, p. 148.
117 *Ibid.*, p. 185.
118 *Ibid.*, p. 114.
119 *Ushinawareta boseiaï, op. cit.*, p. 178.
120 *Ibid.*, p. 194.
121 *Ibid.*, p. 113.
122 See, for example, '*Hoiku no ura de*' ('Care viewed from a different angle'), *Asahi* (journal) 28 October 1988.

5 THE NOSTALGIA FOR YESTERDAY'S MOTHERS

1 Women who were sterile were said to bring the village bad luck. They were called 'women of stone' and it was believed that after their death they went to a special hell reserved them (from Kittredge Cherry, *Womansword*, Kôdansha, Tokyo, 1987, p. 91).
2 From Hiraï Nobuyoshi, *Ushinawareta boseiaï, op. cit.*, pp. 205–6.
3 This is suggested by a son's nickname for his mother: *o-fukuro* ('sack', a euphemism for 'uterus').
4 *Haha no zô* ('Portraits of mothers'), coll. edited by Wakamori Tarô, Sôdo Bunka, 1976. Most abstracts are quoted by Tanaka Kimiko in *Hataraku Josei no kosodateron* (*Educational Theories of Working Women*).
5 In *Futarikko no jidai* ('The era of the two-children family'), Asahi Shuppansha, Tokyo, 1981, p. 30.
6 Takaishi was forced to resign in 1989, following his involvement in the Recruit scandal.
7 Suzuki Michita's (born in 1907) account, in *Haha no zô,* quoted by Tanaka Kimiko, *op. cit.*, p. 54.
8 To tell a women she had put on weight implied that she was financially and psychologically better off and magazines at the beginning of the century (in the Taishô era) proposed recipes to women to help them put on weight.
9 A writer born in 1927, Shiroyama Saburô's account is in *Haha no zô,* in Tanaka Kimiko, *op. cit.*, p. 55.
10 *Ibid.*, p. 59.
11 *Ibid.*, p. 60.
12 Aochi Shin's (essayist born 1909), *ibid.*, p. 55.
13 Nomura Manzô IV's (1898–1978) account. He was a *kyôgen* actor, of comic pieces that are traditionally performed between two separate *Nô* plays. In 1967 he was awarded the title of Living National Treasure. His father was also a *kyôgen* actor. *Ibid.*, pp. 55–6.
14 Account given by the musical critic, Yamane Ginji (born 1906), *ibid.*, p. 56.
15 Account given by Iwasaki Tetsuta (born 1905), *ibid.*, p. 62.
16 *Ibid.*, p. 62.
17 *Futarikko no jidai, op. cit.*, pp. 49–50.

18 As Maurice Pinguet writes: 'Many Japanese men, whose psyche is governed by the mother's wishes, turn out to be ambitious men and even social climbers "without egoism and as though through devotion"' (see 'Nippon no Edipusu' ('The Japanese Oedipus complex'), *Gendai Shisô*, special edition 7, 1984, entitled 'Nippon no Nekko').

19 In 1928 women were barred from working in the mines but in 1933 (due to a shortage of labour) the ban was lifted to allow married women to work there and in 1935 30 per cent of them still went down to the bottom of the shaft. The ban was reinstated in 1938. From *Owareteyuku kôfutachi* ('The tragedy of miners'), quoted by Matsunaga Goichi, in *Nippon no komoriuta* ('Japanese lullabies'), Kinokuniya Shinsho, 1964, pp. 92–3. See also Ishimoto Shidzué's account, *Facing Two Ways*, Stanford University Press, 1984 (especially ch. 11, 'Are miners human beings?', pp. 158–64).

20 From Hara and Wagatsuma, in *Shitsuke, op. cit.*, pp. 57–76.

21 *Ibid.*, 65–9.

22 As Hara Hiroko and Wagatsuma Hiroshi point out, it was not unusual for a young wife living in the country to be registered as a member of the family at the same time as her firstborn. She was therefore not officially considered to be part of the family until she had produced an heir (*ibid.*, p. 199).

23 *Shitsuke, op. cit.*, p. 175.

24 The *ie* was a domestic unit which had a productive and religious function through the perpetuation of ancestor worship. By proclaiming in 1948 that husband and wife were equal, the Civil Code in principle abolished the *ie*, in theory putting an end to the traditional privileges reserved for the oldest son (from P. Beillevaire, 'La famille japonaise hier et aujourd'hui' ('The Japanese family: yesterday and today'), *Sciences Sociales du Japon contemporain*, 7, 1984).

25 From Tanaka Kimiko, *op. cit.*, p. 70.

26 *Ibid.*, p. 68.

27 From *Jinsei no rekishi*, Kawade Shobô Shinsha, quoted by Fugita Shin'ichi, in *O-san kakumei* ('Revolution in childbirth'), *op. cit.*, p. 52.

28 The *hakama* is loose pleated trousers, made of silk, worn by men over their kimono. During the Heian period (794–1185) court ladies wore loose-fitting crimson *hakama*; it was also a kind of uniform for young ladies who came from good families. It is still the standard outfit worn by female university students or even by junior college graduates on graduation day. The *hakama* is still the required outfit worn for certain martial arts such as aikido.

29 For detailed information on all these ceremonies, refer to Yamamura Yoshiaki, *op. cit.*, p. 30, *Shitsuke, op. cit.*, pp. 24–33, as well as Tsuboi Hirofumi *et al.*, *Ie to Josei* ('Women and the family unit'), *Nippon Minzoku Bunka Taikei* ('The structure of popular Japanese culture'), vol. 10, Shôgakkan, 1985 (especially ch. 6 by Aoyanagi Machiko and Oofuji Yuki, pp. 375–414).

30 I met in Tokyo one of the last practitioners of *mushi kiri*, who now practises under the cover of *shôni hari* ('acupuncture for children'). For a detailed study of the term *mushi*, refer to Hara, *Shitsuke, op. cit.* (in particular the section entitled '*Ki to mushi*', pp. 125–32).

31 As Yanagita Kunio and Hashiura Yasuo write: 'Because children were entrusted to men by the gods, it was not impossible to return those who were not needed' (in *San'iku shûzoku goi*, quoted by Fujita Shin'ichi, *op. cit.*, p. 40).

32 From Yanagita Kunio, quoted by Fujita Shin'ichi, *op. cit.*, p. 52.

33 *Ibid.*, p. 52.

34 From Yanagita Kunio, quoted by Fujita S., *op. cit.*, pp. 40–52.

35 From *Nippon no komori uta, op. cit.*, p. 76.

36 Quoted by Fujita S., *op. cit.*, p. 47.

37 *Ibid.*, pp. 39–53.

38 This atmosphere is well portrayed in Imamura Shôhei's film, *The Songs of Oak Mountain* (1983) based on the novel by Fukazawa Shichirô, *Narayama bushikô*, Shinchôsha, 1956 ('The Songs of Oak Mountain', translated into English 1961).

39 This is quoted by Fujita Shin'ichi (*op. cit.*, p. 51) and by Tsuboi Hirofumi *et al.*, *Ie to josei, op. cit.*, pp. 438–9.

40 *Kakure Kirishitan* was the name given to the first Christians. The *kakure Kirishitan* were descended from the early Christians whose faith was secretly passed down over a period of almost two hundred years. On this subject see Philippe Pons, 'Des chrétiens cachés depuis le XVIe siècle' ('Christians in hiding since the sixteenth century'), *Le Monde dimanche*, 9 August 1981.

41 The *kakure Kirishitan* had a fundamental need to believe in their redemption for they carried the burden of the *fumie* – holy images they or their ancestors had had to trample under foot to prove they were not Christians, after Ieyasu had declared in 1613 that Christianity was illegal. See Endô Shûsaku's novel, *Chinmoku*, Shinchôsha, 1966 (*Silence*, Tuttle, 1992).

42 From Yanagita Kunio, quoted in *O-san kakumei, op. cit.*, p. 49.

43 See *Nihon no komori uta, op. cit.*, pp. 70, 71 and 73.

44 *Ibid.*, pp. 48–9.

45 From *Ie to josei, op. cit.*, pp. 440 and 444.

46 From *Shitsuke, op. cit.*, p. 16.

47 *Jizô* is a divinity, the protector of children and pregnant women (see Chapter 6).

48 '*Kajika sukui ni yatta*'; the *kajika* is a melodious stream frog.

49 From *Nihon no komori uta, op. cit.*, p. 76.

50 An *engawa* is a verandah constructed along the south side of the house. A *doma* is an area of earth floor in traditional houses.

51 From Yanagita Kunio, quoted in *O-san kakumei, op. cit.*, p. 48.

52 The *kappa* was a malicious, mythical amphibious creature the size of a child, endowed with the head of a tiger, a beak and a body covered in scales (see also Chapter 6).

53 From *Osan kakumei, op. cit.*, p. 50.

54 See for example the one from the prefecture of Saitama transcribed in *Nippon no komoriuta, op. cit.*, pp. 80–1.

55 From Ohinata Masami, *Bosei no kenkyû* ('Study on "motherhood"'), *op. cit.*, p. 10.

56 From Pierre Souyri, 'Splendeurs et misères de Yoshiwara' ('The glory and misery of Yoshiwara'), *Des villes nommées Tokyo, Autrement*, special issue 8, September 1984, p. 299.

57 From *Nippon no komoriuta, op. cit.*, p. 215.

58 From Jean-Claude Jugon, 'L'Enfant-Dieu: une étude sur les berceuses et les pratiques d'endormissement du jeune enfant japonais dans son milieu' ('The Child-God: a study of lullabies and ways of getting the Japanese child off to sleep in his environment'), in *Les rituels du coucher de l'enfant variations culturelles*, ESF, May 1993 (coll. edited by H. Stork). See also Morisaki Kazue, *Karayukisan*, ed. Asaki Shimbunsha, 1976, and the section entitled 'Karayukisan', in *Nippon no komoriuta, op. cit.*, pp. 202–11; and Lisa Louis, *Butterflies of the Night*, Tengu, 1992, p. 161.

59 From Mariko Asano Tamanoi, 'Songs as weapons: the culture and history of *Komori* (nursemaids) in modern Japan', *Journal of Asian Studies* 50 (4), November 1991, pp. 793–817.

60 Miyamoto Ken's play deals with the subject of *Hahatachi* ('Mothers'): (after having invented a tale) a mother on a pilgrimage admits that she had not abandoned but sold her daughter in Manchuria before boarding the boat that would take her back to Japan.

6 DEMOGRAPHIC MALAISE

1 Taken from *Sei*, a collective work ('The sexuality of Japanese women'), *Group Wife*, ed. Komichi Shobô, 1984, pp. 128–31.

2 *Ibid.*, p. 131.

3 The fact that on average children are born twenty-two months after the wedding day confirms this hypothesis. This is no doubt why the policy current in the majority of companies of women resigning on marriage is still very much associated with giving up work to have the first child.

4 Taken from *O-san kakumei, op. cit.*, p. 237.

5 A decision not unrelated to the fact that abortion is still thought of as a crime. The ministry justified its decision (in the face of accusations from feminists that this was to increase the birthrate) by claiming that a premature baby aged 24 weeks is viable.

6 Pregnancy is calculated as 40 weeks (280 days) from the date of the woman's last period. In Japan therefore week 24 corresponds to the sixth month, while in France it corresponds to the fifth month.

7 Since abortion and giving birth are not considered to be illnesses, they are not reimbursed by social security and health insurances. For example, at the Aiiku Hospital, a delivery with the usual five-day stay, will cost between 700,000 and 1 million yen. At the Seibô Hospital, if there are no complications, the cost of delivery and the usual stay in a six-bed ward will cost 400,000 yen, to which is added 100,000 yen for a private room with shared shower and WC (1992 prices).

8 In *O-san kakumei, op. cit.*, p. 240.

9 The rate in 1978–9 was estimated to be from 50,000 to 80,000 yen; these figures are based on an average of 300 days a year.

10 15.3 women per one hundred thousand die in childbirth against 5.5 cases per thousand of infant deaths. Japanese infant mortality is now the lowest in the world, but Japan is fifteenth (out of sixteen countries) for death in childbirth (taken from Ministry of Health statistics, *Demographic*

Yearbook, 1965–86, and *World Health Statistics Annual*, 1950–86).
11 In Japan abortions are carried out under general anaesthetic by curettage. The vacuum method is not generally used.
12 Taken from *Sei, op. cit.*, p. 131.
13 A laudable action in itself, destined to ease their karmic debt so that they be reunited with Buddha.
14 The monk Kûya Shôin described this legend and although De Visser (*The Bodhisattva Ti-Tsang [Jizô] in China and Japan*, Oesterheld, 1914, Berlin) takes its wider circulation back to the Genroku period (1688–1703) he stresses that there is no mention of it before the beginning of the eighteenth century (taken from Anne Page Brooks, 'Mizuko Kuyô and Japanese Buddhism', *Japanese Journal of Religious Studies*, 1981 (p. 123, n. 4).
15 Taken from *Senzo no hanashi*, Chikuma Shobô, 1946. (See the section entitled 'Sai-no-kawara', pp. 353–5.)
16 Taken from Lafcadio Hearn, *Glimpses of Unfamiliar Japan*, 1894, Tut. Books, pp. 59–61.
17 Bodhisattva is a wise man who passed through all the stages leading to enlightenment except the last which would have made him a Buddha.
18 Anne Page Brooks, *op. cit.*, p. 127.
19 Lafcadio Hearn, *op. cit.*, p. 44 (2).
20 This is also the source of the beautiful wooden painted dolls which originate from Tôhoku (*kokeshi*) whose function could be compared to that of the *mizuko Jizô*. Indeed this is suggested by the distressing association of the words *ko* (child) and *kesu* (to erase).
21 Taken from R. F. Young, 'Abortion, grief and consolation: prolegomena to a Christian response to Mizuko Kuyô', *Japan Christian Quarterly*, winter 1989, p. 34.
22 Taken from Charles Eliot, *Japanese Buddhism*, Routledge & Kegan Paul, London, 1935, p. 22, quoted by Anne Page Brooks, *op. cit.*
23 See Yoshiko Kurata Dykstra, 'Jizô, the most merciful', *Monumenta Nipponica*, XXXIII, 1978, pp. 179–90; see also Alicia Matsunaga, *The Buddhist Philosophy of Assimilation*, Sophia University Press, 1969, p. 235.
24 It is probably no coincidence that the most impressive of these reconstructions can be found on Mount Osorezan, a volcano in the very impoverished region of Tôhoku in north-east Japan, which remains shrouded in snow for five months of the year and which is infamous for the part it played in the 'thinning out of plants', as the *kokeshi* attest (see n. 20). In August, at the time of the festival of the dead, this site is a place of pilgrimage always well frequented by shamans (*itako*) who act as intermediaries communicating with the *mizuko*.
25 This is still valid for although no one is ever caught 'red-handed', little piles of stones can still be found in front of statues of Jizô.
26 Taken from Bardwell Smith, 'Buddhism and abortion in contemporary Japan: Mizuko Kuyô and the confrontation with death', *Japanese Journal of Religious Studies*, 1988, pp. 3–24 (cited p. 17).
27 For detailed information of this subject see Werblowsky, '*Mizuko kuyô* – Notulae on the most important "new religion" of Japan', *Japanese Journal of Religious Studies*, 1991, pp. 295–354 (see especially pp. 334–5).

28 It is with the aim of appeasing these spirits in which no one is interested, that a funeral service where offerings are made, is celebrated during the festival of the dead.

29 This analogy can be found in Werblowsky, *op. cit.*, p. 322. For more information on the *gaki*, see William La Fleur, 'Hungry ghost and hungry people', in *Fragments for a History of the Human Body*, pt I, coll. ed. M. Feher *et al.*, 1979, New York, pp. 270–303.

30 This comparison is reinforced by the fact that *gaki* is a familiar term used to refer to children, equivalent to kid, tot, tyke, youngster, and so on.

31 Although this parallel is not drawn by the anthropologist Ishikawa Jun'ichirô in his book: *Kappa no sekai* ('The world of the *kappa*'), 1985, it is interesting to read his collection of eye-witness accounts from around Japan (see the section '*Watakushi-wa kappa-o mita*' ('I have seen a *kappa*', pp. 19–21). Akutagawa Ryûnosuke wrote a very amusing novel based on this mythical creature entitled *Kappa*.

32 'Amphibious' is a significant detail bearing in mind that this is a characteristic of a newborn baby.

33 Taken from Richard Fox Young's: 'Abortion, grief and consolation: prolegomena to a Christian response to *Mizuko Kuyô*', Japanese Christian Quarterly, 55, 1989, pp. 31–9 (his principal source is Kiriyama Seiyû, the founder of a new religion).

34 A sliding screen comprising a wooden frame with one side covered in translucent paper.

35 See Miura Dômyô, *The Forgotten Child*, Aidan Ellis, Henley-on-Thames, 1983. (The author introduces his name with the title *archbishop*.)

36 Taken from a brochure I found at Chichibu, in the Shiunzan Jizôdera temple.

37 The term *kuyô* refers to carrying out one's duties to the spirits of the departed by offering them food or by performing a memorial service to help them rest in peace.

38 This service is offered by some hospitals. A French woman who suffered a miscarriage when she was six months pregnant told me how someone came to console her the next day by announcing that a *kuyô* had already been said to appease the innocent baby's soul.

39 Chapter 5 described how great a share of the burden the village took in making the decision to commit infanticide.

40 Werblowsky, who retranscribed these inscriptions (*op. cit.*, p. 319), has reason to believe that this promise is seldom kept.

41 The plaque has the unusual feature of being endowed with a statue representing a woman suckling a child, a unique stance in Buddhist statuary. It is one of those rare statues (which belongs to the Edo period when Christianity was banned) representing the Virgin Mary disguised beneath the features of Kannon.

42 Werblowsky rightly states that this mother deliberately pretends to be unaware of the sad fate awaiting them on the banks of the River Sai.

43 The traditional term is *kakekomidera*, meaning a temple closed to men where women can find refuge.

44 Taken from Kobayashi Kazutani, *Mizuko kuyô teradera (tonai)* ('Temples within Tokyo specializing in the *mizuko kuyô*'), Daihôrin, 1979, pp. 15–19 (quoted by Anne Page Brooks, *op. cit.*, pp. 122–3).

45 Werblowsky states that these days fathers are more likely to take their share of responsibility, for example by assisting in the *misuko kuyô* with their partner. My own observations would seem to support this.

46 Taken from Hoshino Eiki and Takeda Dôshô, 'Indebtedness and comfort: the undercurrents of *Mizuko Kuyô* in contemporary Japan', *Japanese Journal of Religious Studies*, 1987, pp. 305–20.

47 Taken from *Shûkyô kôgei* (religious arts), *Mizuko kuyô dera no shôkai* ('An introduction to temples practising *mizuko kuyô*'), 1979, quoted by Anne Page Brooks, *op. cit.*, n. 3, p. 121.

48 Taken from documentation obtained on site.

49 William La Fleur, *Liquid Life*, Princeton University Press, 1992.

50 Or ritual Shintô prayers, of which there is an example (that of the Ishikiri Jinja) in the appendix to Werblowsky's article (*op. cit.*, pp. 341–4). Of course the Buddhist symbols of Kannon and Jizô do not appear but the babies are asked to rest in peace and to work for the well-being of their family.

51 Werblowsky, *op. cit.*, p. 296.

52 *Ibid.*, p. 302.

53 In 'Buddhism and abortion in contemporary Japan: *Mizuko Kuyô* and the confrontation with death', *Japanese Journal of Religious Studies*, 1988, p. 22.

54 Anne Page Brooks, *op. cit.*, p. 137.

7 THE NEW ORDER

1 *Kô shûnyû, kô gakureki, kô shinchô.* The Altman Marriage Bureau launched the catchword *san kô* based on the findings of a survey carried out among its clients who are, of course, looking for the best match possible.

2 *Kao, seikaku, iegara* (in 'San kô, san ryô motomeru josei', *Asahi*, 14 March 1992, Ed. Soir).

3 The two models are so different that the women's magazines carried the following headlines: '*Anata-wa "Momoe gata" soretomo "Seiko gata"?*' ('Are you a Momoe or a Seiko?').

4 Taken from Ueno Chizuko, '*Kodomo-o sutetai onnatachi*' ('Women who would like to abandon their children'), in '*Bosei'-o kaidoku suru* ('Decoding "motherhood"'), coll. Group Bosei Kaidoku Kôza, Ed. Yûhikaku, 1991, pp. 159–72.

5 A *mukoyôshi* is a son-in-law appointed to be the successor of his in-laws, who takes their name and into whose house he moves.

6 In the comic strip – as in the animated version which has been shown on television twice a week for well over twenty years – we never see Masuo argue or even bicker with his in-laws, proof that he makes more of an effort with them than he would with his own parents.

7 A *talento* refers to celebrities who like to take part in 'quiz shows'.

8 She described her life as a busy mother in *Agnes no inochi-ga ippai* ('The very full life of Agnes'), Ed. Shôgakkan, P. and Books, 1989.

9 *Chichi kusai, dasai Ajia no haha*, from Ueno Chizuko, *op. cit.*, p. 160.

10 In *Gendai kazoku to feminizumu* ('The modern family and feminism'), Keiso Shobô, 1989; see especially '*Shinjinrui josei-wa Agnes-o mezasu ka*' ('Is Agnes the new generation's ideal?'), pp. 280–96.

11 Published under the title *Kozure shukkin-o kangaeru* ('Deliberations on taking baby to work with you'), Iwanami booklet, 122, 1988.

12 *Obatarian* is from the title of the comic strip of the same name. This word refers to shameless, egocentric women in their forties, who have lost all their gentleness and charm of old, to become devotees of 'me first!'.

13 Tanaka Kimiko told us that when she asked young mothers-to-be why they wanted to have babies they had replied: 'So that I can give him the sweet name of one of the comic strip heroes'.

14 As of the top executives of Mitsubishi bank (who still had his ageing 90-year-old parents to look after) confided on the eve of his retirement: 'They are taking ages to die!'

15 Yuzawa Yasuhiko is a family sociologist and the author of many books on the question of marriage and the family, including *Kazoku mondai no shakaigaku* ('The sociology of family problems'), Science-sha, 1981 (comments collected during a round table discussion with Madoka Yoriko, Suzuki Katsuko (from the Altman Marriage Bureau) and Mitsuoka Kôji; *Otoko no kekkon nan to onna no kekkon banare* ('Difficulties men encounter when looking for a wife and women's detachment when it comes to marriage'), The Community 97, *chiiki shakai kenkyûsho*, 1992, pp. 10–59).

16 The women questioned were not clients of the bureau.

17 See '*Ajia no hanayome Tôkyô ni ippai!*' ('Tokyo is full of south-east Asian wives!'), *Asahi (Journal)* 26 April 1991, pp. 6–12.

18 The director of the Nippon Seinenkan Marriage Bureau qualified this statement by pointing out that this had happened to her only three times, which still does not exclude the telephone calls she receives from mothers to describe the perfect daughter-in-law or request that their sons be introduced to someone more suitable.

19 This was confirmed by the director of the Nippon Seinenkan Marriage Bureau (see reasons on p. 149).

20 A *miai* is a 'bringing together' with a view to making an arranged marriage. (For more information on this, see Muriel Jolivet, *L'Integration sociale par la voie du mariage* ('Social integration through marriage') *op. cit.*)

21 *Toshikoshisoba* are buckwheat noodles eaten on New Year's Eve (31 December); the number 31 is associated with this expression.

22 *Râmen* are Chinese noodles eaten in a hot soup.

23 This observation refers to a slogan current in the 1970s to describe the ideal husband: 'A car, a house but . . . not the old girl!'

24 Taken from *Asahi* (see n. 17).

25 From 'The quiet revolution: Japanese women today', *Japan Foundation Newsletter*, XIX(3), December 1991, p. 6.

26 The expression *jinshin-baibai* means 'slave trade' or 'wife trade'. For more detailed information, see Mori Katsumi's book, published under this title with the subtitle *Kaigai dekasegi onna* ('Women who emigrate to find work'), Ed. Nihon rekishi shinsho, 1955. See also 'Jinshinbaibai no aika' ('Requiem for the wife trade'), in *Nippon no komoriuta, op. cit.*, pp. 202–19.

27 *Asahi* (see n. 17), p. 9.

28 A private organization 'Help', set up in 1986 in the Shinjuku area of Tokyo, offers to help foreign women in difficulty by providing them with up to two weeks' free accommodation. Single mothers sometimes arrive in search of a refuge until they give birth. There are, however, state-run counselling centres in each prefecture (*fujin sôdan sentâ*) which are there to listen to women.

29 For further information see Dr Sano Kamatarô's book, *Isha-ga susumeru nyô ryôhô* ('Urine as a therapeutic remedy recommended by doctors'), Ed. Tokuma Shoten, 1993. Dr Sano illustrates his book with a photo of himself and his whole team sampling a glass of urine.

30 This is full-time work paid at the part-time rate (see p. 58).

31 In half an hour she earns what it would have taken her a day to earn in the Philippines.

32 '*Yon de shiawase*': she is making a pun with *shi* from *shiawase* (happiness) and *shi* the character used to write the number 4 (which can also be read *yon*). (This play on words is surprising, for *shi* is more often associated with its homonym which means death; in fact many hospitals do not have a room numbered 4.)

33 Taken from an account collected by Ezaki Yasuko and Moriguchi Hideshi, *Zai Nichi Gaikokujin* ('Foreigners who live in Japan'), Shôbunsha, 1988 (see '*Nôson no hanayome I*' ('Farmers' wives'), pp. 90–7).

34 This (*yuinô*) is usually 1 million yen, a sum equivalent to three months' salary. It may or not include the engagement ring. This money, also called *shitaku kin* is considered to be a donation (from the bride's in-laws) to help pay the dowry the bride will bring along with her. Japanese feminists are demanding that this custom be abolished because it gives the idea that the bride is being bought.

35 In *Kindai kazoku to feminizumu* ('The modern family and feminism'), *op. cit.*, pp. 323–5.

36 This expression – a contraction of *Japa*(n) and *yuku* (to go) is a euphemism for the *Karayukisan* model (see Chapter 5) or the *Ameyukisan* (from *America* and *yuku*) which refers to Japanese women who were recruited to go to the United States to work as prostitutes. For further information, see Yamada Waka's fascinating account recorded by Yamazaki Tomoko in *Ameyuki-san no Uta – Yamada Waka no Sûki Naru Shôgai*, Bungei Shunjû, 1978 (*The Story of Yamada Waka – From Prostitute to Feminist Pioneer*, Kôdansha International, 1985); and Sanya Tetsuo's book, *Japayukisan*, Jôhô sentâ Shuppankyoku, 1985, which deals more with the question of Thai prostitutes, and also Lisa Louis, *op. cit.*, ch. 7, 'Women at a discount: *Japayuki-san*', pp. 153–73.

37 For a three-month period which can be renewed only once.

38 '*Nôsanson no hanayome mondai to taisaku*' ('The problem of finding a wife for those engaged in agricultural work and the steps which should be taken'); see Mitsuoka Kôji's comments in *The Community, op. cit.*, pp. 19–9.

39 'Rabbit hutches', which became a catchword in Japanese, was used by Roy Jenkins during the 1979 Tokyo summit when he was the EC Commission president. The term had been used in a confidential EC Commission report on Japanese housing conditions, but was subsequently

leaked. This aroused mixed feelings among the Japanese, who have never stopped referring to it since.

40 *The Community, op. cit*, p. 24.

41 For more information on the subject of the *mazâkon (mother complex)*, see Muriel Jolivet, 'L'empreinte d'Ajasé dans une société marquée par le principe maternel' ('The mark of Ajasé in a society stamped by the maternal principle'), *Bulletin of the Faculty of Foreign Languages and Studies*, Sophia University, 1989, 24, pp. 109–8.

42 Attached to the Altman Marriage Bureau's research department in *The Community, op. cit.*, pp. 25–6.

43 *The Community, op. cit.*, p. 26.

44 A *drive-in* is a fast-food outlet where people can order a meal without getting out of the car.

45 A young woman on what was in fact a very informal *miai* told me that the first question her suitor asked her was: 'And what does your father do?'

46 *The Community*, op. cit., p. 41.

47 Ed. Kôdansha (X Bunkô), 1991 and Kôdansha, 1992.

48 Taken from the report in the *SPA* journal, entitled '*Sex nan'te iranaï genshô*' ('The rejection of sex'), 17 June 1992, pp. 22–31.

49 In 1991 the average age to get married was 28.4 for men and 25.9 for women (taken from *Jinkô dôtai tôkei* ('Statistics on population movements'), Ministry of Health).

50 One student told me (in 1989) that between leaving playschool and going to university he had never had the opportunity of mixing with girls for throughout his schooldays, primary and secondary, he had attended only private single-sex schools.

51 A recurring theme of many television dramas is the intransigence of children as regards their parents' remarrying.

52 See Koyama Tetsuo, '"*Oishii kekkon*" "*tte*" *nan darô*' ('What is a "happy" marriage?'), *The Community, op. cit.*, pp. 60–2.

53 *Hanamuko gakkô* is a title with a somewhat ironic meaning since it is based on the *hanayome gakkô* model. These were domestic science schools which prepared daughters of the rich to become good wives and wise mothers (*hanamuko* means bridegroom).

54 They can also follow an 'à la carte' course, costing 5,000 yen per session.

55 This reply is reminiscent of the one given in another survey (see Chapter 2) where the three main reasons given by men for wanting to get married were: for my social well-being (38 per cent), for my psychological well-being (33 per cent), because it is normal to get married (29 per cent). The replies given by women were: because it makes women happy (34 per cent), because it is normal (25 per cent), for my psychological well-being (22 per cent). Taken from '*Fujin ni kansuru ishiki chôsa*' ('Public opinion survey on women'), published by the Prime Minister's Office, in *Gendai Nihon Josei no ishiki to kôdô* ('Japanese women's standards and deeds'), 1974 (not updated since), p. 33.

56 Questionnaires that I distributed to companies also revealed a need among the male employees to be married by a certain age (see p. 198, n. 4).

57 For further information on this subject, see Muriel Jolivet, 'Carrière et

emploi, les jeunes relèvent la tête' ('Career and employment, the young
raise their sights'), *France-Japon Éco*, 51 (see report on 'Les nouveaux
Japonais'), summer 1992, pp. 11–14.
58 This was still possible up until the mid-1980s. I remember having seen
an artist on television who, when he was asked about his wife's qualities,
said that she was a good mother to him.
59 The Kansai school founder (a former kimono merchant) declared that he
became a master in handling women the day he sold his ten thousandth
kimono.
60 This statement confirms that of Madoka Yoriko's (see p. 165).
61 There are men who find it difficult to talk freely in the presence of
women on such subjects as sexual harassment, sexuality or the art of
becoming an adult male. It should be noted that it was the women who
requested they be admitted to these classes.

8 THE ACHIEVEMENT OF WORKING MOTHERS

1 It seems necessary to qualify this statement – which is contradicted in the
next sentence – for there are many women who definitely do not want
people to think they work because they are needy, any more than they
would wish to suggest that on their husband's salary things are a little 'tight'.
2 Crèches stay open all summer and any 'long' holiday break the carer
might be allowed is limited to five consecutive days.
3 Before the introduction of word-processors, the use of machines able
to type characters required special training which few bosses were in a
position to expect from their secretaries.
4 This bears out the findings of a survey carried out by a frozen food
company which revealed that housewives were their main customers.
There is no doubt that working mothers are looking for ways to
compensate for their absence.
5 Considering that Japan is a high-tech country it is interesting to note that
household appliances are relatively rudimentary (see also Chapter 4,
n. 108).
6 Some paediatricians have special surgery days reserved for particular
vaccinations.
7 The school and university year begins in April, which explains why she
had to wait a year before her child could be admitted. The majority of
crèches do not take babies under the age of 5, 6 or 8 months; these are
admitted depending on the availability of places (in the interim they
often have their full quota of children).
8 *Arubaitu*, from the German word *Arbeit*, refers to moonlighting. It
actually means all those little jobs done by young people and housewives
which are untaxed. It is usually temporary work paid at an hourly rate.
9 Children who have been to a crèche are expected to have 'learnt to eat
everything' (see Chapter 1, n. 27).
10 Taken from '*Gambatte wâkingu mazâ*' ('Keep going, working mothers!'),
Shûkan Asahi Rinji Zôkan (a special issue of the weekly journal *Asahi*),
30 April 1992 (see especially pp. 102–9).
11 See 'Que les femmes sachent se rendre indispensables ouvrira la porte

vers l'égalité' ('The door to equality will open the day women become indispensable'), *France-Japon Éco*, 35, 1988, pp. 44–8.

12 Saitô Satoru is a specialist in problems related to alcoholism, anorexia, bulimia, co-dependence and more recently *workaholism*, which he considers to be just as much a drug as alcohol. He is also the author of *Onnarashisa no Yamai* ('Illnesses linked to femininity'), ed. Seishin Shobô, 1986; *Kazoku izonshô* ('Family co-dependence'), *Seishin Shobô, 1989; Arukoru izonshô* ('Alcohol dependence'), ed. Seishin Shobô, 1989; *Kashoku, kyoshoku* ('Bulimia and anorexia').

13 Quoted by A. Imamura, *Urban Japanese Housewives*, University of Hawaii Press, 1987, p. 107.

14 Extract taken from *Mainichi*, 3 December 1982, quoted by Tanaka Kimiko, *op. cit.*, pp. 92–3.

15 *Itte rasshaï* is literally 'Go and come back!', the customary response being '*Itte mairimasu!*' ('I go and I return').

16 *Kumon* is a very popular *juku* (a private institution which runs parallel to compulsory education, geared to stimulating children) with branches at near every mainline station all over Japan. The children are given homework to do every day, which a teacher then helps them mark twice a week. The method is based on repetition and speed and the children are asked to keep a record of how long it takes them to get through each sheet. There is no minimum age limit since even babies a few months old are considered capable of following the course.

17 A cartoon character extremely popular with the young, *Ampâman* gets his name from the fact that his head is shaped like a roll filled with bean paste (*an-pan*).

18 *Itadakimasu* means 'I take'. This is a polite phrase equivalent to the French 'Bon appétit' pronounced before each meal.

19 Uttered at the end of the meal, *gochisôsama* means 'Thank you for this delicious food!'

20 In Japan people take extremely hot baths at temperatures from 42° to 45°C.

21 *Moomin* is a little Swedish troll whose adventures are described in *Moomin Troll*.

22 This is just not done because there is the risk not only of attracting the envy of others but also the philosophy of the happy medium advocates that happiness should be tempered since pride comes before a fall. Anonymous account published by Wife, under the direction of Tanaka Kimiko, *Kakkazoku no kosodate to shitsuke no môten* ('The educational and behavioural blindspot of the nuclear family'); see '*Kodomo-wa wagaya no takaramono*' ('Our child, our treasure'), 1991, pp. 33–7.

23 Hiraï Nobuyoshi, *Kodomo-o shikaru mae ni yomu hon* ('Think before you reprimand your child'), PHP, 1991, subtitled in English with good reason 'Good humour and an atmosphere of freedom can nourish enthusiasm, initiative and creativity in your children'.

24 Morishita Yuri, another ardent follower of Hiraï's principles, stated, during a symposium (July 1992) to launch the collective work *Kosodate-wa tsurai!* ('What's so difficult about bringing up children!') published by Wife, that if her husband (a psychologist by profession) had not been

there every night to listen to her, she would have had a complete breakdown (Hiraï had neglected to test out his own educational theories).

25 *Esukarêta* or 'escalator schools' are difficult to get into but those who are
selected go straight into the elitist network and are later exempt from
having to take the university entrance examination.

26 These findings are taken from a survey carried out by the Ministry of
Health: *Kekkon to shushan ni kansuru zenkoku chôsa* ('Census on births
and marriages'), of which an extract was published by the *Nihon Keizai
Shimbun*, 5 May 1988.

27 This is a pole traditionally made from bamboo (but now from steel) on
which the clothes are strung to dry.

28 Published in *Kodomo-o shikaru mae ni jomu hon, op. cit.*, pp. 114–15.

BY WAY OF A CONCLUSION

1 Subtitled *Approche thérapeutique du carencé relationnel* ('A therapeutic
approach to inadequate relationships'), Fleurus, coll. 'Pédagogie psycho-
sociale', 1979. I should like to stress that I did not borrow his title when
I translated Kyûtoku's book and that this is pure coincidence, for it is
after having analysed Kyûtoku's (published in the same year) that I first
saw his fascinating study.

2 It was reported in the press that he was born of a 'foreign' mother who
was a *Japayukisan* who went back home with her baby after delivery.

3 *San Francisco Chronicle*, 27 March 1991, 'Study finds widespread hunger
of Children under 12 in US'.

4 This is precisely what Yamada Makoto does in *Kosodate minna
sukinayôni yareba ii* ('Bring your children up as you see fit!') (1990) in
ch. 7 *'Haha to kokoro no kizunaron-o kettobase!'* ('Kick out all those
bonding theories!').

5 There are even *pokkuri dera* where old women go and pray for a speedy
death.

6 In an interview published in March 1993 in the journal *Sukusuku
Akachan*.

7 As opposed to 55 per cent in France. The majority of Japanese women
replied: 'Yes, but I sometimes find it annoying that I never have any time
to myself', and 20 per cent said that they did not enjoy it at all for it got
in the way of what they wanted to do. Taken from the findings of a
survey comparing the education of French and Japanese children,
carried out by the Franco-Japanese Centre for Documentation on
Women (reply to question 37).

8 Nearly all women acknowledge that the carers' experience of, for
example, potty-training proved invaluable.

Bibliography

A SELECTION OF JAPANESE WORKS RELATING TO THE MOTHERHOOD CRISIS

Agnes-chan and Hara Hiroko, *'Kozure shukkin' -o Kangaeru* ('Deliberations on taking baby to work with you'), Iwanami Booklet 122, Tokyo, 1988.

Arichi Tôru, *Nippon no oyako ni hyaku nen* ('Parent–children relationships as observed in Japan over the last two centuries'), Shinchô Sensho, Tokyo, 1986.

Ariyoshi Sawako, *Hanaoka Seichû no tsuma*, Shinchôsha, 1970 (English translation, *The Doctor's Wife*, Kôdansha, 1978).

Doi Takeo, *Amae no kôzô*, Kôbundô, 1971 (English translation, *The Anatomy of Dependence*, Kôdansha International, Tokyo, 1973).

Endô Shûsaku, *Chinmoku*, Shinchôsha, 1966 (English translation, Silence, Tuttle, 1969).

Ezaki Yasuko and Moriguchi Hideshi, *Zai Nichi Gaikokujin* ('Foreigners who live in Japan'), Shôbunsha, 1988.

Fujita Shin'ichi, *O-san kakumei* ('Revolution in childbirth'), Asahi Shimbunsha, Tokyo, 1979.

Fukazawa Shichirô, *Narayama Bushiko*, Shinchôsha, 1956 (English translation, *The Songs of Oak Mountain*, 1961).

Group Wife, (Tanaka Kimiko *et al.*), *Sei* ('The sexuality of Japanese women'), Kei Shobô, 1984.

—— *Kakkazoku no kosodate to shitsuke no môten* ('The educational and behavioural blindspot of the nuclear family'), Tokyo, 1991.

—— *Kosodate-wa tsurai!* ('What's so difficult about bringing up children!'), 1992.

Hara Hiroko-hen, *Hahaoya no shûgyô to katei seikatsu no hendô* ('Mother's occupation and home education'), Kôbundô, Tokyo, 1987 (1985 survey).

—— *Japanese Childhood since 1600* (with Minagawa Meiko) unpublished (an extract was published in German, in *Zur Sozialgeschichte der Kindheit*, Jochen Martin, 1986).

—— *Hataraku onnatachi no jidai* ('The era of the working mother') (with Sugiyama Meiko *et al.*), NHK Books 479, Tokyo, 1985.

—— *Chûshô kigyô no onnatachi* ('Women who work in Tokyo's SMEs') (*Kokusai josei gakkai*, in collaboration with Muramatsu Yasuko and Minami Chie), Miraisha, 1987.

Hayashi Iku, *Kateinai rikon* ('Divorced without being divorced'), Chikuma Bunkô, Tokyo, 1986.

Higuchi Keiko, *Onna no Ko no Sodatekata*, Bunka Shuppankyoku, 1978 (English translation: *Bringing up Girls*, Shoukadoh Pr. Co. Kyoto, 1985, out of print).

—— *Hanamuko Gakkô* ('The school for husbands') (in collaboration with Saitô Shigeo and Itamoto Yôko), Sanseidô, Tokyo, 1990.

Hiraï Nobuyoshi, *Ushinawareta bosei aï* ('The disappearance of maternal love'), Reimei Shobô, Tokyo, 1981.

—— *Yoï ko warui ko* ('The good child and the naughty child'), PHP Kenkyûsho, Tokyo, 1990.

—— *Kokoro ni nokoru Okâsan* ('Mother as she is remembered in our hearts'), Kikakushitsu, Tokyo, 1989.

—— *Kodomo-o shikaru mae-ni yomu hon* ('Think before you reprimand your child'), PHP, Tokyo, 1991.

Hirao Keiko, *Kosodate sensen ijô ari* ('The dissatisfaction of working mothers'), Chôbunsha, Tokyo, 1991.

Ibuka Masaru, *Yôchien dewa ososugiru*, Goma Books, 1977 (English translation, *Kindergarten is Too Late*, Souvenir, London, 1977).

Ikegame Ume, *Ikuji fuan-o koeru kosodate no wa* ('How to overcome anxiety associated with childcare'), Yukkusha, 1987.

Itoh Hiromi, *Ii oppai, warui oppai* ('The good breast and the bad breast'), Tôjusha, Tokyo, 1985.

—— *Onaka hoppe oshiri* ('[Baby's] belly, cheeks and buttocks'), Fujin seikatsusha, Tokyo, 1987.

Iwao Sumiko, Saitô Hiroko, Fukutomi Mamoru *et al.*, *Tanshin Funin* ('Professional transfers'), Yûhikaku, Tokyo, 1991.

Iwao Sumiko and Sugiyama Meiko (under the direction of), *Hataraku hahaoya no jidai* ('The era of the working mother'), NHK Books 456, Tokyo, 1984.

Ishikawa Jun'ichirô, *Kappa no sekai* ('The universe of the *kappa*'), Jijitsû Shinsha, 1985.

Kamata Hisako, Miyasato Kazuko, Suganuma Hiroko, Furukawa Hiroko and Sakakura Yoshio, *Nihonjin no ko-umi, ko-sodate: ima mukashi* ('The Japanese art of bringing children into the world and bringing them up: yesterday and today'), Keisô Shobô, Tokyo, 1990.

Kawaï Hayao, *Bosei shakai Nihon no byôri* ('Japanese society's obsession with motherhood'), Chûô Kôronsha, Tokyo, 1976.

Kobayashi Noboru, *Fureaï no ikuji* ('How to achieve oneness'), TBS Britanika, Tokyo, 1988.

—— *Kodomo wa mirai-he no tabibito* ('Children, these travellers turned towards the future'), Tôkyô Shoseki, 1988.

Kyûtoku Shigemori, *Bogenbyô* ('Illness caused by Mother'), Sun Mark, Shuppan, Tokyo, 1979.

—— *Bogenbyô zoku* ('Illness caused by Mother', part 2), Kyôiku Kenkyûsha, 1980.

—— *Bogenbyô zokozoku* ('Illness caused by Mother', part 3), Sun Mark Books, 1981.

—— *Bogenbyô-o fusegu tame no jyû soku* ('Ten ways to avoid contaminating your child with the mother-sickness'), Sun Mark Books, 1982.

—— *Shin bogenbyô* ('New illnesses caused by Mother'), Sun Mark Books, 1990.

Matsuda Michio, *Ikuji no hyakka* ('Encyclopedia of childcare'), Iwanami Shoten, Tokyo, 1967, 1980, 1983.

—— *Anshin ikuji* ('The art of bringing up children'), Shôgakkan, 1986.

—— *Watakushi–wa josei ni shika kitai shinai* ('I can trust only women'), Iwanami Shinsho 109, Tokyo, 1990.

Matsunaga Goichi, *Nihon no komoriuta* ('Japanese lullabies'), Kinokuniya Shinsho, 1964.

Mitsuoka Kôji, *Nôsanson no hanayome mondai to taisaku* ('The difficulties encountered by agricultural workers to find a wife and steps to be taken'), Nôrin Tôkei Kyôkai, 1987.

Mizuno Mari, *Sekando vâjin* ('The second virginity'), Kôdansha X Bunkô, 1991.

—— *Sekando vâjin shôkôgun* ('The second virginity syndrome'), Kôdansha, 1992.

Môri Taneki, *Shin Emîru* ('The new Emile'), Chikuma Bunkô, Tokyo, 1985.

Mori Katsumi, *Jinshin baibai* ('Wife-trade'), Nihon Rekishi Shinsho, 1955.

Morisaki Kazue, *Karayukisan* ('Those who went abroad (as prostitutes)'), Asahi Bunkô, 1976.

Nichi futsu josei shiryô sentâ (Franco–Japanese Centre for Documentation on Women), *Boshi kankei kenkyûkai* (Study group on the mother–child relationship), *Nihon no kosodate, sekai no kosodate* ('Survey on the education of children in France and Japan'), Japanese edn 1990 (French report 1987).

Nihon fujin dantai rengôhen (coll.), *Fujin Hakusho* ('White Paper on women'), Horupu Shuppankan, Tokyo, 1985.

Nishi Masahiko and Itoh Hiromi, *Papa-wa gokigen naname* (*Papa, You are Cross*!), Sakuhinsha, Tokyo, 1989.

Ochiai Emiko, *Kindai kazoku to Feminizumu* ('The modern family and feminism'), Keisô Shobô, Tokyo, 1989.

Oketani Sotomi, *Bonyû hoiku* ('Breast-feeding'), Shufu no tomo, 1987.

Oshima Kiyoshi, *Taiji kyôiku* ('Foetal education'), Goma Shobô, 1988.

Sasaki Yasuyuki, Takano Akira, Oohinata Masami, Jimba Yukiko and Serizawa Motoko, *Ikuji noirôze* ('Childrearing neurosis'), Yûhikaku Shinsho, Tokyo, 1982.

Satô Hachirô, *Okâsan* ('Mother') (poems, 3 vols), Orion Shuppansha, 1962.

Sugiyama Akira, *Kodomo ni moratta yukaina jikan* ('The wonderful moments children have given me'), Shôbunsha, 1989.

Takuma Taketoshi, *Futarikko no jidai* ('The era of the two-children family'), Asahi Shimbunsha, Tokyo, 1981.

Tanaka Kimiko, *Hataraku josei no kosodateron* ('The educational theories of working women'), Shinchô Sensho, Tokyo, 1988.

Taniguchi Yûji, *Mama kami omutsu-o tsukawanaïde* ('I beg you, never use disposable nappies!'), Siezan Shobô, 1986.

—— *Yamete yokatta kami omutsu* ('What a good thing I stopped using disposable nappies!'), Ikuji Bunka Kenkyûsho Shuppan, 1989.

Tsuboi Hirofumi *et al.*, *Ie to Josei* ('Women and the family unit'), *Nippon no Minzoku Bunka Taisei* ('The structures of popular Japanese culture'), vol. 10, Shôgakkan, 1985.

Tsushima Yûko, *Hikari no ryobun*, 1979 (French translation, *Territoire de lumière* ('Land of light'), Des Femmes, 1986).

Wagatsuma Hiroshi and Hara Hiroko, *Shitsuke* ('Cultural background of childrearing in Japan'), Kôbundô, Tokyo, 1974.

Wakamori Tarô *et al.*, *Haha no zô* ('Portraits of mothers'), Sôdo Bunka, Tokyo, 1976.

Yamada Makoto, *Minna sukinayôni yareba ii* ('Bring your children up as you see fit!'), Tarô Jirôsha, Tokyo, 1990.

Yamamura Yoshiaki, *Nihonjin to haha* ('Japanese and their mothers'), Tôyôkan Shuppansha, Tokyo, 1971.

Yamatani Tetsuo, *Japayukisan* ('Women who came to Japan to work as prostitutes'), Jôhô Sentâ Shuppankyoku, 1985.

Yamazaki Tomoko, *Ameyuki-san no Uta: Yamada Waka no Sûki Naru Shôgai*, Bungei Shunjû, 1978 (English translation: *The Story of Yamada Waka: From Prostitute to Feminist Pioneer*, Kôdansha International, 1985).

Yanagita Kunio, *Senzo no hanashi*, Chikuma Shobô, 1946 (English translation: *About Our Ancestors: The Japanese Family System*, Japan Society for the Promotion of Science, 1970).

Yûki Misae, *Minna nayande mama ni naru* ('We all learn to be mothers on the job!'), Chôbunsha, Tokyo, 1990.

—— *Ni san saiji no mama-wa taihen* ('The trials and tribulations of the mothers of 2 and 3 year olds'), Chôbunsha, Tokyo, 1982.

GOVERNMENT SURVEYS

Nihon no kodomo to hahaoya, Sôrifu Seishônen taisaku hombu (not updated since). A summary was published in English under the title *Japanese Children and their Mothers: International Comparison*, Prime Minister's Office, Youth Headquarters, 1981.

Nippon no chichioya to kodomo ('Japanese fathers and their children'), Sômuchô Seishônen taisaku hombu, Tokyo, 1987.

Atarashii josei no ikikata-o motomete ('The demands of the new women'), Economic Development Agency, 1987.

Kokumin seikatsu hakusho ('White Paper on the life of the nation; towards a society without children; the consequences and how to deal with them'), Economic Development Agency, Press Office of the Ministry of Finance, 1992.

Ministry of health (Kôseishô), *Jinkô dôtai tôkei* ('Statistics on population movements'), 1991.

Ministry of Labour (Rôdôshô), *Shigoto to ikuji dochiramo taisetsu ni shitai* ('The art of reconciling work and children'), Women's Headquarters, 1986.

JOURNALS, NEWSPAPERS, BROCHURES

Gendai no Esupuri ('Esprit d'aujourd'hui', *Sociology Journal*), '*Shitsuke*' ('Childrearing and discipline'), 113, Shibundô, 1976.

—— '*Hahaoya*' ('The mother'), Yoda Akira, Ogawa Katsuyuki *et al.*, 115, Shibundô, 1977.

Recruit centre (brochures), *Working Woman ni kansuru chôsa* ('Survey on working women'), Recruit Research, 1991.
—— *Joshi gakusei-wa nani-o kangaete iru ka* ('What do the female students think?'), 1984 (not updated since).
Asahi Journal, Ajia no Hanayome (report on women who came from Asia to marry Japanese men), 26 April 1991.
Community, Gendai kekkonkô (report on marriage), 97, 1992.
Como, Gyakutai hyakutôban (report on battered child help line) 11, November 1991.
Croissant, report on the falling birthrate, 306, 10 August 1990, pp. 50–72.
Shûkan Asahi, Gambatte wâkingu mâzâ (report on working mothers), special issue, 30 April 1992.
SPA, Sex nan'te irainai genshô (report on the lack of interest in sex), 17 June 1992.
Taiyô, Memento Mori (in Japanese) (report on death), 30 September 1992.

ENGLISH BOOKS WITH REFERENCE TO JAPAN

Cherry Kittredge, *Womansword*, Kôdansha, Tokyo, 1987.
Condon Jane, *A Half-Step Behind. Japanese Women of the 80's*, Dodd, Mead, New York, 1985.
Cook Alice and Hayashi Hiroko, *Working Women in Japan*, Cornell University Press, New York, 1980.
Crihfield Dalby Liza, *Geisha*, University of California Press, 1983.
Hearn Lafcadio, *Glimpses of Unfamiliar Japan*, Tut. Books, 1894.
Hendry Joy, *Marriage in Changing Japan*, Tuttle, 1981.
—— *Becoming Japanese*, University of Hawaii Press, Honolulu, 1986.
Hunter Janet (ed.) *Japanese Women Working*, Routledge, London, 1993.
Imamura Anne, *Urban Japanese Housewives*, University of Hawaii Press, Honolulu, 1987.
Ishimoto Shidzué, *Facing Two Ways*, Stanford University Press, California, 1984.
La Fleur William, *Liquid Life*, Princeton University Press, New Jersey, 1992.
Louis Lisa, *Butterflies of the Night*, Tengu, United States, 1992.
Miura Dômyô, *The Forgotten Child*, Aidan Ellis, Henley-on-Thames, 1983.
Nakano Ann, *Japanese Women: A Century of Living History*, Rigby, Australia, 1986.
Reynolds David, *The Quiet Therapies* (see especially ch. 3, '*Naikan*: Introspection Therapy'), University of Hawaii Press, Honolulu, 1980.
Saga Jun'ichi, *Memories of Silk and Straw*, Kôdenshe International, 1987.
Stevenson Harold, Azuma Hiroshi, Hakta Kenji *et al.*, *Child Development and Education in Japan*, W. H. Freeman, New York, 1986.
Sugiyama Lebra Takie, *Japanese Women*, University of Hawaii Press, Honolulu, 1984.
Wagatsuma Hiroshi, 'Child Abandonment and Infanticide: A Japanese Case', in Jill Korbin *et al.*, *Child Abuse and Neglect Cross-Cultural Perspectives*, University of California Press, Berkeley, 1981.

ARTICLES

Asano Tamanoi Mariko, 'Songs as Weapons: The Culture and History of *Komori* (Nursemaids) in Modern Japan', *Journal of Asian Studies*, 50(4), November 1991, pp. 793–817.

Copeland Rebecca, 'Mother Obsession in Japanese Literature', *Transactions of the Asiatic Society*, 4 series, vol. 3, 1988.

Fox Young Richard, 'Abortion, grief and consolation: Prolegomena to a Christian response to *Mizuko Kuyô*', *Japan Christian Quarterly*, winter 1989, pp. 31–9.

Frager Robert, 'Jewish mothering in Japan', *Sociological Inquiry*, 42(1), 1972, pp. 11–17.

Fujita Mariko, 'It's all Mother's fault', *Journal of Japanese Studies*, 15(1), winter 1989, pp. 67–91.

Hoshino Eiki and Takeda Dôshô, 'Indebtedness and comfort: the undercurrents of *Mizuko Kuyô* in contemporary Japan', *Japanese Journal of Religious Studies*, 14(4), 1987, pp. 305–20.

Iwao Sumiko, 'The quiet revolution: Japanese women today', *Japan Foundation Newsletter*, 19(3), December 1991.

Jolivet Muriel, 'Motherhood in Japan', *Transactions of the International Conference of Orientalists in Japan*, vol. 34, 1989, Institute of Eastern Culture (Tôhô Gakkai).

Kurata Dykstra Yoshiko, ('*Jizô*, the most merciful'), *Monumenta Nipponica*, vol. 33, 1978, pp. 179–200.

O'Connor Thomas, 'Consoling the infants: for whose sake?', *Japan Christian Quarterly*, 50, 1984, pp. 206–14.

Page Brooks Anne, '*Mizuko Kuyô* and Japanese Buddhism', *Japanese Journal of Religious Studies*, 8(3–4), September–December 1981, pp. 119–47.

Rohlen Thomas *et al.*, 'Social control and early socialization', *Journal of Japanese Studies*, 15(1), winter 1989.

Smith Bardwell, 'Buddhism and abortion in contemporary Japan: *Mizuko Kuyô* and the confrontation with death', *Japanese Journal of Religious Studies*, 1988, pp. 3–24.

Werblowsky R. J. Zwi, '*Mizuko Kuyô* – notulae on the most important "new religion" of Japan', *Japanese Journal of Religious Studies*, 1991, pp. 254–95.

FRENCH BOOKS

Des Japonaises ('Japanese Women') (coll.), Des Femmes, Paris, 1987 (translated from Japanese).

Fukumoto and Pigeaire, *Femmes et Samouraï*, ('Women and the Samurai'), Des Femmes, Paris, 1986.

Jolivet Muriel, *L'Intégration sociale par la voie du mariage* ('Social integration through marriage'), DREA, Université Paris-III-Sorbonne nouvelle, 1977 (unpublished).

—— *L'Université au service de l'économie japonaise*, ('How the Japanese economy benefits from universities'), Economica, Paris, 1985.

ARTICLES

Beillevaire Patrick, 'La famille japonaise: hier et aujourd'hui', ('The Japanese family: yesterday and today'), SFS, 16 November 1984 study day, *La Socialité japonaise.*

Jolivet Muriel, 'Le revers de la médaille' ('The other side of the coin'), *Le Monde de l'Education*, 110, November 1984, pp. 18–19.

—— 'Femmes en retrait', ('Women still behind men') *Le Monde*, 14 November 1986.

—— 'Les surprises des crèches japonaises' ('The surprises Japanese crèches hold'), *Le Monde de l'Education*, 132, November 1986.

—— 'Conjuguer travail et maternité au Japon' ('Combining work and motherhood in Japan'), *Projet*, 206, July–August 1987.

—— 'Naître à Tokyo', ('Giving birth in Tokyo'), *Enfants Magazine*, August 1987.

—— 'Dossier sur l'emploi au féminin' ('Report on the jobs women do'), *France-Japon Éco*, 35, 1988, pp. 23–37.

—— 'La vie d'épouse' ('The life of a wife'), in *L'Etat du Japon* ('The State of Japan') (coll.), La Découverte, Paris, 1988.

—— 'L'empreinte d'Ajasé dans une société marquée par le principe mater-nel' ('The mark of Ajasé in a society stamped by the maternal principle'), *Bulletin of the Faculty of Foreign Studies*, 24, March 1990, Sophia University.

—— 'La chasse au trésor' ('The hunt for the treasure') and 'Ne pas trop . . . rêver' ('Don't dream too much'), report 'Emploi et recrutement', *France-Japon Éco*, 42, spring 1990.

—— 'Carrière et emploi: les jeunes relèvent la tête' ('Career and employ-ment: the young raise their sights'), *France-Japon Éco*, 51, summer 1992.

—— 'Un boss, un mari, des gosses . . . et les femmes dans tout ça?' ('A boss, a husband, kids . . . and what about women in all that?') *France-Japon Éco*, 51, summer 1992.

—— 'La contraception au Japon. L'amour à la japonaise' ('Contraception in Japan. Love the Japanese way'), report on 'Les Femmes au Japon' ('Women in Japan'), *Les Voix*, 62, spring 1993.

—— *Les Apparences sont sauves* ('Amour et sexualite'), L'Etat du Japon, La Découverte, 1995.

—— 'Maternal malaise in contemporary Japan as expressed in mythicization of the prewar mother and popular child-rearing theories', *Transactions of the Asiatic Society*, 1996.

—— 'The image of the father and the mother as depicted in the Japanese *manga* (comics)', *Tôhô Gakkai* (Proceedings of The International Conference of Eastern Studies), 40, 1995.

—— 'The maternity crisis in Japan: the country short of children', *Epic World*, 12, 1996.

Jugon Jean-Claude, 'L'enfant-Dieu: une étude sur les berceuses et les pratiques d'endormissement du jeune enfant japonais dans son milieu' ('The child-god: a study of lullabies and ways of getting the Japanese child off to sleep in his environment'), in *Les rituels du coucher de l'enfant, Variations culturelles*, ESF (coll. under the direction of Hélène Stork), May 1993.

Souyri Pierre, 'Splendeurs et misères de Yoshiwara' ('The glory and misery of Yoshiwara'), *Autrement*, Desvilles mommées Tokyo special issue, 8, September 1984, pp. 294–300.

A SELECTION OF GENERAL REFERENCE BOOKS

Badinter Élisabeth, *L'Amour en plus* ('Love in addition'), Flammarion, Paris, 1989.

Brazelton, *Working and Caring*, Addison Wesley, Wokingham 1983.

Czechowski Nicole, Terrasse Jean-Marc *et al.*, 'La mère' ('The mother'), *Autrement*, 90, May 1987.

Delaisi de Parseval Geneviève, Bigeargeal Jacqueline *et al.*, 'Objectif bébé. Une nouvelle science: la bébologie', ('Mission: baby. A new science: babyology'), *Autrement*, 72, September 1985.

Delaisi de Parseval Geneviève and Lallemand Suzanne, *L'Art d'accommoder les bébés* ('The art of accommodating babies'), Seuil, Paris, 1980.

Herbinet *et al.*, *D'amour et le lait* ('Of love and milk'), Stock, 'Les cahiers du nouveau-né', Paris, 1984.

Knibiehler Yvonne and Fouquet Catherine, *L'Histoire des mères* ('The history of mothers'), Montalba, 1980.

Lemay Michel, *J'ai mal à ma mère*, ('Illness caused by Mother'), Fleurus, Paris, 1979.

Olivier Christiane, *Les Enfants de Jocaste* ('Jocasta's children'), Denoël, Paris, 1980.

Pernoud Laurence, *Il ne fait pas bon être mère par les temps qui courent* ('It's not good being a mother these days'), Stock, Paris, 1981.

Raphaël Dana, *The Tender Gift: Breast-feeding*, Schocken Prentice-Hall, Englewood Cliffs, NJ, 1973.

Verny Thomas, *The Secret Life of the Unborn Child*, Summit, New York, 1981.

Von Franz Marie-Louise, *The Feminine in Fairytales*, Spring, Dallas, Texas, 1972.

Index